DATE DUE

NOV 14 1994		
DEC 0 3 1994		
NOV 1 3 1995		
JUN 0 1 2000		

DEMCO 38-297

Uncloaking the CIA

Howard Frazier,
Editor

 THE FREE PRESS
A Division of Macmillan Publishing Co., Inc.
NEW YORK
Collier Macmillan Publishers
LONDON

The Free Press
A Division of Macmillan Publishing Co., Inc.
866 Third Avenue, New York, N.Y. 10022

Collier Macmillan Canada, Ltd.

Library of Congress Catalog Card Number: 77–087573

Printed in the United States of America

printing number

1 2 3 4 5 6 7 8 9 10

Library of Congress Cataloging in Publication Data

Conference on the CIA and World Peace, Yale University,
    1975.
    Uncloaking the CIA.

    "Presentations made at ... the Conference on the CIA
and World Peace, held at Yale University on April 5,
1975."
    Includes bibliographical references and index.
    1. United States. Central Intelligence Agency--
Congresses. I. Frazier, Howard. II. Title.
JK468.I6C64 1975   327'.12'06173   77-87573
ISBN 0-02-915360-3

The poetry on p. 68 is an excerpt from *Let the Rail Splitter
Awake* by Pablo Neruda, translated by Waldeen. Masses &
Mainstream, Inc., 1951. Reprinted by permission of Farrar,
Straus & Giroux, Inc.

This book is dedicated to Dr. Jerome Davis, founder of Promoting Enduring Peace, Inc., whose life has exemplified the kind of democratic values the CIA has violated.

Contents

List of Contributors

Hortensia Bussi de Allende is the widow of President Salvador Allende of Chile and leader of Chileans in exile.

Fred Branfman is a writer and researcher on Laos, where he lived from 1967 to 1971. He has held positions with the Indochina Resource Center and the Tom Hayden for U.S. Senate campaign.

Martin Cherniack is associate director of Promoting Enduring Peace, Inc., and has been active in civil rights, peace, and health-care organizations.

Blanche Wiesen Cook is associate professor of history at John Jay College of Criminal Justice and a writer and editor in the areas of social change and civil liberties.

Frank Donner is an attorney specializing in labor law and civil liberties. He is author of *The Un-Americans* and numerous other works and is preparing a series of studies of political surveillance in the United States.

Stanley Faulkner is an attorney and the author of a number of works on human rights.

Joelle Fishman is a writer, editor, and executive secretary of the Communist Party in Connecticut.

Howard Frazier is executive director of Promoting Enduring Peace, Inc., and has held positions with the federal Office of Economic Opportunity and with consumer organizations.

Patricia Garrett lived in Chile during the entire Allende administration, doing research on social and economic topics.

John L. Hammond teaches sociology at Columbia University and has traveled frequently to Portugal doing research on political sociology and political movements.

Michael J. Harrington is representative from Massachusetts and a leading congressional critic of the CIA and U.S. foreign policy. His activities brought out many of the revelations that led to the investigations of the CIA and other intelligence agencies.

Sokhom Hing is a native of Cambodia who teaches economics in the State University of New York and serves as representative of the group Khmer Residents in America.

Russell Johnson is program consultant for the New England Region of the American Friends Service Committee and has made many trips to Asia.

Mark Lane is an attorney, writer, and lecturer. His work, such as his book *Rush to Judgment,* has helped generate research about the assassination of President Kennedy. He is a professor of law at Catholic University and director of the Citizens Commission of Inquiry.

Ngo Vinh Long is a writer and lecturer on his native Vietnam. He is director of the Vietnam Resource Center and editor of *Vietnam Quarterly.*

Ernest De Maio is a union organizer and official who is now permanent representative of the World Federation of Trade Unions to the United Nations.

Victor Marchetti served with the CIA from 1955 to 1969, rising to the position of executive assistant to the deputy director. He is coauthor of *The CIA and the Cult of Intelligence.*

John D. Marks, a former State Department intelligence officer, is an associate of the Center for National Security Studies and coauthor of *The CIA and the Cult of Intelligence.*

Florencio Merced is a member of the Political Commission of the Puerto Rican Socialist Party and has held positions with other organizations working for the independence of Puerto Rico.

Tony Monteiro is executive secretary of the Anti-Imperialist Movement in Solidarity with African Liberation. He has frequently lectured and written on African developments.

Peter J. O'Connell is a free-lance writer, editor, and researcher, and a college teacher of English and American Studies.

Winslow Peck is a writer and editor for *Counter-Spy* and other publications of Fifth Estate Security Education, Inc. He served as an intelligence analyst for the U.S. Air Force Security Service and the National Security Agency in Turkey and Vietnam.

Jo Pomerance is a writer and lecturer who serves as co-chairman of the Task Force for the Nuclear Test Ban.

L. Fletcher Prouty was for nine years the military officer responsible for the support of the clandestine operations of the CIA.

He is a writer, editor, and lecturer and has been an officer of several corporations and banks.

Kirkpatrick Sale is a writer and editor for many publications. He is author of *SDS* and *Power Shift*.

Adam Schesch lived in Chile during the entire Allende administration, doing research on social and economic topics.

Nicole Szulc is a writer and researcher who lives in Lisbon as correspondent for Spain and Portugal for Pacific News Service.

Preface and Acknowledgments

THIS BOOK IS COMPOSED of presentations made at or prepared in connection with the Conference on the CIA and World Peace held at Yale University on April 5, 1975. All who helped to make that conference a success and this book a reality are owed a debt of thanks. Special thanks are due, of course, to those who made presentations that day and graciously allowed them to be published in this book. The conference was initiated by Promoting Enduring Peace, Inc., Woodmont, Connecticut, and cosponsored by the American Civil Liberties Union, American Friends Service Committee, Center for National Security Studies, Connecticut Civil Liberties Union, Fellowship of Reconciliation, Methodist Federation for Social Action, National Coordinating Committee in Solidarity with Chile, National Lawyers Guild—Yale Chapter, New Haven American Independent Movement, War Resisters League, Women's International League for Peace and Freedom, and World Fellowship of Faiths. Yale Law School and Battell Chapel, the Church of Christ in Yale, made their facilities available for the conference. Arrangements for the publication of this volume were made by Howard Frazier of Promoting Enduring Peace with Charles E. Smith of The Free Press. Rosario Caicedo, Barbara Palumbo, Claudia Cairo Resnick, Eduarda Cavallaro, and Patricia Buck Wolf provided much needed assistance with typing, translation, and other important tasks. The presentations by Florencio Merced and Hortensia Bussi de Allende were made in Spanish by them at the conference and accompanied by English translation. The material by Florencio Merced appears here by permission of Mr. Merced and Susan Cantor. The material by Hortensia Bussi de Allende appears by permission of Sra. Allende and the National Coordinating Committee in Solidarity with Chile, New York, NY. The Spanish original of the passage from Pablo

Neruda at the close of Sra. Allende's presentation may be found in Pablo Neruda, *Obras Completas* (Buenos Aires: Editorial Losada, S.A., 1973), vol. 1, pp. 573–574 (the English translation is by Waldeen and is used by permission of Farrar, Straus & Giroux, Inc., New York, NY). The material by Winslow Peck is taken from *Counter-Spy*, 2, no. 1 (Fall 1974), in which it appeared in slightly different form as "Clandestine Enforcement of U.S. Foreign Labor Policy." Mr. Peck's presentation at the conference was based on this article. Peter J. O'Connell of New Haven, Connecticut, acted as editorial coordinator for the preparation of the manuscript and saw it through production.

Uncloaking the CIA

Introduction

Howard Frazier and Martin Cherniack

UNCLOAKING THE CENTRAL INTELLIGENCE AGENCY has been a major task of the American Left and liberal communities recently. The obfuscations that have characterized government operations for more than a decade are even more gross when the CIA is involved: expenditures are legally hidden; the major press is ridden with willing watercarriers for the Agency (as demonstrated by the censoring of the *Glomar Explorer* debacle and other CIA–Hughes empire connections); congressional oversight committees are controlled by CIA collaborators, such as Representative Lucien Nedzi. Much of the protest against the CIA derives from two pieces of information in 1974: Representative Michael J. Harrington's revelation of CIA expenditures of $8 million on covert activities from 1970 to 1973 to overthrow the government of Salvador Allende of Chile and Seymour Hersh's revelation in the *New York Times* of 10,000 CIA domestic files (a figure that the Rockefeller Commission later upped to 13,000 dossiers, 300,000 personal indexes, and 1,000 organization files).

In an attempt to close this information gap, Promoting Enduring Peace, Inc., initiated the idea of a national conference on the CIA. Promoting Enduring Peace is a nonprofit organization of a religious and educational nature that reprints and distributes articles having to do with world peace, conducts peace seminars and tours in various countries of the world, and presents the annual Gandhi Peace Award. This idea was endorsed by a number of other organizations, and the Conference on the CIA and World Peace was held at Yale University on April 5, 1975.

The conference was, we believe, one of the most significant gatherings yet of critics of the intelligence establishment. Participants included: Victor Marchetti, John D. Marks, Winslow Peck, and L. Fletcher Prouty—all former members of the intel-

1

ligence community; Third World representatives Hortensia Bussi de Allende of Chile, Sokhom Hing of Cambodia, Ngo Vinh Long of Vietnam, and Florencio Merced of Puerto Rico; and prominent domestic critics such as Fred Branfman, Ernest De Maio, Frank Donner, Michael J. Harrington, Mark Lane, Winslow Peck, and Kirkpatrick Sale. The conference was successful beyond the expectations of its sponsors. We were obliged to revise our estimate of people's attention spans as an audience of 1,400 participated in thirteen consecutive hours of speeches and panels presenting what amounted to an electrifying account of the program of what one speaker called "the political police of American capitalism."

A few of the specific items of that program discussed were the following:

> The background to the attempt to censure Congressman Harrington for revealing information about CIA activities in Chile.
>
> The negotiations between ex-CIA officers and arms manufacturers for submachine guns with silencers and unmarked ammunition.
>
> The use of torture.
>
> The wrecking of foreign unions that threaten U.S. corporate interests.
>
> The collusion between the CIA and ITT to destroy Allende's government.
>
> The funneling of $1 million into the 1972 campaign of the then ruling Puerto Rican political party.
>
> The financing of the protests that helped bring down the Allende government.
>
> The printing of manuals on sabotage for Chilean bureaucrats, technicians, and business people.
>
> The obtaining of helicopters so that Marshal Ky could smash his Buddhist opposition.
>
> The backing of Lon Nol's coup in Cambodia.
>
> The obtaining of a Sihanouk imitator to broadcast falsely in the name of the Cambodian prince.
>
> The hiring of "secret armies" in Indochina.
>
> The operation of the Phoenix program in Vietnam, whose more than 40,000 murders (according to South Vietnamese statistics) were directed by William Colby over the resistance of the South Vietnamese government.

The recruitment of mercenaries to operate in Africa.

The funneling of millions of dollars to the Socialist Party of Portugal.

The control of a secret corporate empire.

The infiltration of the universities for CIA research and recruitment.

The keeping of files on domestic political dissidents.

The development of mind-control technology.

The assassination attempts against foreign leaders.

The training of the elite guards of foreign leaders.

The efforts to prevent Jim Garrison from investigating the connection between Clay Shaw and the assassination of John Kennedy.

The splitting of the trade union movement in various countries.

The manipulation of the AFL-CIO.

The CIA's smokescreen that it is mainly involved in gathering information with only occasional sallies into covert political operations and that it is only a defensive response ("counter-intelligence") to the much larger operations of the Soviet KGB is indefensible. Its now notorious practices—corruption, sabotage, assassination—are aimed against the forces of reform and revolution in Third World countries and in the service of the "Pax Americana" of repression and unequal distribution of wealth preferred by American multinational corporations. Hortensia Allende called this peace "the peace of the cemetery." The intelligence establishment's domestic operations show that it has tried out for the role of gravedigger of liberty at home as well as abroad.

This volume contains the most important presentations made at or prepared in connection with the conference. In some instances virtually direct transcripts of speeches have been printed. Victor Marchetti, for example, is forbidden by court order to write anything without CIA review, so his words had to be recorded. Some presentations have been revised for publication for such purposes as including more detail than was possible at the conference or taking into account some developments in the months following it. Where such revisions are extensive, they are noted in the introductory material to the selection. The degree to which events since April 1975 have confirmed the analyses presented at the conference is striking.

As a whole, we believe this book to be a cross-section of the most penetrating kinds of criticism directed at the invisible government that controls so much of our foreign policy—and domestic policy as well. Points of view vary, though most speakers at the conference called for the elimination of the Agency, or at least of its covert operations, echoing Kirkpatrick Sale's evaluation that it would not "automatically cleanse the American system" if there were no more CIA but it would be "an important start, and worth working for." CIA Director William Colby was invited to present his views, but he chose not to appear or to send a representative.

All the speakers shared an understanding that the CIA operates in a larger matrix of conspiracy and surveillance with other institutions of business and government. The destruction of the Chilean economy would not have been possible, as Adam Schesch and Patricia Garrett and Hortensia Allende so clearly show, without the cooperation of private financial institutions, multinational corporations, and U.S.-controlled international agencies such as the World Bank. And it would be a fruitless victory simply to prohibit the CIA from maintaining domestic files while it has informational interlocks to FBI files and other domestic intelligence sources.

One of the most fortunate occurrences in both the conference and this book is the emergence of former insiders as critics. In practical terms only an insider can direct us through the maze of the intelligence bureaucracy. In another sense they demonstrate that even the bunker of Langley cannot be completely secure from humanitarian and internationalist impulses. Politics in the post-Vietnam era will not be identified by "isolationism," a meaningless invention of government phrasemongers who disguise imperialism, murder, and repression with epithets such as "free enterprise system" and "national security." The coming period will involve an active choice on the part of the American people between the greed of the great corporations, whose activities require the CIA, and identification with the emerging demands of the great mass of the world's peoples for a better life. Victor Marchetti predicted that the CIA's next and greatest battleground would be the United States itself. A struggle for the hearts and minds of Americans is under way between the CIA and its critics. The peace of the world may depend on the outcome.

The Problem and the Potential

Michael J. Harrington

■ Michael J. Harrington, a Democrat, has represented the sixth district of Massachusetts in the United States Congress since 1969. Earlier he had served on the Salem City Council and in the Massachusetts legislature. In Congress, Representative Harrington took a prominent role in opposition to U.S. involvement in Indochina. His attempts in 1974 to bring to light testimony about CIA activities against the Allende government of Chile led to his being barred access to the files of the House Armed Services Committee, but in late 1975 a House committee declined to take any further action against him, thus averting a major legal and political clash.

IN SEPTEMBER OF 1974 I was given the dubious privilege of being the subject of the first sustained interest the Congress has shown in the activities of the CIA. That interest consisted of a House Armed Services CIA Oversight Subcommittee hearing conducted by Lucien Nedzi. (Lucien Nedzi, you may recall, was later chosen by the Speaker to chair the House Select Committee on intelligence, the committee that might finally consider the establishment of rational bounds for the activities of the CIA.) The purpose of the subcommittee hearing was for me to explain how the *New York Times* and the *Washington Post* had acquired their stories about CIA intervention in Chile. The committee members were somewhat disappointed because all that I could honestly plead guilty to was my intention: I had been determined that the United States Congress and the American public should ultimately be made aware of what the CIA had done in our name to a democratically elected government.

In a broader sense, I have questioned the responsibility of an elected official who discovers that the CIA has illegally interfered with the domestic politics of another nation. I wanted the House Select Committee to address this issue because the classification process has been seriously abused. The problem with the secrecy system is that it permits those who know about illegal activities to remain silent; in fact, it encourages them to do so. Moreover, it paints as guilty those who do live up to their responsibilities and refuse to take part in the cover-up of illegal activities. The secrecy system simply makes it too easy for elected officials to acquiesce in an institutionalized process that, for example, keeps the truth about illegal covert activities from the American people.

I have had a rather unchanneled interest over a number of years in the issue of the intelligence community. The problem has really been to try to find a way to define that issue as more than a broad discussion of the problems posed by the existence of a secrecy system in a democracy. Rather, at this point, we need a more specific interest to ascertain precisely what we have done—with Chile perhaps the best example. As was true for the impeachment process, however, both the Congress and the American people need consciousness-raising before they are willing to grapple seriously with the general and more difficult issues. And one method of effecting that consciousness-raising, I might add, is the publicity that surrounds revelation of specific outrages.

But this process is itself a slow one. In preparing to testify against the confirmation of ambassadors Shlaudeman and Davis, I checked with the Armed Services Committee to see how many of my colleagues had taken the time, given all the furor, to read the controversial testimony given by CIA Director Colby describing our intervention in Chile. There were only two names on the checkout sheet for the classified testimony: mine on June 4, 1974, and again mine on June 12, 1974.

That revelation gave me some insight into the kind of attitudinal problems that exist in discussions of this issue. Apparently there is a basic, pervasive view perhaps best expressed by President Ford on September 16, 1974. When asked about the operation in Chile, the President responded in a fashion that suggested that our justification in breaking the law lies in the fact that our enemies did it first and do it "all the time." The problem is that that kind of opinion has some rather strange allies supporting it. They do not necessarily come from a southern or rural or "backwater" view of the world either. I think, rather, that they have substantial appeal even at the editorial board level of the *New York Times* and the *Washington Post* and perhaps with much of the public. This situation is precisely the sort of thing that it is going to be extremely difficult to get the Rockefeller Commission or the House Committee to consider at all seriously. In no other way, however, will the country as a whole begin to focus on it.

This sort of thing does have a chance of being reflected in the current Congress, given that it was elected in 1974, the year of a weakened presidency. I do not, however, have a serious expectation that there will be, all of a sudden, a major metamorphosis in the intelligence community.

I think progressive citizens have a difficult but rewarding job ahead. We should take advantage of the opportunities afforded by 1974's occurrences and begin to raise fundamental questions in a way that has some specific meaning. But it should be understood, too, that from an institutional perspective changes are going to be painfully slow in coming. That the *Washington Post*, the *New York Times*, and Evans and Novak all endorsed the *Glomar Explorer* experiment, which probably cost more than all our intelligence in World War II, indicates the attitudinal block we are up against.

What I am suggesting is that we may finally have a foothold for beginning to face an issue that not only fascinates and awes, but also increasingly frightens and disturbs those who consider its implications.

There is one thing we should not underestimate, however, and that is the fact that, just as we have lost some traditional allies whose opinions differ from ours on this issue, we can also expect to gain aid and support from areas and groups that we are not accustomed to having support us. The CIA issue may well cross all the alignments that have characterized the American political landscape for the last half generation. I think that this issue is a populist one and that we can seriously expect support of people from everywhere who will be appalled when they find out exactly what their government has done to other governments in their name.

I do wish, however, to temper the feeling that we have this thing on the run, or that the House and Senate committees or the Rockefeller Commission out of their own volition will go into these areas extensively and in the end make any substantial difference. If by chance any change is forthcoming from them, I think that they will probably have done the right thing for the wrong reasons. My cynicism may be unjustified, but I think that it is possible that change may happen because there is a fatal preoccupation of many people with this kind of avocation. Despite the fact that they know of the danger to their own ability to survive, their fascination with this kind of activity will compel them to go back again to the sources of popular concern and discontent. It will be they, as I told Mr. Colby, who will ultimately lead to the destruction of the covert activities.

We should be aware of the possibility and be prepared to take advantage of the experience we have had recently. If one looks at the way the House handled impeachment—that Dean's testimony lay uncontradicted for months, that the House didn't act until the walls were being pulled down from within—then I think we should be wary of those who think we are already on the way to success.

The United States Congress does not willingly trespass into unknown territory. We do not willingly take risks. And we never, particularly if we are ambivalent about the preservation of an institution, engage in investigative activities that could conceivably go further than our more conservative members would like.

All of these points notwithstanding, it is my firmly held belief that we will not only see success in raising the key issue, but will also gain surprisingly strong support from many people who, once they realize the subtleties of the issue, will find that the kind of CIA activities critics condemn only make our own country more like the countries Americans have considered to be our antithesis.

Now or Never

■ Victor Marchetti served with the CIA from 1955 to
1969, rising to the position of executive assistant
to the deputy director. He is coauthor with John Marks
of The CIA and the Cult of Intelligence (1974). The
CIA brought suit in an attempt to cause substantial
deletions in that book. The courts allowed the book to
be published but ordered certain deletions. The book
as published indicates the portions the CIA wished
deleted but that the courts allowed and has blank
spaces for the deletions sustained by the courts.

THE PUBLIC is finally becoming aware. Even people who once were devoted followers or employees of the CIA are beginning to ask some questions that they would have never asked just a few years ago. But I also think that we should not become too optimistic because we are becoming aware of the problem of the CIA. The CIA is not going to roll over and play dead.

The CIA is powerful, arrogant, and elitist. It was precisely because of this attitude that they got themselves into the trouble that they are in now both strategically and tactically. I do not think that they ever believed that a couple of former CIA and military intelligence people speaking out against the intelligence community could possibly produce enough interest among the public. The CIA never thought that investigative journalists could gather enough information to arouse the public and the Congress. I think that they were absolutely convinced that the various "senior senilities" in the Senate and House could protect them. The biggest shock the CIA ever had was when the Senate voted 82 to 6 to form a special committee to investigate it. But now they are over the shock and are fighting back.

The next big CIA push will be in this country, not overseas. It is not going to be a matter of the CIA penetrating or manipulating foreign organizations or overthrowing foreign governments. Of course, I am sure that they will do that kind of thing, too. They are extremely concerned about Portugal, Italy, the Middle East, Latin America, and many other areas. But I think we are going to see the CIA emphasizing a domestic operation whose primary goal will be to convince the American people that the CIA should go unpunished and uncontrolled.

We have to understand some basic things about the CIA. You cannot think of it in a vacuum. In the first place, it is not the only intelligence organization in the United States government. There are several others, and many of these others are involved in clandestine activities too. Although there is some bureaucratic rivalry between the agencies, there is general cooperation. There are at least sixty government agencies that have intelligence components. Intelligence activities of a clandestine nature have proliferated throughout the country at the state and local levels. This is why the CIA wants to train local police. This is why the CIA has a Domestic Operations Division.

The Domestic Operations Division is an area division. It is just like the divisions responsible for Latin America, for Africa, for Europe, for the Soviet Union, for China, for the Far East, for the Middle East. They call it the Domestic Operations Division, but I think that they should call it the United States Division. It is definitely an area division in the way it works. The difference is that this area is more sensitive and requires more secrecy. Instead of having its offices at CIA headquarters in Langley, Virginia, it has them elsewhere. Instead to having bases in Bogota, Calcutta, or Lisbon, it has them in Boston, Chicago, and Los Angeles. Its domestic operatives act just like operatives overseas would act.

Just think for a minute how an overseas CIA base operates. You can have just five men at a base. But one man may be controlling the minister of the interior or the head of the trade unions. He may have recruited an ex-policeman to be in charge of the goon squad that breaks up demonstrations by rival groups. Another man can be controlling another series of agents. One can be a secretary in some important office; another can be a retired army officer in charge of a surveillance squad; and so on. When you add up, these five men, any contract people who may be attached to them, and the various agents they control may actually amount to hundreds and thousands of people. One man—whether he is overtly with the CIA (that is, under some sort of official cover in some city) or whether he is a "retired" CIA officer (who is, for example, the adviser on public safety to some mayor or governor)—with the right connections in the police department is, in effect, in control of that department.

The CIA has a lot of friends and powerful allies. These people are in Congress, big business, labor, and the media. There are also a lot of CIA alumni spread throughout the country working in police organizations, private security organizations, and a whole variety of pseudointelligence activities. Many of these people will come to the CIA's rescue because the CIA reflects the attitude of people who grew up in World War II and the Cold War, the attitude of people who still think in terms of nineteenth-century solutions to complex twentieth-century problems. Such people think that covert action by the CIA can solve complex economic and social problems. This attitude is prevalent among the most powerful and most influential people in our country. And they are going to come to the aid of the CIA.

The CIA may, if frightened enough, resort to the worst of possibilities, confirm the worst of our suspicions. When you find ex-CIA people in high positions in government agencies dealing with notorious arms manufacturers (people who are making weapons and submachine guns with silencers and ammunition that is completely unmarked), you wonder what such people might have in mind. Could they be readying contingency assassination plans against their opponents? Remember, the Pentagon has already developed contingency plans, such as Project Garden Plot, for a military takeover of our country should the President declare a state of national emergency.

Despite this awful possibility, I do not want to frighten people completely. We will have to deal with a CIA public relations campaign before we will have to deal with any other kind of campaign. We are going to see more and more books coming out favorable toward the CIA. We are going to find the CIA's friends writing nice little articles about the freedom that the CIA should have. We will have certain news magazines controlled by

CIA "groupies" defending the Agency and saying very positive things about it. All the CIA defenders will come together in an organized movement to attack people like John Marks, Philip Agee, Winslow Peck, and myself—everybody and anybody who was once on the inside and has been turned off. They are going to do it in some very devious ways. It is going to be so devious that I am not sure I can cope with them.

I had lunch at one time with a CIA figure who said that they are not going to leave the stage to the Marchettis and the Agees but are going to take them on. There was nothing personal in it, he said. He wanted me to know that he felt that he and I could work together. He felt we could appear together, discussing something like "The Congress Is about to Try the CIA." He had lunch with me in a restaurant owned by CIA people. It is getting so that agents have said to me, "I understand that you are still working with the CIA."

This is just one example of what we are going to have to put up with. There is going to be an all-out campaign. We can be sure of it.

The CIA men are not only arrogant, powerful, and elitist. They are also smart, clever, and ruthless. It is now or never for us and for them. If Congress does not have a real investigation and put some very tight controls on the CIA, we will never get another chance.

Hearing the Screams

John D. Marks

■ John D. Marks, a former State Department intelligence officer, is an associate of the Center for National Security Studies. He is coauthor, with Victor Marchetti, of The CIA and the Cult of Intelligence, which the CIA attempted to censor.

WHAT THE CIA HAS DONE around the world is quite impressive when you add it up over the years. Starting in the late 1940s, the CIA tried to organize resistance movements in Albania, Poland, and the Ukraine, although it made no headway. It was much more successful in organizing and subsidizing anticommunist political parties, labor unions, newspapers, and politicians all over Western Europe. But as the European situation stabilized in the early 1950s, the CIA increasingly turned its attention to the less developed countries of Asia, Africa, and Latin America.

In 1953 the CIA overthrew the Iranian government and restored the Shah to power—something to be remembered as oil prices rise. In 1954 the CIA mounted a counterrevolution in Guatemala and installed a new regime. In 1958 the CIA tried to overthrow the Sukarno government in Indonesia but failed. President Eisenhower lied openly about that intervention. In 1961 the CIA tried to overthrow the Castro government in Cuba at the Bay of Pigs and failed miserably. The CIA, however, continued for most of the decade to support guerrilla operations against Cuba, to sabotage the Cuban economy, and to organize at least half a dozen assassination attempts against Castro, some involving the Mafia. (The CIA's use of the Mafia has shocked many people and caused some wonderful arguments about which organization has more honor.) In Chile the CIA tried to

13

stop Salvador Allende in the 1958 elections, the 1964 elections, and the 1970 elections, failing in this last case. Finally, the Agency "destabilized" Allende's government in 1973. In Indochina there was continued CIA intervention from the early 1950s to the present. In fact, there is not a country in the Third World where the CIA has not intervened in one fashion or another over the years. We all know this reality very well.

That is why I want to concentrate on two stories. The first one is told by Philip Agee. Agee is a former CIA operative who now resides in England and has written a book called *Inside the Company: CIA Diary* (New York: Stonehill, 1975), which is the most detailed account of what the CIA actually does in specific countries. He minutely describes the CIA's operations in Ecuador, Uruguay, and Mexico. Agee was in Uruguay—the country where the movie *State of Siege* was set—from 1964 to 1966. He was the CIA's contact man with the local police and intelligence services. He was the person who recruited CIA agents in the Uruguayan secret police and gave them money and helped in their training.

At one point in 1965 Agee passed on to the head of the Montevideo police intelligence division the name of a local leftist leader, which Agee had learned through his own intelligence sources. A few days later Agee was in the office of the Montevideo police chief. They were talking about the normal business of the day when Agee started to hear moans from down the hall. He knew immediately what those screams were: a man was being tortured. At that point Agee had the terrible feeling that perhaps the man he had just fingered to the Uruguayan police was the person being tortured down the hall. He did not want, however, to say anything because he felt that he might hurt the delicate relations between the CIA and the Montevideo police force. At the same time the police chief was similarly embarrassed, and he kept ordering a subordinate to turn up a radio that was playing in the room. After the radio got louder and louder, the meeting was finally ended. Two days later Agee found out that the tortured man was indeed the local leftist he had fingered to the police force.

This is the firsthand account of a CIA operative who was on the spot. So far no one has challenged Agee's facts. Many people have challenged his politics and motivations, but nobody has dared to challenge his facts, even the CIA.

Now I want to report a portion of a recent interview that I had with another ex-CIA operative. This person had served in Latin America and Vietnam and talked to me very frankly about his experiences. Before I start, I should explain what the Provincial Interrogation Centers, or PICs, were. These were large buildings that the CIA constructed in every Vietnamese province, complete with interrogation rooms, detention cells, offices for the American and Vietnamese employees, and so on. Nothing has been changed in the interview except a few words that protect the identity of the CIA man who is talking.

CIA Operative: I never personally thought in terms of morality. I received a directive: this is what has to be accomplished, and I was graded on achieving objectives. Get it done. Now if someone had made out an assignment to kill somebody, I certainly would have worried about the morality of that. But if I were working against Che Guevara, what the hell! Whatever he was doing was totally illegal. So I would do everything I could do to get him, even if it were illegal. Which is the greater illegality?

John Marks: That seems to be an attitude which is rather common in the CIA: that everything is for the greater good and for the national security.

CIA Operative: Again, I can't think of ever setting out or even wanting somebody to be hurt or maimed or killed. There were illegalities, but they were little illegalities. And if someone got hurt, generally speaking, it would be when we didn't have pure control of the operation. And by that, I mean when we were using the police, because with these people, their mentality is different than ours. They're totally brutal. They used to publicize those PICs over in Vietnam; they were under our jurisdiction and control. And they drove me up a damn wall! Spending half of my time going from PIC to PIC, and, by God, I had those things neat and clean and orderly. And then the next thing I'd find is that in one province some Vietnamese had gotten the hell beaten out of him. That was never authorized or directed. We would raise all kinds of hell, and it was like talking to a stone wall.

These people [the Vietnamese] just have the mentality that

force and might make right, and they totally hate and dislike one another. They're going to beat the hell out of each other. The CIA assumed an awful lot of blame. Our only responsibility was to set these things up. Of course, we had the functional jurisdiction to provide funding and advice to the PICs, which were operated by the Special Branch police. We did have some power over the Special Branch too, since we were supporting and financing them. But the torture, there were times when we even didn't know about it. We'd hear about it because some newspaperman was floating through the area, and somehow he'd find out. We'd read about the torture in the paper, and we'd get a cable from Saigon asking: What in the name of God is happening in your damn PIC now? But we never, as an agency, instigated either torture or violence.

Now there were times when we knew the way certain policemen were. Guatemalans are vicious, and they'll stand somebody up in a basement, or put him in cold freezing water, and so on and so forth. And maybe the Brazilians use their electronic devices and so forth. We would know that. We would tell them not to. They would say, "All right, we're not going to do it." But we [the CIA] were not going to be present during these interrogations. Again, because I don't like to see that sort of thing. If I am there, they're not going to do it in all probability. And as soon as I leave, they're going to haul the guy back. They'd tell me: "We talked to him for two hours." Hell, they'd keep him for twenty-four hours. We would know this. We do try to get them to change their techniques and procedures, but they're not going to change. They never have, and they never will. And they know damn well that if they ever get thrown out of power, they are going to undergo the same treatment because of the revenge motive. In some of these countries, it's been working back and forth for a hundred years and will always continue to do so. But by the time it gets publicized, because the Agency is maybe supporting, financing, or even advising a given group, whatever that group does, then its sins come back to haunt the Agency. And it really isn't fair, and that's how most of us would look on it when we were involved.

This ex-CIA man is giving a terrifying example of the "clandestine mentality" that is so common in that agency. He is to-

tally separating his own personal mentality from the acts that the CIA and its agents are committing in the name of our "national security." He is the kind of person who should be eliminated from positions of power and influence. He is also the kind of person who is not going to tell the truth to a Senate committee. Yet he is a man who loves his children, who mows his lawn. If you would speak with him, you would find him reasonably charming. In other words, he is a human being, not a mindless automaton. But he completely separates his work for the CIA from any sense of personal morality. This is a very important distinction.

The time has come for the rest of us to take on some responsibility for these kinds of actions, which are being committed in our name all over the world. We can keep our radios turned up only so loud, then eventually we have to hear the screams. The time has come to eliminate the clandestine portion of the CIA, to make the United States subject to at least a minimum standard of international law and decency. Defenders of the CIA argue that while the Soviets have their secret police, the United States cannot give up its own similar weapon in the international struggle. I would remind you that bacterial warfare is a very effective weapon in international struggles but that the United States has decided, for reasons of its own, that germ warfare is below the minimum standard of decency on which we will operate. The "dirty tricks" and covert actions of the CIA are also below that minimum standard. The sooner the United States gets out of such activities, the better.

Strongarm of the TNCs

Ernest De Maio

■ Ernest De Maio was a union organizer in Connecticut, Pennsylvania, and the Midwest in the 1930s. He has been district president and general vice-president of the United Electrical, Radio and Machine Workers of America, vice-president of the Illinois state CIO, treasurer of the Illinois CIO Political Action Committee, and a member of the Radio and Radar Division of the War Production Board. He is now permanent representative of the World Federation of Trade Unions to the United Nations.

IF WE ARE TO UNDERSTAND the CIA, we must first take a look at the socioeconomic system that spawned it. Our society is a system based on the exploitation of the many by a few who own and control the capital goods that produce the nation's wealth and the financial institutions that are its lifeblood. These powerful few with their great economic resources control the political life of the nation. They maintain a shadow government that makes the basic decisions that are relayed to the executive and legislative branches of the overt government through henchmen placed in strategic positions throughout the federal apparatus.

This situation is reflected in the interlocking relationships between the major industrial and financial corporations and government. Such interlocking is the major reason for corruption in government. The purpose of government as conceived by the Founding Fathers was to promote the general welfare. The

shadow government has prostituted this into promoting the welfare of the generals—General Electric, General Dynamics, and the Pentagon brass.

Over the years government has gotten beyond the reach of the people. Unable to influence the government, frustrated and alienated, voters are avoiding the election polls like the plague. They have been the victims of presidential lies and deception. As if witnessing shades of imperial Rome, they have seen the White House put on the auction block. CREEP [Committee to Reelect the President] was Nixon's bagman. It collected from the major corporations for presidential favors at the expense of the people.

This corruption did not, however, go unnoticed or unchallenged. There were courageous men and women in the universities, the arts and sciences, and the trade unions. They spoke out, organized, and held meetings. But their ranks were infiltrated by government agents. Paid informers fingered the brave and testified that they were subversives, agents of a foreign power, or part of a vague catch-all called the "communist conspiracy." How many will recall that even President Eisenhower was called a card-carrying Communist and the Supreme Court a part of the Communist conspiracy? The mass media turned the witch hunt into a Roman cricus. Lives and careers were destroyed.

After over forty years of surveillance and investigations by the FBI, I can't get too excited about the fact that the CIA has also gotten into the act. But I'm not dismissing the CIA. I believe that neither the CIA, the FBI, the IRS, the Army, nor any other agency of government should be allowed to do the dirty work of the transnational corporations (the TNCs) if we are to remain a free people. The transnational corporations not only dominate the U.S. scene, but also have extended their tentacles throughout most of the world.

The most important historical development in recent years is the rise of the once-colonial nations that have cast off their imperialist oppressors. They have established political independence. In many of these new nations, however, the old imperial masters still control the economy. The raw materials, utilities, transport, and such industry as they have are controlled by transnational corporations based mainly in the United States. For example, anyone familiar with the economic history of

South America, its trade and payments patterns, knows that the major U.S. corporations have bled that continent white. Our government, fronting for these corporations, has used its military power to keep it that way for years.

In this "enlightened" age, however, the U.S. government does not necessarily resort to naked military power. There are other options. Military intervention only occurs after other efforts have failed. We train military officers from other countries, corrupt them, and then use them to overthrow governments their people have elected to power.

Chile, though, was something out of the ordinary. Democracy was strongly entrenched, and the military tolerated civilian control. The Chileans were trying something new. They sought to achieve control of their economic and political destiny by peaceful means through the electoral process. Despite considerable CIA interference, Salvador Allende, at the head of a Marxist coalition, won a plurality of votes in a tight three-way election. Nothing that ITT and the copper trust did could keep Allende out of the presidency. This experiment in peaceful change was aborted by the intervention of the U.S. government. The CIA was used to destabilize the Allende regime.

Chapter 11, Article 1 of the Charter of Economic Rights and Duties of States, adopted by the United Nations over U.S. objections, reads as follows:

> Every state has the sovereign and inalienable right to choose its economic system as well as its political, social and cultural systems in accordance with the will of its people, without outside interference, coercion or threat in any form whatsoever.

Article 2, section 1 states:

> Every state has and shall freely exercise full permanent sovereignty, including possession, use and disposal, over all its wealth, natural resources and economic activities.

Needless to say, these principles did not guide our government in Chile. Where the imperial right of U.S. transnational corporations to exploit other peoples is involved, our government will do whatever has to be done to preserve that dubious right.

The details of what the CIA did or let happen in Chile; the

assassination of generals who stood in the way; the bribing of others to carry out the coup; the slaughter, arrest, and torture of thousands will be told by others. There are, however, a few points I would like to make. After the coup, *all* political parties —right, center, and left—were banned. The Congress building is now the national headquarters of the military police. All opposition newspapers have been closed down. The universities are run by the military. The escudo during the latter days of the Allende regime exchanged at 500 to the U.S. dollar. On March 3, 1975, the *New York Times* reported that the escudo had again been devalued to 2,900 to the dollar. This action is an official devaluation for foreign purposes of 580 percent in eighteen months. When we think of the distress caused by 12 percent inflation in this country in 1974, we can only guess at the mass misery that prevails under conditions of almost total impoverishment in Chile.

A reliable yardstick to measure the degree of democracy that exists in any society is the existence of trade unions that effectively defend and advance the interests and welfare of the workers. We now know that the CIA did some of its most destructive work in the Chilean trade unions. It corrupted leaders and financed strikes against the Allende government. Its objective was not simply to make apolitical unions under the aegis of the American Institute of Free Labor Development, the infamous industry- and CIA-financed AFL-CIO front for the building of class-collaborationist unions in South America. Its purpose, aided, abetted, and financed by the CIA, was to wreck a friendly government.

The consequences to the workers have been an unrelieved disaster. The honest trade union leaders were arrested, tortured, and murdered. Others were driven underground or exiled. Union headquarters were padlocked. Now the unions cannot function. The corrupt CIA-supported unionists who struck against Allende are not leading strikes today against far worse conditions. The ruling junta has been trying to set up a labor front with them without success.

There have been several CIA-engineered counterrevolutions in Latin America. But none has been as savage in its consequences as the Chilean coup. It seems that we are engaged in the reprehensible business of trying to drown revolutionary ideas in blood. It hasn't worked in Southeast Asia. It didn't work in Greece or Portugal. It isn't working in Spain. And it won't work in Chile.

What is happening in the world today is not the falling of dominoes. It is the growing resentment and reaction of the peoples of the world against our TNC-run government. The corrupt code of sharp business practices is a poor and unworkable substitute for the high principles of the Founding Fathers of our country.

The events in Chile have added a new dimension to the age-old struggle of peoples for political, economic, and social emancipation. It has already lowered the tolerance levels of acceptable opposition in the ongoing struggle for the minds of the people. The immediate reaction in Peru to the Chilean developments was to close down the opposition press. In Portugal the irresponsible ultraleft and right suspected of CIA connections have been restricted.

When the U.S. government failed to redeem its pledges to aid in the reconstruction of North Vietnam, when it continued to aid the Thieu regime in its violations of the Paris Peace Agreement, when it continued its reactionary role in Cambodia, the revolutionary forces of Southeast Asia responded in what they believe from long and bitter experience to be the only language the U.S. government understands.

The demise of our client states is predictable. What bothers me most is this question: If we permit the CIA and other agencies of our government effectively to deny to other people their democratic rights and aspirations, how long do we retain them for ourselves? When our government engages in economic warfare, subsidizes the opposition press, organizes strikes, disruption, and mass demonstrations, it is crippling the normal democratic process and the economy of countries. It prevents the small adjustments in policies and application that resolve day-to-day problems and keeps them from becoming big, unwieldy, and explosive. If we have contempt for the legal process in other countries, can we maintain respect for the law here? Watergate was bringing home to the American people what our government practices abroad.

The shadow government is conducting an unannounced subliminal campaign. The general outline of its propositions is that democracy is slow and cumbersome. It questions whether democracy can survive the conditions created by modern technology. It suggests that what is required to meet the problems posed by current realities is an authoritarian state, a euphemism for fascism. Some say we should strengthen the presidency. To what point? Dictatorship?

The only form of government that works for the people is democracy. It is hardly necessary to recount the transient glories of Mussolini's Italy, Hitler's Germany, Salazar's Portugal, the colonels' Greece, and Franco's Spain. The handwriting is there for all to see. There is no future for fascism.

Democracy works. But it has been a long time since it has been effectively used. Democracy has been shelved. What we have is the inefficient government of, by, and for the transnational corporations. They have used their power to lower the living standards of the people. They have idled production facilities and millions of workers at a time when there are vast unmet personal and social needs. They have thwarted union organization and corrupted much of it. They have given us endless preparation for war. They have drafted our youth to die in brushfire wars to defend the vital interests of the TNCs. In their mad drive for maximum profits, they have created conditions that not only reduce their profits, but also threaten the stability of their own economic and social system.

When we go after the CIA, we are taking on the strongarm agency of the power structure. In this continuing endeavor we shall have to control and curb the monopolies and their transnational operations. They have the power of the government. We have the potential support of the people. It is an unequal contest. With history and the people on our side we cannot lose. In this desperate struggle the monopolies have already lost the battle for the minds of the people. This is why they resort to infiltration, entrapment, disruption, provocation, and terror.

No matter whether terror is physical or psychological, it is the weapon of the defeated. The monopolies cannot win, we cannot lose. The long journey begins with a single step. That step was taken some time ago. We must dedicate ourselves to mobilize the democratic forces of the people, to bring back to America government of, by, and for the people. In the untiring pursuit of this objective, we shall establish the basic prerequisite of enduring peace.

Crimes against
the People

Joelle Fishman

■ Joelle Fishman is executive secretary of the Communist Party in Connecticut and a member of the Central Committee of the Communist Party of the United States. She has been a writer and editor for several publications and is a correspondent for the Daily World. Her campaigns for the offices of congressional representative and mayor of New Haven achieved minor party ballot status for the Communist Party in Connecticut.

THE CIA CRIMES committed against the people of Latin America, Africa, and Portugal are the acts of a government body doing the bidding of ITT, Kennecott, Anaconda, and other corporations desperate in their attempts to maintain control of the people of the world.

It is now documented public knowledge that following the election of Salvador Allende in 1970, the CIA undertook to engineer economic chaos and military takeover in Chile at the cost of many lives and much bloodshed. The struggle for the freedom of Chilean political prisoners, for elementary rights for trade unions, and for an end to U.S. military and economic aid to the Chilean junta is a struggle against the CIA tentacles of U.S. imperialism. President Ford has called the CIA intervention in Chile "in the interest of the U.S." Of course, we know that it was not in the interest of the people of the United States to spend millions to destroy the Popular Unity government.

Rather, it was in the interest of those multinational corporations that had been nationalized in Chile.

The immediate possibility of a people's government, responsive to the needs of the people and not to U.S. monopolies, plus the existence of socialist Cuba, motivated the monopolies to prepare the coup in Chile, just as the strength of Cuba led to the Bay of Pigs invasion and unsuccessful attempts on the life of Fidel Castro.

In December of 1972 President Allende made an eloquent speech to the United Nations General Assembly exposing the machinations of U.S. corporations. I shall quote from it briefly:

> Before the conscience of the world I accuse ITT of attempting to bring civil war in my country, the greatest possible source of disintegration of a country. That is what we call imperialist intervention. . . . The aggression of the great capitalist enterprises is intended to prevent the emancipation of the working class. . . . Chile is a nation which has attained the political maturity to decide by majority vote to replace the capitalist economic system by the socialist. . . . It is my duty to inform this Assembly that the reprisals and economic blockade that have been employed in an attempt to produce a chain reaction of difficulties and economic upsets represent a threat to domestic peace and coexistence. . . . It cannot hope, however, that any political or judicial power will in the long run deprive Chile of what is legitimately its own.

The ruthless acts of the CIA are continuing now in Portugal. The Portuguese have charged that U.S. Ambassador Frank Carlucci has tried to engineer a Chile-style coup against their government and is continuing his attempts with a group operating out of Spain. At the same time the newly independent African countries that were formerly Portuguese colonies are also being infiltrated in order that coups can be staged against their governments. Nathaniel Davis, who was U.S. ambassador to Chile and helped direct the CIA coup by the military, is now U.S. assistant secretary of state for African Affairs. And just as the CIA interfered in the democratic elections in Chile, the CIA financed the Popular Democratic Party candidates in Puerto Rico in order to protect the powerful imperialist interests in that country.

The CIA
in Puerto Rico

Florencio Merced

■ Florencio Merced is a member of the Political Commission of the Puerto Rican Socialist Party. He was president of the University Federation for Independence in Puerto Rico from 1958 to 1970. He directed the work of the Pro-Independence Movement, predecessor of the Puerto Rican Socialist Party, in San Juan from 1971 to 1975. He participated in the Fourth Conference of Non-Aligned Nations in 1973 and has headed delegations of the Puerto Rican Socialist Party to Cuba and other countries, and to the United Nations.

PUERTO RICO, my homeland, is a Latin American country militarily intervened in by the United States government since 1898.

The geographic area of our national territory is just a little over 9,000 square kilometers. It would be a grave error, however, to conclude from this fact that the occupation of our island is of minimal importance to the United States government.

North American capital investment in Puerto Rico surpasses $9 billion. The fabulous profits obtained from these investments are far greater than those that would be obtained from similar investments within the United States national territory. In more concrete terms, Puerto Rico constitutes the United States' fifth largest market in the world and its second largest market in the Americas. The economic interests of United States capital in our country constitute more than a third of all North American interests in Latin America as a whole.

One of the most important functions served by the political and military intervention to which Puerto Rico is subjected is our economic exploitation. But we would again be wrong if we were to limit our judgment of the importance of our colonial condition for North American capital to the aspect of economic exploitation alone.

North American imperialism has for years used Puerto Rico as a launching point for penetration throughout the rest of Latin America and the world.

North American intervention in our country is of such magnitude, and the prevailing system of such a nature, that we can affirm that Puerto Rico is among the countries where the greatest number of North American intelligence and repressive agencies operate. United States Army and Marine Corps intelligence agencies also operate there. Federal courts operate openly, and practically all of the laws passed by the United States Congress are applied in our country. We should also add to these the colonial administration's intelligence agencies, its courts, and the rest of its repressive apparatus. The colonial administration's repressive intelligence apparatus is at this very moment receiving millions of dollars from the North American federal government through programs established by the Law Enforcement Assistance Act.

We used to joke about our luck by saying that the Federal Bureau of Investigation operated in Puerto Rico because they considered us North American territory and the Central Intelligence Agency also operated in Puerto Rico because they considered us foreign territory. Now we are not sure. After the discovery of the existence of the Domestic Operations Division of the Central Intelligence Agency and its activities in the United States, it is possible that the CIA as well as the FBI agree that our island is "a territory pertaining to the United States government." What is really important is that we Puerto Ricans continue to consider ourselves as a Latin American nation in which the United States government has intervened.

The Central Intelligence Agency as well as other intelligence agencies and instruments of repression used by the federal government in Puerto Rico act in every way possible to stop the development of our people's struggle for national independence and all that this struggle represents in terms of social justice.

The seriousness of the Central Intelligence Agency's operations in our country does not lie merely in the fact that it involves an intelligence agency. Intelligence agencies exist all over the world and will go on existing as long as there are causes and interests that make them necessary. The main problem concerning the Central Intelligence Agency is not centered on the systems and methods that it uses but rather on whom it serves, even though these methods and means are determined precisely by the interests of those whom the Agency serves.

The Central Intelligence Agency in our country serves the power and interests that benefit by colonial intervention at the expense of the lives and jobs of Puerto Rican workers. At the same time, as we mentioned previously, Puerto Rico is used as an operations center with respect to the rest of the world, especially Latin America. Remember the "Showcase of Democracy" image of Puerto Rico sold to the Latin American continent? The deterioration of our economy and of the prevailing system when seen alongside the uninterrupted development of Cuba has nullified this role.

Our reality as a Latin American people, our situation as a link between Latin America and the United States, and the active struggle for independence taking place throughout our country and in the United States and becoming stronger during the present decade provide the setting that explains the Central Intelligence Agency's intense activity in Puerto Rico.

If we understand the interests served by the Central Intelligence Agency and the threat represented to these interests by the struggle for Puerto Rican independence, then it will be easy to understand why this agency operates in our country.

One of the first things the CIA does, wherever there are certain given conditions, is support the political parties representing the status quo and protect the interests served by the Agency. An eloquent example is the aid and support offered by the CIA to Eduardo Frei's Christian Democratic Party in Chile.

In our country it is a known fact that the CIA supported the Popular Democratic Party (PPD) in the 1972 elections. The CIA channeled about a million dollars into this party's electoral campaign, and the Popular Democratic Party won the elections. The cover-up for this maneuver was made possible by the celebration of a telethon in which the Popular Democratic Party supposedly collected more than $1.5 million in less than ten hours. Any way you want to look at it, it's impossible to collect that amount of money in that period of time with that kind of fund-raising activity in our country. It was later determined that the bank account used by the CIA to provide these funds was located in a bank in the Bahamas.

Once a government or colonial administration that has been backed by the CIA is established, the Agency guarantees that its policy is implemented by placing its own agents and creating its own connections within the government. There should be no doubt in our minds regarding the confession made by José Figueres, ex-president of Costa Rica, to the effect that he collaborated with the CIA for more than twenty years, even while acting as president of his country.

In Puerto Rico, to cite only one case, Governor Roberto Sánchez Vilella's first assistant during his 1964–1968 administration was a CIA agent. It is no longer a secret that Juan García Passalacque, a prominent Puerto Rican lawyer and professor, carried out that function while acting as special assistant to said governor. Ex-governor Sánchez Vilella himself has mentioned in private the problems he confronted resulting from CIA intervention during his administration.

In spite of all the CIA and other intelligence and repressive agencies' activities, our struggle for independence is becoming stronger, broader, and more extensive. Aware of this fact, the CIA has increased its activities against the independence forces.

The CIA's practice of falsifying documents concerning organizations that it combats is widely known. This practice has been used in Puerto Rico since the beginning of the 1960s. Before the election boycott carried out by the Pro-Independence Movement, predecessor of what is now the Puerto Rican Socialist Party, documents favoring electoral participation and signed by a group of Pro-Independence Movement members appeared. It was immediately verified that these documents were false and that the supposed group did not exist. Also in 1967 documents falsely bearing signatures of the Youth of the Pro-Independence Movement were found to be in circulation on an international scale.

Upon many occasions journalists have been angered by and have protested against the CIA's use of their profession as a front for its operations. In Puerto Rico the CIA does not only use the journalism profession but also completely controls news agencies. The only news agencies operating in our country are United Press International and Associated Press. The United Press International offices in San Juan are not allowed to publish anything occurring in the United Nations regarding Puerto Rico without specific permission from its New York office. This situation is obviously not simply a matter of a certain news agency's particular way of operating. It is a result of the CIA's penetration of the news world.

We might add that the main newspapers in the country have not taken part in the censorship of news of happenings regarding Puerto Rico in the United Nations. We shall return briefly to the CIA's contacts in the mass media when we talk about the CIA's operation within the trade union movement.

At times there are jobs that official instruments of repression should not, cannot, or do not want to do. The CIA intervenes in these cases. The aid given by this agency to the rightist organization *Patria y Libertad* in Chile is widely known.

The CIA has sponsored paramilitary groups in Puerto Rico. These groups originated from exiled Cubans and some extreme rightist organizations made up of Puerto Rican youth. The independence movement and its organizations have been victims of more than 125 armed attacks in the last four years, attacks by means of firearms, bombs, arson, and other methods.

Far from being uncertain of the CIA's participation in these attempts, the Puerto Rican Socialist Party has positive, concrete proof of its participation. We have publicly denounced various organizations by name as CIA fronts. In the case of the exiled Cubans, we have publicly pointed out one of their number employed by a government agency as the CIA agent in charge of coordinating his group's clandestine activities with another CIA agent. The latter agent is also responsible for the coordination of some sectors of Puerto Rican youth connected with the pro-statehood New Progressive Party (PNP) and Young Americans for Freedom.

There are two important points about these armed attacks. The first is that nobody has been accused and condemned for them, including for the bombing of a legal public meeting of the Puerto Rican Socialist Party on January 11, 1975, in which two workers died. The second is that these attacks are not directed only against independence organizations. All of the Latin American countries with diplomatic representation in

San Juan who have renewed diplomatic relations with Cuba have also been bombed.

As for infiltration into leftist organizations and the creation of and support for shadow, divisive, and provocative groups, we find the more direct participation of the FBI as well as the more sophisticated participation of the CIA.

Finally, we want to denounce an intelligence operation being developed by the CIA in Puerto Rico at this time against the development and unity of the trade union movement.

Puerto Rican professor Wilfredo Matos stated in an article in our daily newspaper *Claridad:*

> We must study the experiences of other countries to understand how the United States Central Intelligence Agency intervenes in worker movements.
>
> Let's take a look at the example offered to us by the recently published book entitled *The Politics of Heroin in Southeast Asia* by Alfred McCoy.
>
> The place is France; the year, 1947. The French CGT was leading a general strike which was at the brink of paralyzing the whole country. The Communist Party was the party with the greatest influence within the CGT. Shortly after the beginning of the strike, the sector belonging to the French Socialist Party (a social-democratic party, non–Marxist-Leninist) broke away from the CGT forming a new central called Worker Power. According to McCoy's quotation of Thomas Braden, previous director of the international division of the CIA, which appeared in the May 20, 1967, edition of *The Saturday Evening Post,* the CIA was behind the Worker Power group and also behind the French Socialist Party.

Later in his article, Professor Matos comments:

> Are we perhaps immune to the CIA's actions? Aren't there the given conditions in our country so that our growing worker movement might also suffer the dissociating jolts prepared by the CIA, working in the interests of yankee capitalism as well as the bourgeois parties—the PPD and the PNP? Everyone knows that the organized worker movement in Puerto Rico has experienced tremendous growth within the past few years. New trade union leaders have appeared, working closely with older leaders who have remained faithful to the interests of the working class. Witnessing the

deterioration of capitalist projects in the colony, the working class has received a sound jolt accelerating its awakening. A working class Party has appeared and a structure which brings together different trade unions in an effort to increase the worker's capacity to act against their employers has arisen—of course we are referring to the United Workers Movement.

Here we want to add that the CIA, in attempting to divide the workers' movement and minimize the Puerto Rican Socialist Party's influence, has counted on the agents it has placed within the commercial daily press. As a matter of fact, there is more than one journalist having ties with the Agency who works actively in this way.

We are at present studying the possibility of the CIA's involvement in the attempt to create a trade union organization parallel to the United Workers Movement. This objective of the Latin American Workers' Confederation is being pushed in Puerto Rico by their representative there, a Cuban exile who came from Venezuela.

There are still more aspects and angles of CIA activity in Puerto Rico that we have not discussed. It would be impossible to cover everything in a short presentation. Besides, we are far from being experts and do not have the necessary means to be able to follow each and every step taken by the CIA. It is difficult if not impossible even for the experts and, therefore, far more difficult for us. I can, however, assure you that when we talk about CIA activities in our country, we are talking about something that has perhaps been studied little, but is very strongly felt. Those of us who struggle for structural change in Puerto Rico constantly come in contact in one way or another with CIA activity. We are not always able to decipher that activity, but we often detect it.

Our colonial situation, as well as any other colonial situation in the world, is a threat to world peace. CIA activity in Puerto Rico is proportionately an equal threat to world peace.

The Stinking Fish

Stanley Faulkner

■ Stanley Faulkner is an attorney in New York City.
A member of the International Association of Demo-
cratic Lawyers, he has designed litigation against
the CIA and is attorney for Luis Corvalan and Jose
Cademartori, political prisoners in Chile. He is the
author of "The War in Vietnam: Is It Constitutional?"
(Georgetown Law Journal, June 1968), Apartheid (with
Deep Ford; published by the African National Congress,
1974), Violation of Human Rights and International
Law in Chile (International Commission of Enquiry into
the Crimes of the Military in Chile, 1974), and War
Crimes (National Lawyers Guild, 1974).

THE MILITARY TAKEOVER in Chile has smothered that country
with a blanket of lawlessness by the ruling junta. There exists
in Chile today complete and total disregard of the rights of the
people. The very roots and foundation of a democratic government have been destroyed. It would be impossible to describe
fully how the people of Chile have been affected by the military
junta. In December 1974 and January 1975 alone, 1,500 people
were arrested without the charges against them being made
public.

The evidence now known clearly establishes that the CIA
played a major role in undermining the duly elected government of Chile. More than $8 million for clandestine activities
by the CIA was used in 1970–1973 to overthrow the Allende
government. This use of United States taxpayers' money was
approved by the 40 Committee headed by Secretary of State
Kissinger. Considering the exchange rate on the black market in

Chile, $8 million would have been really equivalent to more than $40 million.

The CIA secretly financed trade union groups for strike purposes as early as March 1972. Strike benefits were provided to support such strikes. We well remember the fifty days when there was a truckers' strike in the fall of 1972. The evidence now is that this strike also was supported through the CIA. This strike was followed by the strike of middle-class shopkeepers and a taxi strike, also amply subsidized.

The use of the CIA in subverting the political independence of a country is not new. There was the overthrow of Mossadegh in Iran in 1953 and Arbenz in Guatemala in 1954. Senator Fulbright, while Chairman of the Senate Foreign Relations Committee, put it this way: "This is a very old problem. The involvement of the CIA in other countries has been well known for years. There is not much news in that." I ask, if it was so well known, why didn't he do something about it?

And why did President Ford defend the CIA after revelations of its Chilean activities came out? Tom Wicker, writing in the *New York Times* of September 20, 1974, stated:

> The disclosure that the Central Intelligence Agency financed the series of strikes that preceded the overthrow of President Allende in Chile ought to make Gerald Ford hide his face. Either he has been conned by the CIA into grossly misleading the American people and giving his approval to international gangsterism, or he did it on his own.

Despite Ford and Kissinger's pronouncements, the truth is that all forms of the media operated freely during the Allende government. There was no censorship of the press, radio, or television. *Time* in its issue of September 30, 1974, called President Ford's remarks an "anachronistic, cold-war view of national security reminiscent of the 1950s." *Time* stated that Ford

> left the troubling impression, which the Administration afterward did nothing to dispel, that the U.S. feels free to subvert another government whenever it suits American policy.

Three United States government documents have been unearthed revealing State Department knowledge of and participation in CIA activities affecting the 1970 election in Chile and after. The first document was dated August 31, 1970, and dealt with the CIA recommendations for investing amounts ranging from \$350,000 to \$900,000 for covert activities in support of anti Allende forces.

The second document was dated September 4, 1970, the day Allende won the election by a slim vote. There was a proposal to bribe members of the Chilean Congress, who under the Chilean constitution would have to ratify the election and choose the president, not to vote for Allende. The 40 Committee recommended that \$350,000 be spent for this purpose.

The third document was dated July 25, 1973, just seven weeks before the coup that brought the junta to power. This document was a recommendation by the CIA for financing anti-Allende political parties, including a special amount of \$350,000 for the Christian Democratic Party and \$200,000 for the National Party.

Professor F. H. Bradley, late Fellow of Merton College, Oxford, wrote many aphorisms. I have selected the following: "Where all is rotten, it is man's work to cry 'stinking fish'."

The Case of Chile

Adam Schesch and Patricia Garrett

■ Adam Schesch, Ph.D. candidate in history at the
University of Wisconsin, and Patricia Garrett, Ph.D.
candidate in sociology at the University of Wisconsin, lived in Chile during the entire Allende administration. Adam Schesch did research there on popular
organizations in industries, housing projects, and
shantytowns and on political parties and their organizing tactics. Patricia Garrett did research on
Chilean women, agrarian reform, election results, and
the economic policies of the Allende government. Following the September 1973 coup that overthrew the
Allende government, Schesch and Garrett were arrested
and held in the National Soccer Stadium, where they
witnessed beatings and executions. The presentation
given by Adam Schesch at the Conference on the CIA and
World Peace was based on the experiences and research
of himself and Ms. Garrett.

U.S. GOVERNMENT and business operations overseas against popular movements actually consist of two diametrically opposed
operations: insurrection and repression. That is, they overthrow governments, and prop them up. In most cases the same
agencies carry out both assignments.

The operations are complex. They involve more than just
a few "cloak and dagger" operatives. With the backing of
several public and private agencies, including the CIA, they can
be shifted from a "solo" to a full "orchestra." The CIA role has
to be studied in connection with other government organizations, the multinational corporations, and their front groups.
Within the host society the operations include and affect more
than just a few individuals. Large numbers of people in differ-

ent socioeconomic strata of the target society are used one way or another in these operations.

Chile illustrates these points. The following description is developed mainly from personal observations. We lived and worked in Chile as academic researchers from November 1970 to September 1973. We are among the few Americans who were there from the beginning to the end of the Allende government. The point of view of this presentation is from the inside (of Chile) looking out. Documentation in detail for this overview can be found in three issues of *NACLA's Latin America & Empire Report*, published by the North American Congress on Latin America: "Chile: Facing the Blockade" (January 1973); "Chile: The Story Behind the Coup" (October 1973); and "U.S. Counter-Revolutionary Apparatus: The Chilean Offensive" (July–August 1974).

For the following discussion we have divided the U.S. intervention into economic, political, and military components.

Economic Intervention

Economic intervention can be divided into two stages. The first stage was concerned with the general destabilization of the Chilean economy as a whole. The second stage was directly related to the creation of the immediate preconditions for the coup that overthrew President Allende and the Popular Unity government in September 1973.

1. INVESTMENT CREDITS

U.S. banks organized an immediate boycott of Chile as soon as Salvador Allende entered office in 1970. Only five of thirteen international banks gave any credit at all. The lines of credit dropped from $230 million to less than $30 million within two months of the beginning of Allende's term of office.

2. MANIPULATION OF COPPER PRICES

A deliberate campaign was inaugurated to drive down the price of copper in 1971. Rumors were spread that the Chilean supplies were far greater than they were. (Chile is one of the four largest exporters of copper.) In 1971 the price of copper fell from $0.65 a pound to $0.48 a pound. Each penny drop in price meant a loss of $14 million in revenue to Chile.

3. BLOCKAGE OF SPARE PARTS AND MACHINERY

We witnessed the deliberate campaign to cripple day-to-day activities in Chile as we commuted to work on Santiago's buses. Most of the buses came from the U.S. By 1972 between one-quarter and one-third of Santiago's buses were out of commission because of the refusal of U.S. suppliers to sell the needed parts. This refusal occurred despite Chile's offers to pay "cash on the line" in *advance* of delivery. The problem was only partially solved by the creation of a dummy corporation in Mexico to purchase parts from that country for reshipment to Chile and by burdensome purchases of new buses from Argentina.

At the same time the copper companies struck back at nationalization by blocking attempts to replace worn machinery and purchase spare parts at the copper mines. Because most mining equipment came from the U.S., this situation had a crippling effect. Chile could not replace U.S. machines with European or Soviet equipment. In the end Chile literally had to cannibalize parts and machines from older mines in order to keep the more efficient mines going.

4. LEGISLATIVE SABOTAGE OF THE BUDGET

The opposition parties, who were heavily subsidized and encouraged by the U.S., engaged in a campaign to sabotage the Popular Unity government's social welfare programs and/or force the government to spur inflation through deficit spending. They carried out this campaign by a deliberate refusal to finance the budget. In Chile a measure can be passed without arranging for financing the expenses. The government was forced to choose between cutting such things as the defense, welfare, and education plans and so on or using the printing press to print money. In the first year of the Popular Unity government only three-fourths of the budget was actually backed by new revenues. In the second year only one-third and in the third year only one-fourth of the budget was covered. These percentages go far beyond legitimate opposition.

5. ORGANIZATION OF A BLACK MARKET IN GOODS, ESCUDOS, AND DOLLARS

The United States played an important role in the creation of an extensive black market in goods and dollars in Chile. It provided sophisticated training programs for business and professional people through the American Institute for Free Labor Development (AIFLD), giving Chilean business a capacity to launch an organizational and propaganda campaign that it had never demonstrated before.

The black market included three major elements. First, the wholesale, transportation, and retail networks were altered to channel large percentages of certain goods to large and small clandestine warehouses and hideouts in the countryside. The withholding campaigns were combined with a skillful psychological warfare campaign to create shortages in products ranging from tires, to soap, to baby bottles, to life-saving drugs. Second, smaller merchants and distributors were financed through a clandestine banking system organized in late 1972. Third, the U.S. fomented a black market in dollars for the purpose of supporting its own activities in Chile, including financial support to specific black-market, boycott, and strike campaigns. Under these circumstances one dollar could purchase the equivalent of ten dollars' worth of goods or services. As the government never gained control of more than one-quarter of the major distribution networks, it was unable to stop the disastrous campaign.

6. CAMPAIGNS OF ECONOMIC SABOTAGE

The first attempts to cripple the economy physically occurred during 1971, when owners of large estates deliberately destroyed or dismantled for sale abroad large quantities of agricultural machinery and slaughtered or moved to Argentina tens of thousands of diary and beef cattle. In 1972 and 1973 the economic sabotage campaign was systematized. Manufacturers deliberately spoiled or damaged large quantities of production and consumer goods. For example, the government found 25,000 baby-bottle nipples dumped into a river. *Patria y Libertad*, an extreme right-wing organization, published and distributed a "civil resistance" manual. It gave concrete advice to bureaucrats, technicians, and business people about sabotage techniques in their different kinds of work. It should be pointed out that Gandhian or other traditions of civil disobedience did not exist in Chile. The information on World War II resistance movements that was spread about the country came only from outside the country.

One reason why workers pushed for nationalization of monopolies stemmed from the owners' deliberate attempts to hold back productive capacity, refusal to install on-hand new machinery, and so on.

7. STRIKES AND BOYCOTTS BY BUSINESS AND PROFESSIONAL GROUPS

In a country with a long tradition of constitutional and civilian-led government, a coup d'état would have been rejected unless it had some substantial civilian support. In September–October 1972 and July–August 1973 the pro-coup civilian leadership launched an effort both to paralyze the country's economy and to demonstrate mass support for a coup. The "strikes" that took place were almost totally of business and professional groups. Not a single medium or large industry ever shut down. The organizations that went on strike received extensive training and financing from the U.S. through AIFLD, the multinational corporations, and the CIA. The most important material damage was done by the transport owners. The truckers' strikes received several million dollars' worth of aid each time. Politically, the worst damage was caused by the partial strike in one copper mine—whose workers had strong ties to the parallel unions organized by AIFLD.

The damage to the economy of each attempted stoppage was enormous. The October 1972 attempt alone cost the country between $50 million and $75 million outright. It also was a major cause of the decline in the 1973 harvest because fertilizer and seed shipments were disrupted.

CONCLUSION

There is no doubt that the Popular Unity government made a number of economic mistakes of its own. It did not, for example, eliminate traditional problems with bureaucratism, incompetence, and political bickering. At the same time, given hard data on production increases and so on, it is clear that the Chilean economy would never have broken down without the external boycott and the clandestine internal intervention. Politically the U.S.-inspired and U.S.-backed economic warfare was a major factor in bringing much of the middle-income sectors over to the side of the coup.

Political Intervention

By its very nature political intervention is hard to uncover. In the case of Chile a significant number of specific incidents of U.S. political intervention have come to light that can be absolutely verified. At the same time a number of important "leaks" and hearings in the United States have revealed a general intention to intervene in Chile on the part of the U.S. government. The major missing link between the specific incidents and the general intentions is a coherent and concrete plan of intervention. Although this plan is still missing, its broad outlines can be reconstructed from a number of important published studies done for the Defense Department during the 1960s on the mechanics of overthrowing governments.

Since 1960 private corporations, various research institutes on university campuses, and government research centers have completed studies concerned with fomenting subversion, as opposed to putting it down. Various works specifically relevant to Chile can be found in the immediate by-products of Project

Camelot, a notorious multicountry, multistudy investigation of social upheaval and how to cope with it.

Though Project Camelot was officially disbanded, certain aspects of the original research design were obviously pursued. The POLITICA game, published by Abt Associates of Cambridge, Massachusetts, was designed to provide a planning exercise for intervention in any of the three "common" political situations of most Latin American countries. As reported by *NACLA's Latin America & Empire Report* on page 20 of its July–August 1974 issue:

> The game was set up with 35 groups and individuals as the players who were judged to be the crucial factors in acting out any political situation. Spread throughout the country they included: the military, a conservative political party, a liberal party, a national liberation movement, the middle class, latifundistas, students, a foreign embassy, and an industrial bourgeoisie among others. The players could vote, enter into coalitions, communicate, engage in business, revolt, strike, participate in terrorist actions, bribe and deceive. The military could revolt. The government could close the university, tax, order the military to act.

POLITICA's utility is complemented by other studies designed to provide practical information on such diverse subjects as terrorism, psychological warfare, and the planning and execution of a coup d'état.

The POLITICA game and various other similar studies provide a coherent framework for a series of events that took place in Chile in 1970–1973. As in the economic intervention the political subversion by the U.S. can be divided into two stages. In the first stage the political warfare was aimed at alienating specific sections of the population from the government and weakening the internal coherence of the progressive parties in the Popular Unity coalition themselves. Once a general climate of alienation had been created, the political warfare campaign sought to create an atmosphere of social and political insecurity that would provoke and justify an intervention by the armed forces.

The following types of activities are in rough chronological order of their occurrence. Activities were intermingled at any one time, however.

1. INFILTRATION OF LEFT SPLINTER
GROUPS AND PARTIES

After the coup the betrayal of dozens of worker and peasant leaders showed that the CIA and Chilean parties had had some success in infiltrating the parties of the Popular Unity government. Their greatest success, however, lay in the manipulation, and possibly the creation, of various tiny ultraleftist organizations during the Popular Unity government.

In May 1971 a group called Vanguard of the People (VOP) assassinated Edmundo Perez Zukovich, a former vice-president of Chile and a leader of the major centrist opposition party, the Christian Democratic Party. The assassination came just after a major Popular Unity victory in the nationwide municipal elections. This victory was interpreted as a mandate for the Popular Unity government to continue the program that had brought economic recovery and general prosperity to the then stagnant Chilean economy. VOP, composed of no more than a dozen persons, had suspicious origins and had no base of support at all.

As a result of the assassination of Edmundo Perez Zukovich, the tentative cooperation between the Christian Democrats and the Popular Unity coalition was abruptly terminated. After this event government initiatives in the area of agrarian reform and nationalization of the large monopolies were disrupted on a number of occasions by splinter group seizures of tiny farms and small factories. Although many were undoubtedly the work of people who wanted to speed up the process of change, others had more suspicious characteristics. One incident involved the seizure of the farms of four generals one week before an election in the province where their farms were located. The incidents were utilized by the opposition to create fears among the thousands of tiny merchants and farmers that the government intended a general expropriation of all private property in Chile. As in other countries, there were some indications of participation by individuals with ties to the criminal underworld and the various agencies of repression.

During the same period of time a number of seemingly irrational splits occurred in minor parties. Although there were three Marxist parties in the Popular Unity coalition of six parties and although there were also two already established ultraleft parties outside the coalition, several new splinter groups suddenly blossomed. In at least one case, that of the *Partido Comunista–Bandera Roja,* an ultraleft group with less than fifty members, there was no obvious source of the huge amount of money spent by the group in the period of its organization. Such new groups spent most of their time attacking the Popular Unity coalition and little time on the right-wing opposition.

2. PSYCHOLOGICAL WARFARE CAMPAIGNS IN THE MASS MEDIA

The mass media in Chile were not known for especially creative journalism or advertising campaigns. Articles and ads were fairly obvious, and in terms of style, old-fashioned. Yet, surprisingly, the opposition newspapers and radio stations were able to initiate a number of sophisticated psychological warfare campaigns at the end of the first year of the Allende presidency.

The first campaign concerned supposed shortages in a wide variety of products. It was clearly linked to the creation of a well-organized and well-financed black market. The announced shortages ranged from toilet paper to life-sustaining medicines such as insulin. The amusing incident on the Johnny Carson show that provoked a run on toilet paper in the U.S. is similar to the not-so-amusing rumor campaigns in Chile.

The major goal of the psychological warfare in Chile was to create sharp social divisions in the population. The main targets were the white-collar workers, small merchants, small farmers, and professionals. Three separate examples will serve merely to illustrate the magnitude of this effort. In 1971 the government began to purchase shares in the country's only paper manufacturer. Artificial shortages had been created, and luxury paper goods were being produced instead of basic necessities. The Right made a major effort to prevent the paper plant takeover under the banner of "preserving freedom of expression." The struggle was portrayed as a fight between Communist dictatorship and democracy. This portrayal was made despite the government's plan to put control over distribution of newsprint in the hands of private boards drawn from the journalists' union and newspaper owners.

During the 1973 election campaign the Christian Democrats pushed an elaborate ad campaign called "This I How to Destroy the Middle Class." It stressed the relative increase in prices of major nonessential items like luxury housing and gold jewelry. It left out the government's success in building large numbers of prefabricated housing and new public housing complexes and omitted the spectacular increase in the price of gold on the international market. Later on the opposition launched an immense campaign to discredit the government's proposed educational reforms, which concentrated on eliminating functional illiteracy and expanding technical educational facilities at the expense of subsidizing exclusive private schools in the upper-income sector.

3. CREATION OF MASS OPPOSITION ORGANIZATIONS

The most important effort made by the CIA and the Chilean Right to show mass popular opposition to the government focused on women. The campaign to create a seemingly broad women's movement was modeled on a similar campaign in Brazil in 1963–1964. Traditionally, proportionately less women voted for the Left than men. The opposition tried to show that the Popular Unity programs were threatening women's traditional role in the home and the traditional values centered around "family, home, and religion." At the same time it capitalized on the growing practical difficulties associated with the developing black market and the government's attempts to distribute basic necessities at controlled prices and in an equitable manner.

The campaign to mobilize women began when the economic boom of 1971 was still going strong. That December the Right organized the march of the "empty pots and pans." Though all observers on the scene agreed that most women demonstrating came from the wealthy western district of the city and photos showed an extraordinary number of well-dressed women in proportion to the whole, the event was billed as a mass protest of hunger. Despite all efforts, women in the housing developments and shantytowns were not drawn in. The gold-plated pot on a charm bracelet or pin that became popular in 1973 said a lot about the social origins of the "empty pots" movement. Despite the upper-class character of *Poder Femi-nino,* the opposition mass media made enormous efforts to project a massive rejection of the government by women. This effort continued even after the women's vote for the Left in the 1973 elections rose 10 percent; that is, the Left won more new votes among women than among men.

Later women were used in more violent ways. Various confrontations involving small groups of women took place in the months before the coup. One involved a deliberately pro-vocative confrontation between a woman and the constitution-alist commander in chief of the armed forces, General Carlos Prats.

The other major effort to organize a mass base in support of a coup involved the business and professional associations of Chile. Using the American Institute for Free Labor Develop-ment, ostensibly a labor union–oriented organization, literally hundreds of business and professional people were trained in techniques of boycotts, demonstrations, lockouts, and work stoppages. The preparatory phase ended in September 1972, when the taxi and bus owners and small merchants shut down their operations, supposedly in protest over rising costs.

At that moment the major professional and producers' as-sociations, similar to U.S. organizations such as the National Association of Manufacturers, joined in ostensible support of the economic grievances. Within just a few short days, however, the original declarations of solidarity had turned into virtual declarations of sedition. The manufacturers, large estate owners, and doctors' groups were not interested in a solution to grievances, only in situations that could provoke a coup.

The actual development of the various work stoppages or lockouts by the different professional and owners' associations revealed the role of the U.S. and the political use to which the ostensibly economic protests were being put. In the case of the small merchants, a majority of those who had closed down wanted to reopen their shops after just a few days. In both October 1972 and July–August 1973, gangs of toughs from the ultraright traveled throughout Santiago forcing stores to shut down. When local representatives of the smallest merchants tried to work out practical solutions with the government for their problems, they were intimidated by the professional and industrial organizations that had supposedly gone out in support of their initial lockouts.

The country could not be paralyzed, however, unless the transportation network could be shut down. Because the publicly owned railroads continued functioning, the trucking and bus owners were the focus of attention. In both the 1972 and 1973 transportation stoppages, ultraright paramilitary organizations coerced small owners into participating. This effort was reinforced by paying the owners a daily fee not to work. Large amounts of dollars flowed into Chile to pay this subsidy. The amount was so great that the ratio of escudos to dollars actually stabilized and even went down—for one of only two times in the entire three-year period 1970–1973. That is, dollars lost some of their value.

Parallel to this effort, U.S. agents and their Chilean friends were attempting to shut down factories, mines, and other essential services. The artificiality of the entire effort was never more clearly revealed than in the October 1972 strike. Despite the fact that AIFLD and other U.S. agencies had worked intensively in Chile during the Alliance for Progress years during the presidency of Eduardo Frei in the mid-1960s, virtually the entire organized working class rejected the calls for support of the stoppages.

4. ELECTION MONEY

The easiest method of overthrowing the government was the constitutional process of impeachment of the president. In order to achieve this end, the opposition had to win a full two-thirds control of the Senate and Chamber of Deputies. It began to lay the groundwork for impeachment in a series of by-elections beginning in 1972. From the very beginning large amounts of money flowed into Chile to support the election campaigns of the opposition. This practice had roots in earlier elections, such as in 1964, when over $20 million was funneled from the U.S. through the German Christian Democratic Party on behalf of Eduardo Frei of Chile's Christian Democrats.

CONCLUSION

In summary, the political warfare campaign was a carefully orchestrated and entirely artificial attack on the government. It was aimed at the middle-income, "law and order" sectors. Although U.S. involvement in many aspects of the campaign has been exposed, the overall planning still needs to be studied. In particular a major effort must be made to investigate research firms, such as Abt Associates, Inc., which produced the POLITICA game, and the various authors of the studies on how to overthrow a government. (Some information on Abt is contained in the July–August 1974 issue of *NACLA's Latin America & Empire Report*.)

Despite all these provocations, the Chilean Popular Unity government never stepped outside the law or repressed democratic rights. To the very end, the right-wing press was able to print and broadcast totally inflammatory and seditious material. One of the ironies of this situation—given the U.S. justification for the coup—was that the success of the political warfare campaign largely depended on the Popular Unity government's respect for democratic forms.

Military Intervention

1. CONTINUED MILITARY AID TO THE ARMED FORCES

Despite the ostensible worsening of relations between the U.S. and Chilean governments, the U.S. continued to give Chile substantial amounts of military aid and provide training for large numbers of Chilean officers. During the three-year period of the Popular Unity government, large numbers of officers participated in advanced training programs in Panama, Florida, and Colorado. It is clear that through these continued contacts, the U.S. was able to assure the pro-coup military of U.S. support for their efforts and concrete help after the coup was successful. In addition, the U.S. made advance arrangements for active involvement in specific aspects of the coup itself.

6. TERRORISM

Once it became clear that there was significant backing for the Popular Unity government, the U.S. and the Chilean elite had to prepare for a violent solution to their problem. In terms of political warfare this solution involved the use of terrorism. At the time of Salvador Allende's election, the Right did not have an efficient instrument with which to launch a major terrorist effort. They tried to provoke an early coup by assassinating the constitutionalist commander of the armed forces, General René Schneider. The act was performed by an informal nucleus of terrorists drawn from the sons of the major conspirators.

After this attempt to provoke a coup failed, the U.S. stepped in and provided the technical expertise and money for the creation of a proper paramilitary terrorist organization. Enough information has been discovered to establish the strong links between *Patria v Libertad* and American and Brazilian operatives. This organization was created with the expressed intention of being the shock troops in promoting the social and political chaos needed to justify the coup. The organization of training camps in Bolivia, the formation of clandestine radio communications networks, and the construction of an elaborate system of specialized terrorist cells culminated in the terror campaign of July–August 1973. In two months *Patria y Libertad* was responsible for general harassment, more than 500 separate incidents of bombings, and several assassinations. These murders included that of one of the chief military aides to President Allende and the head of the Santiago branch of the small truckers' associations opposed to the truck stoppage.

One of the more macabre aspects of the Chilean military dictatorship's effort to justify the coup is its publication of a list of political murders during the Popular Unity government. Of the approximately seventy people murdered during the three-year period, those killed by leftists of any stripe—including the VOP murders—are only a handful. The vast majority of the victims of political murders were peasants and workers killed by *Patria y Libertad* or similar local right-wing terrorist organizations in the countryside and provincial cities.

During the Popular Unity years the amounts of money spent by the U.S. to influence elections began with modest sums and increased as the mid-1973 congressional elections approached. Early in 1972, for example, money was siphoned off from a $50,000 Ford Foundation grant to a Catholic University institute to finance ostensible "research" on Christian Democratic land reform in the very provinces where Raphael Moreno, a former conservative Christian Democratic agricultural minister, was running for a vacant Senate seat.

In the March 1973 election campaign all financial stops were pulled out. In addition to incredible amounts of advertising—even more than in a typical United States campaign—the Christian Democrats attempted to distribute huge quantities of "food baskets" to lower-income residents of housing developments and shantytowns. The campaign ended rather abruptly when the government traced the baskets back to black-market warehouses.

It is important to remember that even a few million dollars had the impact of tens of millions of dollars in a situation where one dollar could buy from $7 to $10 worth of goods and services on the black market.

5. FAILURE IN THE CHURCH

In September 1972 the Right tried to launch a "rosary campaign" as part of the October 1972 boycott and work stoppages. This campaign was one of the few clear-cut attempts to bring the Catholic Church into the struggle. In previous years attempts had been made to involve the church in Alliance for Progress programs. As a result of historic conditions and the contacts made by younger priests with the popular sectors, the reformist ideology of the Frei era had unforeseen results. It sparked the creation of a Christians for Socialism movement. The Popular Unity government made concrete efforts to demonstrate its respect and appreciation for the church's humanitarian efforts and its willingness to work with the church in solving concrete social programs. As a result, even the more moderate hierarchy refused to get drawn into a crudely antipopular alliance.

2. PARAMILITARY WARFARE

As time wore on, it became clear that the Popular Unity government had significant support in the armed forces. This support included constitutionalist officers as well as officers who had become sympathetic to the general nationalist and populist aims of the Popular Unity program. In addition, it became more and more clear that a substantial part of the population was willing to fight to defend the government.

Under these circumstances the coup planners decided that a backup force outside the military was needed. *Patria y Libertad* and the youth organization of the right-wing National Party were marked for more extensive duties in the event of a long struggle. In the aftermath of an attempted coup in June 1973, the government uncovered the basic paramilitary structure of *Patria y Libertad*. It involved a network of urban guerrilla warfare cells. The paramilitary network depended heavily on foreign support. Its training and armament have been traced back to specialized training camps in Bolivia and Texas. In Texas the International Police Academy ran what can only be called a school for terrorists, one in which students learned bombing and sabotage techniques. Most of the instructors in the Bolivian camp were veterans of training programs in the Panama Canal Zone and various counterinsurgency training camps. The entire operation was coordinated from abroad by two retired Chilean officers, General Alfredo Canales and Major Arturo Marshall. These two officers were retired by President Allende after openly seditious acts.

3. TECHNICAL ADVICE ON MAKING THE COUP

One of the most curious things about the Chilean coup involves lack of previous experience in the mechanics of coup making. Chile had not had a coup since the 1920s and had not fought a war since the 1890s. Yet the armed forces were able to execute what was probably the most complicated and difficult coup in the postwar Third World. One of the answers to this anomaly may reside in a paperback, *Coup d'Etat* (New York: Fawcett World Library, 1969), by Edward Luttwak. Luttwak, identified in a *New York Times* article on terrorism as a Defense Department consultant, is a right-wing commentator in the United States. His book is "a practical handbook—a brilliant guide to taking over a nation" according to the publisher. The book details the preconditions, strategy, planning, and execution of a coup. Like the POLITICA game, the book is structured in such a way as to make it highly adaptable for any specific situation.

The book alone would probably be a decent or acceptable manual for highly trained professionals. Yet NACLA has detailed in its articles, which have yet to be refuted by U.S. government sources, how the United States organized a veteran team of coup makers in its Santiago embassy. Veterans of such coups as those in Guatemala (1954), Brazil (1964), and the Dominican Republic (1965) began arriving as early as 1971. The last members arrived shortly after the March 1973 elections, which demonstrated increased popular support of the government and eliminated the possibility of Allende's impeachment. Information on the coup team members reveals that virtually every aspect of the political and military phases of the coup was covered by a veteran activist in labor, mass media, paramilitary groups, or armed forces organization.

4. ACTIVE PARTICIPATION IN THE COUP ITSELF

At this point, many of the details on the coup itself are still sketchy. Evidence published in Argentina suggests that the planes actually used in the precision bombing attack on the presidential palace were U.S. planes using "smart bombs" and piloted by foreigners. At the same time units of the U.S. Navy were stationed off the major port, Valparaiso, ostensibly to participate in joint naval exercises. In fact, U.S. Navy personnel played a key role in communications coordination during the coup.

There are a number of other details that have come out since the coup. The actual importance of participation by U.S. personnel on the day of the coup itself should not, however, be overestimated. Impartial international experts had rated the Chilean armed forces as the second best trained military in

Latin America. Once certain specialized techniques and materials had been passed on, there is no need to assume massive U.S. participation. Such participation might risk public exposure, and the Chileans were quite capable of executing the coup by themselves.

General Conclusions

1. What is important about the U.S. intervention in Chile is the preparatory phase. Without active U.S. financing, training, and supplies, the coup could clearly never have been successful, though undoubtedly it would have been tried at some point. The Popular Unity government was winning the people to socialism and successfully transforming the economy. The old elite and the other vested interests had everything to lose by its success.

2. Since the coup a huge repressive apparatus has been installed. The same organizations and individuals who organized the overthrow of the Popular Unity government are now being used to keep the new government in power.

3. The U.S. involvement in the overthrow of the democratic government of Chile is a serious warning for United States citizens. The investigations of the CIA have shown that the people behind the Chilean coup have few scruples about similar activities in the U.S. Chile teaches us that it *could* happen here.

4. The massive and complex nature of the intervention discredits the notion that U.S. counterrevolutionary activities are simply the work of a few "cloak and dagger" operators. Any serious investigation must look at the multinational corporations and other government agencies including the Defense, State, Commerce, and Labor departments, as well as private foundations and the international operations of the AFL-CIO.

5. Finally, in a more general vein, the question of Chile once again poses the question of who makes our foreign policy and whom it serves. Even a brief review of the nature of the Popular Unity government and the military dictatorship that followed shows that the coup was not in the interest of 95 percent of the American people.

6. At the same time, Chile, as did Vietnam, once again teaches a lesson about political struggle. If a movement represents the genuine aspirations of the great majority, it cannot be suppressed. Today in Chile, 80 percent of the population totally opposes the junta. The Left has been restructured, the trade unions reorganized in secret.

"El pueblo unido jamás sera vencido": "The people, united, will never be defeated."

The Facts about Chile

Hortensia Bussi de Allende

■ Hortensia Bussi married Salvador Allende in 1939. She assisted him in his four campaigns for the presidency of Chile, to which he was elected in 1970. During the Popular Unity government, which he headed, Sra. Allende was active with women's organizations, promoting their participation in the political process and supporting the establishment of child-care centers. She escaped from her house while it was being bombed during the September 1973 coup that overthrew the Popular Unity government and in which President Allende died. She now resides in Mexico City but devotes most of her time to traveling around the world to denounce the violations of human rights in Chile under the junta and to work for the liberation of her homeland.

IT APPEARS AS A CRUDE IRONY of history that the United States, this great nation, which was the first to gain its independence in the Western hemisphere under the banner of the people's right to self-determination, should now be known—because of the actions of its leaders—as the champion of intervention and the supporter of puppet regimes opposed to the people's will.

The chapter concerning CIA and North American imperialistic intervention in Chile is by no means closed. It is just beginning. Each day we know of new facts that up to today have been hidden from the North American people and from international public opinion. It is necessary that these so-called "secrets" be known. It is necessary that the mysteries that envelop the monstrous maneuvers executed by the great economic interests and hidden from the noble and generous people of the United States be revealed. It is to these people, who are not implicated in this affair, which was perpetrated by the monied interests, that I appeal. I ask the people of the United States to insist that the intervention in and responsibility of the U.S. government for the fascist massacre that exists in Chile be made known and denounced. The intervention of the U.S. government started long before the military coup in Chile, not just in September 1973. The object was to prevent Salvador Allende's victory. It was done behind the back of the North American people and of Congress.

Today President Allende's constant denunciations have proven to be true. In 1972 in his speech before the United Nations, he declared:

> My country is the victim of a grave aggression, and has been since the very moment of our electoral triumph on September 4, 1970. We are affected by the development of powerful external pressures which tried to prevent the installation of a government freely elected by the people, and attempted to defeat it ever since. They have intended to isolate us from the world, strangle our economy, paralyze our commerce in our main export product, copper, and prevent our access to sources of international financial aid.

He continued:

> We are conscious that when we denounce the economic and financial blockade, such a situation is not easily understood by the international public opinion, not even by some of our own countrymen, because it is not a declared, open aggression, without disguise, before the face of the world. On the contrary, it is always an underground attack, indirect, but nonetheless damaging for Chile. We find ourselves faced with forces which operate in the shadows, without a flag, with powerful weapons, posted in the various places of influence.

Unfortunately this dramatic warning fell on deaf ears. In order for it to come to light and draw attention, it has been necessary to kill a president, massacre 30,000 Chileans, imprison 100,000 people, and abolish all civil liberties. President Allende in his last words from inside the government palace enveloped in flames said it once again:

Foreign capitalism and imperialism, allied with reaction, have created such a climate that the Armed Forces have broken with their traditions—those traditions which General Schneider had taught them and Commander Araya reasserted—both victims of the same social sector, of those same people who today will stay in their homes waiting to reconquer power, through the actions of others, in order to continue to defend their profits and privileges.

The tragic experience of underdeveloped countries shows that the intensity and scope of CIA action is in direct relation to the magnitude and strategic importance of North American interests and the level of development and organization of the liberation movements. In Chile the two conditions developed simultaneously. That accounts for both the old and the new strategy of the CIA, extending into almost every national activity. With the CIA's history in Chile now partially revealed to the public, one can begin to reconstruct the abominable trail of North American aggression against our people. [Documentation for the charges made in the following reconstruction can be found in: Pío García's collection, *Las fuerzas armadas y el golpe de estado en Chile* (Mexico, D.F.: Siglo Veintiuno Editores, 1974); Armando Uribe's *Le livre noir de l'intervention américaine au Chili* (Paris: Editions du Seuil, 1974); Germán Marín's forthcoming work for Siglo Veintiuno Editores, *Una historia fantástica y calculada: la CIA en el país de los chilenos;* and *NACLA's Latin America & Empire Report* issues of January 1973, October 1973, and July–August 1974.]

1964: The CIA turns over $3 million to the Christian Democratic Party in order to help the presidential campaign of Eduardo Frei against the popular candidacy of Salvador Allende.

1969: On the eve of another presidential election, the CIA distributes $500,000 "in order to maintain those individuals who would sustain the anti-Allende forces."

1970: Another $500,000 is handed over to the leaders of the political parties opposing the candidacy of Allende.

— A meeting to analyze the possibilities of an Allende victory takes place with John A. McCone, a director of ITT and former director of the CIA, and Richard Helms, then director of the CIA, both in attendance.

— Henry Kissinger convokes an extraordinary meeting of the 40 Committee in which the CIA is authorized to distribute $400,-000 among the press, radio, and television companies opposed to Allende.

— On September 14 Harold S. Geneen, president of ITT, proposes his plans to Kissinger to intervene in Chile, saying that he is "prepared to help economically with sums up to seven figures, for operations that will preserve the interests of ITT in Chile."

— On September 15 the State Department authorizes Edward Korry, ambassador to Chile, to do everything possible to prevent Allende's assumption of the presidency.

— At the end of September Richard Helms, director of the CIA, instructs William V. Broe, of the CIA Clandestine Services Division for the Western Hemisphere, to meet with Edward Gerrity, vice-president of ITT. In the meeting they study "possible actions to apply economic pressure" intended to prevent the ratification of Salvador Allende as president of Chile by the National Congress.

— Between September and October the CIA spends $350,000 to bribe Chilean legislators to vote against the imminent ratification of Allende as president.

— In October General René Schneider, commander in chief of the Army, is assassinated. The purpose of the crime is to provoke the intervention of the armed forces and thus stop the congressional ratification of Allende. Among the plotters we find a CIA agent born in Chile and residing in Venezuela who makes a special trip to Chile during the conspiracy.

— After Allende takes office, a meeting takes place between John McCone and William Broe to examine "contacts with selected members of the Chilean Armed Forces who would be able to lead some type of uprising."

— Judd Kessler, an Agency for International Development (AID) official in Santiago, in a memorandum to Deane R. Hinton, CIA economic analyst in the U.S. Embassy in Santiago, dated October 2, presents the diverse long- and short-range North American options for the destruction of the Popular Unity government.

— The National Security Council, with authority over the CIA, approves the anti-Chile policy of the "invisible blockade."

— In Chile John B. Tipton and James E. Anderson are put in charge of directing the network of agents infiltrated into the parties of the Left and of the Right in accord with the following outline:

Clandestine operations group: Robert J. O'Neill, Val Moss, Donald H. Winters, and Fred Shaver.

Work group against Cuba, socialist countries, and foreign residents in Chile: Allen D. Smith, Franklin Tonini, and Arnold M. Isaacs. (Note: North American residents in Chile were controlled by consular officials.) In addition to those mentioned, Harry Shlaudeman (now ambassador to Venezuela), John B. Tipton, Keith Wheelock, and Joseph F. McManus were also part of this network.

— Raymond Warren, local chief of the CIA, arrives in October. The network formed under his direction includes, among others, the following:

Group for operations in communications (propaganda and psychological warfare): G. Claude Villareal, Paul L. Good, Denis A. Allred.

Paramilitary operations group (with links outside of Chile): Leo G. Karpoff (Bolivia), David McGrath (Rio de Janeiro), Robert L. Taylor (Bolivia), Claris R. Halliwell (Sao Paulo).

Military intelligence group (Defense Intelligence Agency; worked with the CIA): Lawrence A. Corcoran, William Hon, James Switzer, Adrian Schreiber, and John Carrington (with the Air Force; later decorated by junta leader Pinochet for his participation in the bombardment of the government palace and other targets during the coup).

— At the end of 1970 the 40 Committee, presided over by Henry Kissinger, authorizes the CIA to distribute $5 million for a "destabilization effort" against the government of President Allende, to be used between 1971 and 1973.

1971: In January a special committee is formed under the auspices of ITT to pressure the U.S. government and influence international credit agencies to move in directions that would threaten Chile with economic chaos.

— Deane R. Hinton, specialist in the field of economic intelligence, plays an important role in coordinating the campaign for economic chaos as director of AID in Chile. In 1971 he is called to the U.S. to fill a position on a subcommittee of the

National Security Council charged with defining government
policy regarding the nationalization of North American interests abroad. Later Hinton became Ambassador to Zaïre.
— In February President Nixon declares that the election of a
socialist president in Chile can have profound implications for
the Interamerican system.
— In March Howard C. Edwards is arrested by the Chilean
police for his possible involvement in an international maneuver to cause a reduction in the price of copper. Edwards had
participated in the Bay of Pigs invasion and had worked in
Czechoslovakia during the 1968 occurrences.
— Frederick W. Latrash, AID official who participated in the
overthrow of Jacobo Arbenz in Guatemala in 1954 and in the
destruction of the Nkrumah government in Ghana in 1966, is
named political director of the U.S. Embassy in Santiago.
— *Patria y Libertad,* or "Fatherland and Liberty," an ultra-
rightist paramilitary organization, is formed in Chile under the
operational experience of the CIA.
— The American Institute for Free Labor Development
(AIFLD), under the leadership of Robert J. O'Neill, country
program director for Chile, contributes to the formation of the
Confederation of Chilean Professionals, a group that was to
play a decisive role in the truckowners' and merchants' strikes
of 1972 and 1973.
— Edmundo Perez Zukovich, ex-minister of the interior in the
Eduardo Frei government, is assassinated in June with the evident purpose of creating conditions for a coup d'état. The Organized Vanguard of the People, a group supposedly of the extreme
left, was responsible for that assassination. The group was actually infiltrated by Panamanian elements serving the CIA.
— Vice-president of ITT, William R. Merriam, writes to Peter
Peterson, executive director of President Nixon's Council on International Economic Policy and assistant to the President for
international economic affairs, reiterating proposals intended
to suffocate the Chilean economy through the rejection of international loans and suspension of the importation of copper and
other goods. This policy was intended to create sufficient economic chaos to stimulate the intervention of the armed forces.
Merriam proposes that the CIA collaborate in this process.
— Secretary of State William Rogers meets with representatives of Anaconda, Ford Motor Company, First National City

Bank, Ralston Purina Company, and ITT. In the get-together
it is proposed to embargo spare parts and materials for Chile
and cut off all forms of North American aid.
— The United States changes its ambassador in Chile. The
position is filled by Nathaniel P. Davis, who began his career as
an official of the Office of Strategic Services (OSS), precursor
of the CIA. He had formerly been assigned to Czechoslovakia,
the Soviet Union, and Bulgaria and had also been in Chile as
head of the Peace Corps there in 1963. Immediately previous
to his new appointment in Chile, he had been ambassador to
Guatemala, a post he had assumed immediately after the ab-
duction and execution of his predecessor, John Gordon Mein.
   1972: On March 21, U.S. journalist Jack Anderson reveals
the plans of ITT and the CIA against the Popular Unity government.
— The same journalist makes public a secret cable from Ambassador Nathaniel Davis to the State Department that suggests
that in preparation for a military coup it is first necessary to
create "a discontent so profound that a military intervention
would be warmly received."
— The U.S. corporations operating in Chile resort to economic
sabotage. Ford Motor Company suspends its activities and closes
its plant. General Motors does likewise shortly thereafter. Ralston Purina is brought under state control when it becomes
clear that it is not paying customs taxes and is violating the
law of international exchange.
— Kennecott and Anaconda obtain the embargo of Chilean
products in the U.S. and freeze the accounts of the various
Chilean governmental agencies in New York, some of which
include those of the state copper corporation and the Production Development Agency.
— It becomes increasingly difficult for Chile to get parts and
replacements for U.S.-produced machinery. The result is that
21 percent of the taxis and 31 percent of the public transportation become immobilized.
— Kennecott brings suit in France to block the payment for
copper sales to the government of Chile. Private U.S. banks cut
Chile's access to credit from $200 million to $35 million. They
suspend all credits to suppliers.
— Wolf Research and Development, a "privately" owned U.S.
corporation, proposes to Chile a series of research programs in-

volving remote sensors placed in NASA satellites as part of the ERTS and Skylab programs. The application of this technology for supposed research consists of terrain information photographs, espionage flights, and air detection of mineral deposits.

— Enno Hobbins, formerly editor of *Life* Magazine, and Alvaro Puga were CIA agents on the staff of *El Mercurio*. Part of the $400,000 approved by the Forty Committee for anti-Allende propaganda went to finance *El Mercurio*.

— In October General Cesar Ruiz Danyau, commander in chief of the Chilean Air Force, travels to the United States, invited by his U.S. counterpart, General John Ryan. From this trip the Chilean Air Force obtains a $5 million credit. In contrast, the Popular Unity government itself in three years received only $3 million in credits from the United States.

— In 1972 no more than 13 to 20 percent of Chilean imports came from the U.S., compared with about 40 percent in preceding years.

— In the financial arena, the percentage of short-term credits that Chile received from the U.S. was reduced from 78 to 6.6 percent.

— On October 11 the first owners' strike is declared, preceded by a commercial shutdown and followed by the truckowners' lockout. These seditious activities are intended to paralyze the economy of the entire country for several weeks. This action coincides with the Western European embargo of Chilean copper as a result of Kennecott's legal maneuvers in France. The CIA, as has since been revealed, actually financed the owners' shutdown, inundating the black market with dollars.

— In December, Jorge Guerrero, secretary of the National Command for Gremial Defense, which directed the owners' shutdown, is invited to Washington by AIFLD.

1973: Alexander Zanders, ex-agent of the CIA, informs Chilean authorities of the preparation of a military coup against the Popular Unity government. He reveals the so-called Centaur Plan. Zanders accompanies his denunciations with conclusive evidence, including intelligence reports and taped material.

— At the request of the CIA, the U.S. government provides $200,000 and $350,000 respectively to finance the activities of the National Party and the Christian Democrats.

— President Allende's naval attaché, Commander Arturo Araya Peeters, is assassinated on July 27, by members of the ultra-rightist group *Patria y Libertad*, organized by the CIA two years before.

Also on July 27, a new truckowners' strike starts and will grow to include merchants and professionals. Simultaneously a wave of terrorist actions spreads over the nation. A high-tension tower is blown up while President Allende is addressing the country on TV and radio. *Patria y Libertad*, backed by the CIA, does not conceal its responsibility in this affair. The Chilean Naval Intelligence Service contributes to the effort with logistical advice.

— Michael Townley, a North American citizen and member of the Peace Corps in Chile during President Frei's government, returns to Chile as a CIA agent to collaborate with *Patria y Libertad*. He takes charge of a five-man brigade that carries out a sabotage operation at a power plant in the city of Concepción. Although they fail in their objective, they kill the plant's night watchman, Tomás Henriquez. Townley then manages to escape to Argentina and from there flies to the United States.

— Pablo Rodriguez, head of *Patria y Libertad*, visits the United States and makes contacts with Watergate burglars Bernard Barker, Frank Sturgis, Virgilio Gonzales, and Eugenio Martinez, who had participated in the espionage and robbery of documents from the Chilean Embassy in Washington a year earlier.

— On May 15 the Union of Professional Employees from the El Teniente Copper Mine starts a strike. The mine had been expropriated from Kennecott. This strike was directed by Guillermo Medina, who was advised directly by AIFLD, as well as by *Patria y Libertad* leaders such as Manuel Fuentes Weddling, presently press attaché to General Gustavo Leigh.

— On June 29 a tentative coup is defeated. It is led by Armored Regiment No. 2 and by civilians from *Patria y Libertad*. Pablo Rodriguez and other leaders of this fascist group seek refuge in the embassy of Ecuador and leave Chile. It is thought that the June 29 attempted coup was mounted as poorly as it was because of a failure of communication between the CIA, directly linked with *Patria y Libertad*, and the DIA, the Pentagon's Defense Intelligence Agency, which was working with the Chilean military traitors.

— In August the CIA is authorized to invest an additional $1 million in Chile. It has been maintained that this allocation was canceled when the coup took place. The truth is that the

sum was spent—as has since been acknowledged publicly:
$250,000 went for a radio station and thousands of dollars were
used to finance public relations trips of junta officials shortly
after the coup. The rest is not yet accounted for.
— In September ships from the U.S. Navy arrive in Chilean
waters to participate with the Chilean Navy in the joint maneuvers called "Operation Unitas."
— At the same time, thirty-two U.S. observation and battle
planes land in Mendoza, Argentina; fifteen of the planes leave
forty-eight hours after the coup. Simultaneously 150 North
Americans described as "specialists in air acrobatics" arrive in
Chile.
— On September 9, President Nixon is informed about plans
for the military coup in Chile.
— September 11. The military coup takes place. The Popular
Unity government is overthrown; President Allende is murdered; and a fascist dictatorship is installed.
— The fact that U.S. warships from the Unitas maneuvers
were standing by ready to help in case they were needed in
carrying out the coup is disclosed.
— Another fact is revealed and denounced: namely, that on
the day of the coup a WB-575 plane was operated in Chile by
Majors V. Duenas and T. Schull from the U.S. Air Force. This
plane was a flying electronic control station, serving to coordinate the communications of the putschists.
— The German magazine *Neue Berliner Illustrierte* of December 25, 1973, states that it has a confidential U.S. Army document, taken from a vault at Fort Gulick, Panama, outlining a
plan to destroy the Popular Unity government. The U.S. plan
revealed in Germany has characteristics very similar to the
events of September 11.
— Chile's National Department of Investigations comes into
existence under the Defense Ministry with the collaboration of
the CIA and the DIA and with the help of Brazilian and German
experts such as Walter Rauff, former Gestapo officer and the
man responsible for developing Hitler's mobile gas-extermina-
tion units.

What you have heard is a very short resume of open North
American intervention in Chile's internal affairs through 1973.
What has occurred since the coup is more widely known. No

events in recent time have so wounded international sensitivity as the barbarism taking place in my country. These events have been unanimously repudiated in every corner of the world. No government is so completely discredited and morally isolated as the military junta of Chile.

In 1974 the putschists' thirst for blood extended even beyond the frontiers of Chile to Buenos Aires, Argentina, to carry out the cowardly assassination of General Carlos Prats and his wife. The Gestapo methods, adopted through the CIA, now boomerang on their own practitioners. For example, the disappearance of General Oscar Bonilla, presumed successor to dictator Pinochet, carries the trademark of the methods used by Hitler to eliminate his possible competitors.

As grotesque and repugnant as is the role played by the fascist junta, we have absolute confirmation of the participation of the CIA and imperialism in the liquidation process against the longings of a people for liberation. As surely as the responsibility for such deeds falls upon the previous U.S. administration and especially upon Nixon, President Ford has also astonished world public opinion by declaring that the policy was carried out "in the best interests of the Chilean people, and certainly, of the United States." That is to say, that the government of the United States openly proclaims the right to intervene by whatever means, no matter how illicit, dirty, or criminal they may be, in the internal processes of the peoples of this hemisphere, wherever and whenever its financial interests make it seem advisable.

In September of 1974 when President Ford confessed the North American intervention in Chile, he argued that it was done to help save the communications media of the opposition parties. For his part, Henry Kissinger told the U.S. Senate that "the activities of the CIA had as their object the prevention of the establishment of a one-party government by a minority President." The question arises: Where is the concern of Mr. Ford and Mr. Kissinger now when in Chile all political parties have been suppressed, all public liberties abolished, the National Congress closed down, and the country converted into a showcase for concentration camps?

The attempt to justify this intervention has been based on what is called a need to defend democracy. This argument lacked any basis at all during the years of the Popular Unity government, but democracy certainly needs defending today in face of the junta's fascist dictatorship. Nevertheless, we observe that the only industrialized country whose government helps that tyranny—politically, financially, and militarily—is the United States.

From what has transpired, one can only conclude that the true objective of the U.S. interventionist policy has been to install a fascist-style government that would ensure what the transnational companies call "the social peace" in a "climate favorable to foreign investment." The "peace of the cemetery" created by the military junta is exactly the "social peace" sought after by those same transnational corporations.

It is clear that the intervention practiced in Chile is only one single case in a general policy of intervention and collusion between the U.S. government and the interests of North American investment abroad, especially those of the multinational companies: ITT, Kennecott, Anaconda, etc., etc. This pigheaded, policelike conduct carries the implicit objective of installing fascist regimes in underdeveloped countries and not only violates the recognized norms governing relations between states institutionalized in the Charter of the United Nations but also clearly contradicts those ideals for which the people of the United States have fought ever since their independence.

This conflict between the real interests of the North American people and the policy of foreign intervention explains the deceptive practices of the U.S. government. In the effort to justify this duplicity to the citizens of the United States, the leaders of the government find themselves in increasingly clear and difficult contradictions. How can the U.S. government possibly convince its people that the barbarism and terror in Chile is compatible with the ideals and interests of the great majority of North American citizens? Are the interests of the U.S. people served in any way by the brutal destruction of the Popular Unity government in Chile? That government was a democratically elected, constitutional one whose margin of votes had even increased in the last elections prior to the coup in 1973.

How can the North American government try to convince its people that the association between the CIA and ITT—a corporation that collaborated with the Nazis even as U.S. soldiers were dying in the fight against fascism during World War II—can contribute to the strengthening of democracy either in Chile or the United States? When will the president of the United States put an end to support of the fascist military junta and the offers to it of financial credits and military aid beyond anything ever dreamed of by our government of Popular Unity? How can the U.S. government convince its people that in order to fulfill the ideals of Abraham Lincoln, it is necessary to help those sinister forces that seek to establish fascism on a world-wide scale, making no exception of the United States?

The reaction of the U.S. people to the revelations of CIA activity both abroad and within the United States shows us that there is a reserve of moral power that can prevent abdication of those ideals of liberty that have been fought for by generations of U.S. citizens. It appears that the North American people are beginning to understand that it is impossible to help fascism abroad without becoming exposed to those same forces inside the United States.

In order to legitimize the shameless violations of mutual respect between nations, whether they be powerful or not, the U.S. president has thrown the Charter of the United Nations in the wastebasket and tries to raise the law of the jungle to the plane of international relations. The peoples of Latin America and Southeast Asia have been the victims of practices in the bloody tradition of Nazi fascism. Today the United States has the sad privilege of breathing new life into those traditions.

At least imperialism has begun to pay a price for unleashing its aggression against the Popular Unity government presided over by Salvador Allende. The price is the awakening and strengthening of the consciousness of many peoples and governments about the direct threat of fascism as a new pattern of domination in our epoch. With that consciousness we have witnessed the extensive and profound growth of a movement in solidarity with the Chilean people. This movement represents an answer to a terrible outrage against the human rights and destiny of a small nation and expresses, furthermore, the recognition that we are dealing with a situation that endangers all of humanity.

The Chilean drama not only encompasses the contradictions of Chilean and Latin American society, but those of the Third World in general. In the case of Chile we have the subjugation, although momentary, of a nation that has carried forward a process of emancipation. This tragedy points out to us that it is the nations of the Third World that are, and will continue to be, the principal targets of imperialist aggression.

We address the people of the United States. We wish to take this opportunity to thank you for your efforts to unmask the aggression being waged against the Chilean people. We would also like to express, in a very special way, our recognition of the efforts of those fine North Americans who have demonstrated their convictions in effective solidarity with the victims of the tyranny.

In a responsible manner, we would also like to offer the warning that when fascism is flushed from our country, the Chilean people will disown and reject absolutely whatever accords, whatever pacts, whatever treaties have been agreed to by the military junta with whatever state or international organization.

Finally, it is our duty to appeal to the conscience of the North American people to prevent the continued support of your government for the most bloody regime that has been known in the history of Latin America, the dictatorship of Augusto Pinochet. The North American people cannot continue as accomplices in a policy contrary to their own best interests. Consequently, the demand must resound for the suspension of all military aid and credits to the junta, against any renegotiation of the external debt, and for the defense of human rights in Chile.

Confronting this tangible danger of fascism, the so-called silent majority must convert itself to an active, thundering majority for democracy.

As Pablo Neruda said in *Let the Rail Splitter Awake:*

> It is your peace that we love, not your mask.
> Your warrior's face is not handsome.
> You are vast and beautiful, North America.
> Your origin is humble like a washerwoman's,
> white, beside your rivers.
> Shaped in the unknown,
> it is your peace of honeycomb that is most sweet.

The fight against fascism in Chile is a fight against the dangers of fascism all over the world. That is why we can say, with all certainty and conviction, "We shall overcome."

The CIA and
the Vietnam Debacle

Ngo Vinh Long

■ Ngo Vinh Long is a specialist on Vietnam, his native land, and China. He is author of Before the Revolution: The Vietnamese Peasants under the French and a three-volume series, Vietnamese Women in Society and Revolution. He has also contributed over a hundred articles to various publications. At present he is director of the Vietnam Resource Center, which publishes a monthly newsletter and many booklets, and editor of Vietnam Quarterly, an international journal devoted to the study of Vietnamese society. On the verge of the fall of the Saigon regime, Mr. Long at the Conference on the CIA and World Peace discussed the CIA role in Vietnam.

VIETNAM "BOASTS" a long and certainly very active history of CIA involvement. This history began with the activities of the Office of Strategic Services (OSS), the CIA predecessor, during World War II. Before 1945, because of the need for intelligence on the Japanese as well as information on missing American airmen, the OSS maintained frequent contacts with Ho Chi Minh and his fellow Vietnamese revolutionaries. After the death of President Roosevelt, the OSS began to sabotage the Vietnamese resistance and revolution. For example, according to Edward Hymoff's *The OSS in World War II* (New York: Ballantine, 1974), as early as 1945 the OSS was already training many counterrevolutionary Vietnamese agents such as Phan Quang

Dan, deputy premier of the Thieu regime. Over the years as head of the Refugee, Resettlement, and Land Development Program under Thieu, Dan caused untold suffering to millions of people and death to tens of thousands of others by carrying out to the letter the American plans for massive forced relocation and by stealing peasants' lands and siphoning off refugees' funds.

In 1946 the OSS financed Vietnamese Kuomingtang leaders to run in municipal elections against both Ho Chi Minh and Emperor Bao Dai. After the CIA was formally created in 1947, its agents went everywhere in Vietnam and contacted Vietnamese individuals and groups, including members of the resistance against the French, in an attempt to buy them off. For example, in early 1948 three CIA operatives toured the Mekong delta to make contact with resistance groups against the French. One of them, Arthur Doyle, sought out some Catholic leaders of the resistance and offered to help them in all matters. (See Le Tien Giang, *Cong Giao Khang Chien Nam Bo, 1945–54.* Saigon, 1972.)

After the French defeat at Dienbienphu in 1954, CIA activities in Vietnam grew by leaps and bounds. In the two decades after the signing of the 1954 Geneva accords, CIA operatives carried out every trick in their book in the country. They sabotaged the accords. They conducted "black propaganda" against the Vietminh regime. They conspired to install Ngo Dinh Diem as "President of the Republic of Vietnam" against the stipulation of the Geneva accords and through a rigged referendum in which only Diem was allowed to run. They paid tens of millions of dollars to the sect leaders who opposed Diem to get them to allow him to remain in power. They poured in tens of millions of dollars to help Diem build a gigantic prison and police system. They built the Confederation of Vietnamese Labor—the AFL-CIO of Vietnam—into a huge counterinsurgency and repression network. They helped devise and carry out the massive relocation of the rural populations of Vietnam through programs like the "agrovilles," the "strategic hamlets," the "new-life hamlets," and the "new new-life hamlets" in order to control the population and deprive the "revolutionary fish" of the popular "water" that supported them. They murdered tens of thousands of Vietnamese civilians, whom they suspected as Vietcong, through assassination and black propaganda programs such as the so-called "counterterror," the Provincial Reconnaisance

Units, and the Phoenix program. They deposed and murdered Vietnamese puppets and henchmen they no longer needed. They helped rig elections in order to maintain dictators they favored. They stirred up hatred between Vietnamese and minorities such as the mountain tribesmen, the Chinese, and the Khmer people. They created conflicts between the various religious communities. They bought off religious leaders to create strife within the religious communities themselves. These are only a few of the many CIA activities in Vietnam that have been documented.

But documented activities represent only an infinitesimal proportion of the real extent of CIA operations in Vietnam. The reason for this fact is that CIA covert activities in Vietnam have been leaked little as compared to those in other countries. Too many high CIA agents have risen through the ranks because of Vietnam. It is not likely that they would allow their careers to be jeopardized by disclosure of their activities there. William Colby (director of the CIA), Ted Schackley (head of covert activities for Asia), George Carver (head of Intelligence Estimate), and James Delaney (one of the highest officials at the CIA Asia desk)—to name but a few—are all "old Vietnam hands." Colby was the director of the "pacification" program and Schackley was the CIA station chief in Vietnam during the years of direct American involvement.

CIA activities in Vietnam did not abate with the withdrawal of American troops after the signing of the Paris Peace Agreement in 1973. On the contrary, CIA operations increased. They have done everything possible to sabotage the implementation of the Paris Agreement. In fact, it is not an overstatement to say that since 1973, CIA agents have been running the Vietnam show. The reason is that the State Department has been paralyzed as a result of Kissinger's personal-style diplomacy. Kissinger has tended to rely heavily on CIA agents rather than on career State Department officials.

Among the CIA agents conducting American foreign policy in Vietnam—besides the big shots already mentioned—are Allen Carter (director of the United States Information Agency), Frank Scotton (USIA Vietnam desk), Thomas Polgar (CIA station chief in Saigon), Douglas Pike (assistant to Kissinger on Indochinese Affairs working under Winston Lord), Everett Baumgartner (USIA motion picture officer for Asia), and a horde of others who staff most of the USIA positions and who are political officers at the U.S. Mission in Saigon and its various consulates around the country. Frank Scotton was the originator of the Provincial Reconaissance Units program, the predecessor of the Phoenix program. For years he worked closely with John Paul Vann, the famous CIA operative who specialized, among other things, in black propaganda, which involved him in murder, forgery, and outright deception of the American press in order to discredit the National Liberation Front (NLF) in particular and the opposition to American intervention in general. Everett Baumgartner was Colby's deputy and used to oversee pacification efforts in the central provinces of Vietnam. Any person who has the faintest knowledge of the pacification program would know what disasters have visited the Vietnamese people as a result of such efforts. Baumgartner was also in charge of the Phoenix program in that area. Douglas Pike has been a CIA propaganda expert for years. He published three books and many articles that made him the "authority" on the Vietcong before he was included in Kissinger's personal staff. The disastrous influence of Douglas Pike over the course of American policy in Vietnam during early 1975 will be discussed shortly.

Although it might be an interesting academic exercise to make a listing of CIA operatives and their activities in Vietnam, it is essentially a job that will lead to no end. For example, many career diplomats and professional soldiers who served in Vietnam also worked with the CIA. Philip Habib, the U.S. undersecretary of state for Pacific Affairs, for example, worked with the CIA when he was in Vietnam. In 1966 it was Habib who authorized the loan of U.S. helicopters to Marshal Nguyen Cao Ky for carrying marines into Danang to smash the Buddhist opposition there. Rather than indulge in such academic exercises, let me instead point out how CIA activities since mid-1974 brought about the predicament in Vietnam in the spring of 1975.

In the summer of 1974 in the face of stepped-up counterattacks by the National Liberation Front/Provisional Revolutionary Government (NLF/PRG), a movement in the U.S. Congress to cut aid to Saigon, and President Nixon's imminent impeachment or resignation, there was widespread agreement among American officials and CIA agents that President Thieu should be replaced in Saigon because his faithfulness in carrying out the Nixon doctrine and the widespread corruption of his regime had clearly made him a liability. A number of CIA agents as well as State Department officials, therefore, went to Capitol Hill and hinted to some congressmen and senators that Thieu could be replaced and that aid to Saigon did not necessarily mean aid to the Thieu regime. These hints caused some concern to a few senators, who began to ask questions about the consequences of Thieu's overthrow.

When Ambassador Graham Martin was asked during testimony before the Senate on July 25, 1974, about the effects of a replacement of Thieu, he assured the senators that "constitutional" replacement of Thieu "would be managed easily" and that he did "not anticipate that any change in individuals would cause any deviation from the present thrust of the Government of Vietnam." In July and August many American officials and CIA agents also visited prominent political and religious figures in Saigon and, in order to feel them out, implied that there might be a change in leadership in Saigon. Among these American visitors was Douglas Pike. In early September Pike was lifted from a relatively insignificant USIA job to become Kissinger's assistant on Vietnam.

Perhaps prompted by these events, on September 5, 1974, the Catholic Anti-Corruption Campaign issued "Indictment No. 1," accusing Thieu of six specific charges of corruption. Quoting Father Thanh, the Campaign's chairman, the October 7, 1974, issue of the *Washington Post* stated that the reasons for the Catholic actions were that "South Vietnam also needs a clean government so 'our allies will trust us' and will send foreign aid and investment." For about two months thereafter, South Vietnam was convulsed by an extremely well organized and well financed campaign against corruption. There were also daily rallies and demonstrations, the larger ones organized by the Catholics. A number involved tens of thousands of Catholic faithful.

During this period CIA agents flocked to South Vietnam. Phillip A. McCombs reported in the November 2, 1974, *Washington Post* that "a significant number of CIA agents has come to Saigon during the past two months of protests . . . renewing contacts in both the opposition and the government to report on developments." The U.S. Embassy in Saigon publicly encouraged a coalition of conservative forces within the Catholic, Buddhist, Cao Dai, and Hoa Hao churches to give the appearance of widespread popular backing for Thieu's successor regime (*Hoa Binh*, September 27, 1974).

The Buddhist Church jumped on this suggestion, sent their people to meet with representatives of the other three religions, and publicly called upon the four religions "to take the responsibility upon themselves as a force rallying the people to demand peace and to force all the warring parties to sit down and nego-widespread popular backing for Thieu's successor regime (*Hoa Binh*, September 27, 1974).

Many Third Force (neither pro-NLF/PRG nor pro-Thieu) groups joined in the demonstrations and rallies called by the Catholics in order to make their views heard. The Catholics, however, were worried that participation by Third Force groups would have the effect of upstaging them, expanding the focus of their opposition, and making the situation too fluid for them to control. CIA agents (General Edward Lansdale, the infamous hero of *The Ugly American*, among them) came back from Vietnam in early October and recommended that the plan to have Thieu replaced should be called off unless everyone was sure that Thieu could be replaced peacefully in a very short time.

On October 18, 1974, Nguyen Van Chau, secretary general of the Vietnam Pax Romana and former deputy commander of the cadre training center in Vung Tau, arrived in Washington under the auspices of the U.S. State Department. Chau spent ten days in Washington at the homes of his CIA friends. During this time he visited with many officials and politicians in the U.S. government and told them that as the representative of the Catholic Anti-Corruption Campaign, his message was that Thieu should not be forced to leave too soon. He argued that the Campaign wanted Thieu to stay in power until the October elections so that he could be used as a focus for galvanizing the Campaign and training Catholics in political struggle so that they would be able to deal with the communists later on. Chau admitted that the Catholic movement in the local areas was not firmly organized and that there was still a lack of talented and able cadres. The Campaign, he said, needed more time to organize itself to control the transfer of power. (When faced with these and other statements by Chau, Father Thanh issued a public statement denying that Chau was a member of the Campaign, adding, however, that "he is a very close friend of mine who knows my position very clearly and would never say anything contrary to my thinking" (*Dai Dan Toc,* December 5, 1974).

On October 21, 1974, three days after Chau's arrival in Washington, the U.S. Embassy in Saigon issued a six-page statement of wholehearted support for Thieu, denying that it supported any of the dissenting political groups (*Washington Post,* January 19, 1975). This statement was followed by a warm message of support from President Ford on the occasion of National Day, November 1. According to the *Post,* "Thieu appeared in public that day, ebullient." On the very next day, Thieu embarked on a series of political repressions that resulted in the arrest and death of many Third Force members and the flight underground of the rest.

The Catholics immediately ceased all public activity and became increasingly anticommunist in their public statements. For example, on November 13, Father Thanh emphasized in a press conference: "We're anti-Communist. We have never taken advantage of the Catholic Church" (*Chinh Luan,* November 14, 1974). On November 17, he read a statement that, in effect, spelled out the Campaign's political platform and plan of action. In the statement he compared the NLF/PRG to maggots, saying that the corrupt Saigon regime was just like a rotten corpse giving life to the communist maggots. For that reason, Father Thanh said that there had to be a change in the leadership of the Saigon regime but that the regime itself should be maintained intact with all its paraphernalia such as the constitution, which outlaws the legal existence of the Communists. At the same time the Catholics, U.S. officials, and CIA agents began devising plans for replacing Thieu quietly in the upcoming presidential elections scheduled for October 1975 so as to install a more "acceptable" government in Saigon, one which the United States could support without risking too much domestic dissension. If, however, Thieu agreed to go peacefully before October, they would conduct an election in which there would be five or six slates to give the appearance that there is indeed democracy in South Vietnam. They would then conduct a runoff election between the two top "votegetters." The "winner" would be the one able to get more than 50 percent of the votes. This situation would show that the new regime really had the support of the people.

Of course, all of these intrigues were for the purpose of sabotaging the Paris Peace Agreement. The Agreement states that the tripartite National Council of Reconciliation and Concord will "decide the procedures and modalities" of elections. But the Catholics and CIA agents wanted to organize an election under the provisions of the Saigon constitution. On November 19, 1974, Colonel Vo Dong Giang, NLF/PRG spokesman at the Two-party Military Commission in Saigon, held a press conference in which he criticized Father Thanh and his Campaign for trying to maintain the Thieu regime, for following American policy, and for refusing to move toward peace as called for by the Paris Peace Agreement and as desired by the Vietnamese people. The colonel also called on the United States to respect and implement the Agreement.

Perhaps partly because of the realization that the Catholics would not want to move toward peace by having Thieu replaced and partly because of the Ford administration's push for more aid to Saigon, the NLF/PRG began to mount a series of counter-attacks against Thieu's forces in an attempt to point out that when forced into a military confrontation Saigon forces would not be able to stand up in spite of all their military gadgets. Both the Thieu regime and the Ford administration jumped on these attacks in order to ask for more aid. Democratic Senator Hubert Humphrey maneuvered through a foreign aid bill that authorized $450 million in "economic aid" to the Saigon regime for fiscal year 1975, $100 million more than the amount authorized for fiscal 1974.

According to a Saigon paper (*Dien Tin*, January 16, 1975), 90 percent of U.S. economic aid to Saigon has been used to maintain the war. For this reason the NLF/PRG, among others, must have interpreted this action by Congress as a renewed commitment to the Thieu regime. The NLF/PRG therefore increased its military pressure, and by early January eight districts and a province fell. But the United States and the Saigon ruling circles refused to learn the lesson of these events. After the NLF/PRG forces relaxed their military pressure to wait for a response from Saigon toward some kind of a political solution, Father Thanh said publicly that the Communists had been lucky enough to take a few isolated districts and towns but would never be able to take over more heavily defended areas.

Meanwhile, in mid-January CIA agents briefed many people

in the Senate about their "heartland policy." They maintained that the Saigon army had high morale and was fully equipped but overextended and for that reason could meet with defeat by selective and concentrated attacks from the Communists. They thought that such defeat would have the effect of lowering the morale of the Saigon forces while raising domestic opposition to increased support to Saigon. They recommended withdrawal to the coastal areas and abandonment of some Central Highlands provinces to preserve the strength of the Saigon troops. It was pointed out that such withdrawal had the advantage of providing tighter control of populous areas, making it possible to conduct and control the upcoming elections free of communist sabotage. Also for the purposes of convincing congressional leaders of the morale of the Saigon troops and the need for increased aid, the White House and the various agencies suggested that a congressional fact-finding delegation pay a visit to Saigon.

While in Saigon some members of the congressional delegation were briefed by CIA agents about the possibility of having to give up some Central Highlands and central coastal provinces so as to create a "balance of forces" that would enable the Saigon regime to put up an effective stand against the NLF/PRG. As reported in the April 7, 1975, issue of *Far Eastern Economic Review,* while accompanying the delegation to Saigon, Philip Habib, the U.S. undersecretary of state for Pacific Affairs, also outlined to Thieu this option of withdrawal from the Central Highlands. Thieu was not enthusiastic about this fallback option at the time. Some congressional leaders, however, became convinced after a few days of conversations with CIA agents and other U.S. officials as well as Saigon political personalities that the morale of the Saigon troops was high and that they were well-trained. Even Representative Pete McCloskey, a veteran dove, came back from the tour impressed and said repeatedly in many interviews that he would recommend continued aid to Saigon for three more years.

Perhaps in reaction partly to the attitude of American officials and the Saigon ruling class and partly to the attitude of the congressional delegation, the NLF/PRG again mounted military pressures after a month's lull. Aided by the uprisings of mountain tribesmen, NLF/PRG forces surrounded Banmethout, Kontum, and Pleiku and pushed Thieu to carry out hastily the

American plan of withdrawal to the coastal areas. This fallback option was the straw that broke the camel's back and led Saigon to abandon one province after another because its troops simply refused to put up any kind of a fight.

Meanwhile, CIA agents keep themselves busy with public-relations maneuvers such as so-called "humanitarian aid" to refugees and orphans, who actually are the victims of CIA activities that sabotaged the establishment of peace in Vietnam in the first place.

The CIA
against Cambodia

Sokhom Hing

■ Sokhom Hing, a native of Cambodia, is assistant professor of economics at the State University of New York College at Old Westbury. Since 1970 he has served as a spokesman for the group Khmer Residents in America.

CIA ACTIVITIES IN CAMBODIA cannot be examined, analyzed, explained, or exposed apart from the goals of U.S. foreign policy in general. Nor can the overthrow of Prince Norodom Sihanouk's policy of peace, independence, and neutrality for Cambodia by the CIA-supported Lon Nol clique be explained on easy conspiratorial grounds alone. Nor can these matters be explained solely on the basis of a simplistic economism that attributes the downfall to economic mismanagement.

The CIA was born in an atmosphere of Cold War tension. Its raison d'être is to serve the U.S. government in the conduct of foreign policy, especially when the United States cannot get its own way through proper diplomatic channels. The strategy of U.S. foreign policy is global. Right after World War II, the United States emerged as the major Western power, replacing the declining British. Because of its expanded productive capacity and advanced technology and science, the United States had been able to produce tremendous quantities of goods and services, including sophisticated weaponry to supply most of its Western allies and others in the war. In the process the United States became able to shape part of the world according to its

image. The "oneness" of national security and business interests
has ever since been put in the forefront of U.S. foreign policy.

Another force has also emerged at the opposite pole from
the United States—the USSR. Although devastated by the German fascists in World War II, the Soviet Union was able to
rehabilitate its wrecked economy and become a major world
power. With its advanced knowledge in science and technology,
the Soviet Union has reached the status of an industrial state.
In 1949 China also became an independent socialist state, after
a protracted revolutionary war of national liberation.

In the early 1950s the world was divided into two camps:
the capitalist camp, as represented by the United States, and the
socialist camp, as represented by the USSR and the People's Republic of China. Between these two camps emerged numerous
new states freshly broken away from the colonialist yoke. After
hundreds of years of foreign domination, suppression, and exploitation, these new, young nations wanted to be free and independent and did not intend to align themselves with either
major force. Their main desire was to secure some relative internal stability, security, and unity so that they could develop
their economies, left backward by colonialism, according to the
aspirations of their own people.

Cambodia was one of those countries. Cambodia fought and
won her independence from France in 1953. With the overwhelming approval of the Cambodian people, the Royal Government, guided by Prince Norodom Sihanouk, declared in 1953
that Cambodia would stay neutral and nonaligned. At a later
date, Cambodia's emphasis on neutrality was made clear to the
world when the Royal Government issued the following draft
statement:

> The Royal Government of Cambodia, being resolved to fol-
> low the path of peace and neutrality in conformity with the
> interests and aspirations of the Cambodian people, as well
> as the principles of the Geneva Agreements of 1954, in or-
> der to build a peaceful, neutral, independent and prosperous
> Cambodia, solemnly declares that:
>
> 1. It will resolutely apply the five principles of peaceful co-
>   existence in foreign relations, and will develop friendly
>   relations with all countries on the basis of equality and
>   reciprocal respect for independence and sovereignty;

2. It is the will of the Cambodian people to protect and ensure respect for the sovereignty, independence, neutrality
   and territorial integrity of Cambodia. . . .
7. It will accept direct and unconditional aid from all countries that wish to help the kingdom of Cambodia to build
   up an independent and autonomous national economy on
   the basis of respect for the sovereignty of Cambodia;
8. It will respect the treaties and agreements signed in conformity with the interests of the Cambodian people and
   the policy of peace and neutrality of the Kingdom, in particular the Geneva Agreements of 1954 and 1962.[1]

The draft statement was not well received by the U.S. government. John Foster Dulles, then Secretary of State under the
Eisenhower administration, openly declared that neutrality was
immoral and dangerous. At the Overseas Press Club of America
on March 29, 1954, Dulles stated, as reported the next day in
The New York Times:

> The United States has shown in many ways its sympathy
> with the gallant struggle being waged in Indo-China by the
> French forces and those of the Associated States. And Con-
> gress has enabled us to provide material aid to the estab-
> lished governments and to their peoples. Also our diplomacy
> has sought to deter Communist China from open aggression
> in the area.

It is unmistakably clear that Dulles, as U.S. foreign policy
maker, was interested in extending the area under U.S. domination so as to preserve and enhance U.S. interests. This was done
at the expense of other states' independence, sovereignty, security, and welfare. The U.S. government would side with the colonialists and the local dictators and reactionary elements as long
as they cooperated with the U.S. global strategy of containment.

By 1954 the United States and its allies had already established a military pact in Southeast Asia, SEATO. Dulles put tremendous pressure on the Royal Government to accept SEATO
and its "umbrella of protection" against communism. In May
1955, agreements were concluded with the U.S. government
under which the latter was responsible for making payments
to the Cambodian administration and army and U.S. military
personnel engaged in the training of the Cambodian army were
to enjoy extraterritoriality. The U.S. government continued to

pour aid into Cambodia in the hope that the Royal Government would change its mind and make a compromise with the United States on matters concerning SEATO.

In January 1956, Prince Sihanouk went to Manila at the invitation of Philippines President Magsaysay. During his stay in Manila, Prince Sihanouk was pressured by Senator Manglapus of the Philippines to accept SEATO membership. He was also approached by a CIA covert operative named François Baroukh. Baroukh tried to persuade Prince Sihanouk to deliver a speech favorable to SEATO. He refused. In his book *My War with the CIA*, Prince Sihanouk said:

> My first experience with CIA intervention in Cambodian affairs dates back to late 1955, when Allen Dulles, then head of the CIA, visited me in Phnom Penh. Prior to this, his brother, the late John Foster Dulles, had called on me in his capacity as Secretary of State, and he had exhausted every argument to persuade me to place Cambodia under the protection of the Southeast Asia Treaty Organization. I refused, because such arrangement was contrary to the pledge of neutrality accepted by Cambodia at the 1954 Geneva Conference, and which I was to reaffirm at the Bandung Conference in April 1955.[2]

Faithful to the principles of neutrality and nonalignment, Prince Sihanouk made trips to the Soviet Union, Czechoslovakia, Yugoslavia, and Poland and established diplomatic and trade relations with them during 1956–1957. He also went to the People's Republic of China, and in 1956 Cambodia recognized China. At this juncture the U.S. government began to put greater pressure on the Royal Government to change its foreign policy. When open diplomacy did not work, the U.S. government resorted to the law of the jungle by relying on the CIA to help organize plots and assassination attempts against Prince Sihanouk and sabotage within Cambodia as well as trying from outside to overthrow the Royal Government.

Robert McClintock was the first U.S. ambassador to Cambodia. He was known to be an experienced agent of the CIA. William Donovan was U.S. ambassador to Thailand until 1954. Donovan had been director of the Office of Strategic Services, the forerunner of the CIA. Donovan's successor in Bangkok was John F. Peurifoy, another CIA covert operative, who had masterminded the coup in Guatemala that overthrew the Arbenz government. In the Philippines, President Magsaysay was elected in 1953 with the help of a CIA operative, an Air Force colonel named Edward Lansdale. Later Lansdale was sent to Vietnam to help bolster the regime of Ngo Dinh Diem. Diem won the election in 1955 with 98 percent of the vote. In short, the U.S. government had a network of covert operations in Southeast Asia, and Cambodia was practically surrounded.

Inside Cambodia the CIA succeeded in making contact with Cambodian rightists, some of whom occupied high offices in the Royal Government, such as Sirik Matak, Lon Nol, Son Ngoc Thanh, Dap Chhuon, and Sam Sary. The CIA tried to consolidate these links and isolate Prince Sihanouk. At the same time Cambodian progressives were the targets of the CIA. In 1958 Nop Bophann, the director of a progressive newspaper, was cowardly assassinated in daylight in the center of Phnom Penh near a military barracks. Prince Sihanouk vehemently condemned this criminal act. In 1959 Prince Sihanouk was the target of an assassination attempt by a man named Rat Vat, who was apprehended by the security police and later confessed that he was sent by the CIA. He was executed. In September 1958 SEATO members met in Bangkok, calling for strong action against Cambodia. The plan was called the Bangkok Plan. According to Malcolm Salmon, the Bangkok Plan was approved by the late President Eisenhower. Salmon also says:

> In its maximum form, the Bangkok Plan involved the forceful overthrow of the Cambodian government, the assassination of Prince Sihanouk, the abolition of the Cambodian monarchy and the establishment of a Diem-style "republic" throughout Cambodian territory. In its minimum form, it involved the dismemberment of Cambodia with the formation of a so-called provisional Government of "free" Cambodia comprising the provinces of Battambang and Siem Reap (bordering Thailand), the central province of Kompong Thom, and the provinces of Stung Treng and Kratie (bordering South Vietnam). Success of the minimum Bangkok Plan would have opened up a corridor through Cambodia territory from South Vietnam to Thailand, encircling and isolating neutral Cambodia and preparing the ground for civil war. Under maximum and minimum plan alike, Son Ngoc Thanh was to be president of the new Cambodian government, Sam Sary prime minister, and Dap Chhuon, minister of defense.[3]

Ngo Dinh Diem of South Vietnam and Sarit Thanarat of Thailand and CIA operatives helped execute the Bangkok Plan. The three Cambodian collaborators were Son Ngoc Thanh, Sam Sary, and Dap Chhuon. While working inside Cambodia, Sam Sary and Dap Chhuon were supposed to contact the South Vietnamese representative to Cambodia, Ngo Trong Hieu, Diem's man in Phnom Penh. Son Ngoc Thanh had the task of setting up armed groups along the Cambodian-Thailand border. According to Salmon, Thanh had two senior Thai military men and a sum of $1.2 million in U.S. money placed at his disposal for this purpose.

The plot was discovered by the Royal Government. Sam Sary fled to Saigon and later died. On February 21, 1959, Royal Army troops went to Siem Reap to arrest Dap Chhuon. In *The Second Indochina War* Wilfred Burchett wrote:

> The rebel headquarters was raided in time. Large stock of arms, a quantity of small gold ingots for buying collaborators, and incriminating documents were found. Dap Chhuon was wounded by one of his own men in the surprise attack and, according to accounts later, he asked for a highranking officer to whom he wanted to make a statement on the background of the plot which would have incriminated Lon Nol. The latter, then head of the Cambodian army, sent someone to finish off Dap Chhuon with a bullet in the head.[4]

In this plot an American of Japanese descent, Victor Masao Matsui, was involved. He was a CIA agent stationed in the U.S. Embassy in Phnom Penh. He worked very closely with Ngo Trong Hieu, the South Vietnamese ambassador to Cambodia.[5]

From 1954 until diplomatic relations were broken in 1965, there were at least twenty-seven known CIA covert operatives registered as diplomats at the U.S. Embassy in Phnom Penh. During the period from 1961 to March 18, 1970, Cambodia had to deal with a multitude of provocations and subversive activities on the part of the CIA, with Lon Nol, Sirik Matak, and Son Ngoc Thanh as collaborators.

Son Ngoc Thanh, a politician who collaborated with the Japanese militarists during World War II, worked closely with the U.S. Special Forces (Green Berets) stationed in South Vietnam and in Thailand. The Green Berets trained Son Ngoc Thanh's troops, called Kampuchea Khmer Krom (KKK). These KKK troops were recruited in South Vietnam among the Cambodian minority living there. When Lon Nol staged the coup d'état on March 18, 1970, that overthrew Prince Sihanouk, Son Ngoc Thanh sent his troops from South Vietnam to Phnom Penh to support the coup. This action was part of the agreement worked out between Lon Nol, Son Ngoc Thanh, and the CIA a few months before the coup. In a Dispatch News Service International report of October 12, 1971, T. D. Allman, an Oxford University scholar, wrote:

> In a recent series of interviews with this reporter, Son Ngoc Thanh indicated that at least some Americans, in an official capacity, supported plots to overthrow Sihanouk in the crucial months of the last half of 1969 and the first quarter of 1970.
>
> Among the facts emerging from the conversations with Son Ngoc Thanh, who is considered a prime candidate to become the first President of the fledgling Khmer Republic: —In early 1969, the U.S. government, working through agents attached to Son Ngoc Thanh's staff of exiled anti-Sihanouk partisans, gave assurances of U.S. support for anti-Sihanouk moves in Cambodia, including a two-pronged invasion of the country.—February 1970, when Sihanouk left Cambodia for France, members of the Lon Nol entourage were considering deposing Sihanouk, but were apprehensive that communists would launch a retaliation attack. U.S. CIA personnel promised to do "everything possible" when asked to support Thanh's Khmer Krom troops should the retaliation attack occur.

These are the proofs that the U.S. government, through CIA covert operations, was directly involved in the coup that destroyed Cambodia's principles of peace, neutrality, and independence. Before the coup the CIA contacted Lon Nol at the American hospital in Paris and encouraged destabilization efforts in order to create economic and political chaos inside Cambodia, especially in Phnom Penh. The CIA also sent an American cargo ship, *Columbia Eagle,* to carry munitions to the seaport of Sihanoukville two days before the coup. The ship was closely guarded, but it was photographed low in the water when it arrived and high in the water when it left, indicating that its cargo had been unloaded. On the day of the coup reporters in Phnom Penh were surprised to find Lon Nol soldiers armed with U.S. M-16 rifles not previously in the Cambodian arsenal. Six weeks after the coup, the U.S. invaded Cambodia to help Lon Nol, thus plunging Cambodia into the Indochina war.

U.S. Intervention in Cambodia and the Philippines

Russell Johnson

■ Russell Johnson is program consultant for the New England Region of the American Friends Service Committee. From 1961 to 1965 he directed the Quaker International Conference and Seminar Program in South and Southeast Asia. Since that time he has made repeated visits to that region. He has also visited Cuba and China.

I FIRST BECAME ACQUAINTED with Prince Norodom Sihanouk of Cambodia in the early 1960s. I can remember talking with him in Phnom Penh in those days when Cambodia was a beautiful, peaceful kingdom, and he was working for, in effect, a noncommunist, nonviolent, and nonaligned method of social change. He talked very freely about the 1959 plot to assassinate him in which the governor of Siem Reap province was used by the CIA. But fortunately for Sihanouk, President De Gaulle tipped him off because the French were not happy about the American intrusion in what had been their domain. When I had a chance to visit with him in Peking in 1971, Sihanouk told me that the CIA had obtained someone with a high-pitched voice identical to his and was broadcasting in the name of the prince into the occupied areas of Cambodia. This item is a very interesting little example of all the different, clever ways and means that the CIA has used to try to discredit legitimate revolutionary movements and to bolster U.S. allies.

In June of 1970, three months after the overthrow of Sihanouk and at a time of widespread protest in the United States, a friend who was working with Lon Nol said to me in private conversation in Phnom Penh: "When is your government going to give us the aid that has been promised us? We are getting a little desperate." The reason the Lon Nol regime was getting "a little desperate" is that it had had a commitment made to it, but because of the outrage in this country—among the people and in the Congress—the CIA and the Pentagon were having to play it very cool. What they counted on was that opposition would die down, as it did, and that they then could begin to move back into Cambodia. And that is what happened.

What this fact means for the American people is, I think, eternal vigilance. One of the areas to be vigilant about is the Philippines. In 1898 the United States took over several territories from Spain: notably Cuba, the Philippines, and Puerto Rico. I had a chance to visit Cuba in 1969. As I traveled around for thirty days, examining their revolution and trying to do a little homework on what had happened that led to it, I found that there were several key factors. One was that there was a privileged ruling elite that was completely self-serving and self-aggrandizing and indifferent to the welfare of most of the people. A second was that though there was a fairly substantial middle class—perhaps 15 to 20 percent of the population in Cuba—the bulk of the people either lived in slum areas in the cities or in the countryside, virtually neglected, penniless, and ignored by the ruling elite. The third factor was foreign exploitation, mainly by American corporations, of the resources of Cuba. It was that background that led to a revolution, the toppling of a tyrannical regime in an essentially Roman Catholic country, and the coming into power of a communist leadership.

This, essentially, is the present situation in the Philippines. I think that the Philippines is going to pose the next major crisis for American policy in Southeast Asia. As powerful interests in our country are now being forced out of Indochina, the stake that they have in the Philippines is going to become more and more important. Admiral Noel Gayler, the chief of our Pacific command, in an interview in the March 25, 1974, *U.S. News & World Report* spoke very emphatically of the great importance strategically of the more than twenty-seven different military bases that our government has in the Philippines, including the Subic Bay naval base, which is our largest naval base outside the North American continent, and Clark Air Force base, which is our largest Air Force base outside the North American continent. Today under the regime of President Ferdinand Marcos, who declared martial law and brought democracy to an end in the Philippines in September of 1972, there is no longer any freedom for the people.

Yet there is tremendous privilege for American, Japanese, and other multinational corporations that invest in the Philippines. They can take out their capital gains. There are no taxes on them. There are no trade unions to worry about any longer. There is a vast pool of unskilled labor. There is no opposition press. There are no opposition congressmen. So for an executive of, say, the Ford Motor Company, it would make sense to invest in the Philippines because profits would average five times as great on operations there as on operations in the United States. This situation also holds true in Taiwan, South Korea, and so on. I am calling attention to the Philippines because there is now almost $3 billion of American investment in banks and businesses there. (Chase Manhattan Bank had a meeting with its board of directors there in the fall of 1974. They said that it was because of the "growing importance of the Philippines in the bank's operations in Asia.")

There are three types of rebellion facing the Marcos regime. There is full-scale war going on now in the southern islands of Mindanao and the Sulus. The war is being waged by the Moslem minority, who have always been treated like second-class citizens by the Christian north. This area is another part of the world where, as with American Indians, there is a new generation rising up to wage armed resistance. In the case of the Moslem Filipinos, they are receiving weapons from Libya and other places.

In the northern islands there is the New People's Army. They are Maoist-oriented communists. They are not the Huks of the post–World War II period but a new group begun by university teachers and students who packed up and went off into the hills à la Fidel Castro, in one case taking along most of the weapons of the big armory in the Philippines military academy with them. Now they are waging essentially political struggle. But they are also preparing for armed struggle.

The major opposition to Marcos is within the Catholic and Protestant communities. One Catholic priest, Father Edicio de la Torre, is now in prison, and there are reports that he has been tortured. There are many other priests and nuns who have been held and tortured in the prisons of the Philippines.

The tragedy for us in this country is that we have not heard about these occurrences yet. Although I cannot document CIA activity in the Philippines, all that I have learned supports the view that there is an operation going on there similar to those described as occurring in other countries. It is no coincidence that the American diplomat who headed up the so-called secret war in Laos, William Sullivan, is now our ambassador in the Philippines. American warships have been seen shelling rebel-held positions. War planes have been seen ferrying Filipino troops and equipment into battle. And the Green Berets have been there on training missions.

There is, however, the possibility for action to prevent something like another Vietnam in the Philippines because Marcos is still very conscious of his image in this country. His is not so repressive and brutal a regime as that in South Vietnam under President Thieu or that in South Korea under President Park. Many of the major opposition leaders have been put in jail, but there is a chance of new opposition leadership coming up. Getting acquainted with the organization called the Friends of the Filipino People (11 Garden Street, Cambridge, Massachusetts 02138) is a good way for people in this country to become informed about developments in the Philippines.

We should also learn something from the people of Cambodia and the people of Vietnam—it is a long, long struggle (it may take generations) to liberate a people. Most progressive Americans have been too spoiled and have given up too early. Even though the Vietnamese and Cambodians are very modest and humble people, we have a lot to learn from them about what it takes to wage a struggle for liberation. And that's what Americans are now into.

The Secret Wars of the CIA

Fred Branfman

■ Fred Branfman was educational adviser to International Voluntary Services in Laos from 1967 to 1969, a writer and researcher in Laos from 1969 to 1971, director of the U.S. antiwar group Project Air War from 1971 to 1973, and codirector of the Indochina Resource Center from 1973 to 1975. In 1975 and 1976 he was policy coordinator of the Tom Hayden for U.S. Senate campaign in California. As the Indochina war reached its climax, Mr. Branfman made the following presentation at the Conference on the CIA and World Peace.

I WILL TRY to give a brief overview of the aspects of CIA activities in Indochina that I think are most relevant for us as Americans.

What the CIA has done in Indochina is the most ambitious experiment in history to control the political behavior of entire populations. I have never felt comfortable with the word "genocide." I think it has very specific connotations for most people. It is what the Nazis did to the Jews. Precisely because U.S. leaders could not practice that kind of genocide—the systematic extermination of an entire people—in Indochina, they turned to the beaviorial control techniques that I shall discuss.

In what follows, think about the kind of mentality that U.S. leaders showed in Indochina. The CIA is only an example. The entire executive branch, as we know from the Kissinger papers ("National Security Study Memorandum #1," which was revealed by Daniel Ellsberg), was fully aware of what the CIA did in Indochina. The kind of mentality that the CIA officials had in doing what I am about to describe is fully shared by all our national leadership. This mentality has direct implications for all of us. As I go on, think about how it works, how it regards other human beings, how it is controlled.

I'd like to speak about three broad areas: (1) CIA activities on the ground in Laos; (2) CIA involvement in the air war in Laos; (3) certain aspects of the CIA police intervention in South Vietnam. I shall focus largely on this last area.

CIA Involvement on the Ground in Laos

What the CIA did in Laos was very simple. It created an army of its own, an army paid, controlled, and directed by American CIA officials entirely separate from the normal Laotian government structure. This army was originally made up of Meos. After the Meos were destroyed, however, large numbers of Thais were brought in. There were also Burmese, Laotians, Chinese, and Filipinos. In fact, some troops from every people in Southeast Asia were brought into Laos as part of what became known as "the secret army." The CIA trained the secret army; directed it in combat; decided when it would fight; and had it carry out espionage missions, assassinations of military and civilian figures, and sabotage.

The CIA also put a great deal of emphasis on psychological warfare. The question of psychological warfare is very interesting. Americans were told in the early 1960s that the core of our program would be to win "hearts and minds" in Indochina. A tremendous attempt was indeed made to do this through land reform, education, and the rest. To make a very long story short, the attempt failed. By the time Richard Nixon came into office, the whole "hearts and minds" concept was scrapped. Instead of changing people's attitudes, the emphasis shifted to controlling their behavior. We couldn't affect how they thought, but we could try and control their political behavior. We could control it, for example, by penning them in as refugees, carrying on assassination programs, and the like.

The paramilitary ground activities carried out by the CIA can be discussed at length. I have talked about them for two hundred pages in a manuscript on the CIA in Laos. Let me give you just one example. There was a fellow in northwest Laos. He was a near legendary CIA agent who went out there in the late 1950s. He set up a camp in Nam Ou, right near China. Between 1965 and 1970 this man, using thousands of anti-communist tribesmen, would send intelligence-gathering teams into China and carry out combat operations against the Pathet Lao. The teams that went into China would not only surveil, tap telephone lines, and so on. They would carry out "snatches." They kidnapped people and brought them back where they tortured them to get information.

This agent typified one aspect of the CIA in Laos. There are many stories I could tell about him, but I will tell just one. In the late 1960s a friend of mine was a pilot for a private CIA airline. The agent threw a box on the airplane one day and said, "Take this to Landry in Udorn." (Pat Landry was the head of the CIA in Udorn, coordinating the Burma-Thailand-Laos-North Vietnam theatre.) My friend started flying the plane and noticed a bad odor coming from the box. After some time he could not stand it anymore and opened up the box. Inside was a fresh human head. This was a joke. The idea was to see what Pat Landry would do when someone put this box on his desk. You cannot throw a human head in the wastepaper basket, you cannot throw it in the garbage can. CIA paramilitary activities were and are being carried out by people, like this agent, who have gone beyond the pale of civilized behavior. There are hundreds of these people now working in the Third World. This fact is, of course, not just a disgrace, but a clear and present danger.

Another story I want to tell briefly concerns a friend of mine named Ron Richenbach, an Agency for International Development (AID) official who exposed the CIA secret army in 1968 to Senator Kennedy's subcommittee on refugees. He then went back to Laos in a private capacity and found that all the Americans working there were furious at him for having blown the whistle. Richenbach had committed the grave error of complaining about the fact that as a result of CIA activities in Laos, the Meos were being exterminated as a people.

One day he went into a soup shop and, horrified, saw a man

named Vince Shields, who was the head of the CIA at Long Chien, the secret CIA base in northern Laos. Of course, Ron was very worried. He hoped he would not be noticed, but Shields called him over. They started to talk, and Richenbach was amazed to find that Shields was very friendly. He finally could not stand it anymore and said, "Look, aren't you angry at me?" Shields said,

> No! Listen, you've got the right story. Of course we're destroying the Meo people, but it doesn't bother me very much because I've never pretended that I'm here to help the Meo people. I work for the United States government. It's only these AID people who are all confused and think they're here to help somebody. I'm not angry at you. Frankly, I respect your conscience. I'm glad you did it.

And so we have two CIA types, the technician—the cool, calm character who directs these programs without any emotion—and the other type, those who have been there a long time and have become totally brutalized in the process.

What about controls on CIA paramilitary activities? When people bring up the question of congressional control of the CIA, they should be reminded of the Thai troops in Laos. In 1970 it was revealed that the United States had something like 5,000 to 10,000 Thai troops fighting in Laos in the pay of the CIA. So Congress passed a law expressly forbidding that. The CIA simply ignored the law. Not only did it keep funding the Thai troops already there, but it even increased the number to 20,000. In effect, the CIA simply said, "Well, these people are no longer Thai troops. They are volunteers to the Laotian government. Since we pay the Laotian government, that is O.K." In fact, they did not even observe that nicety. The CIA continued to pay them itself.

This situation is a very dramatic example of the fact that even when Congress tries to stop CIA secret paramilitary activities on the ground, they find they cannot.

CIA Involvement in the Air War in Laos

I can sum this situation up by saying that the United States dropped two million tons of bombs on Laos, as much as was dropped on both the European and Pacific theaters in World War II. The majority of these bombing raids were targeted by CIA officials, not Air Force officials. The CIA officials worked at Udorn Air Force Base. They were a special team of photo reconnaissance people who, because they were CIA, because the CIA had men at Udorn, and others on the ground, bureaucratically decided what would be bombed. In Laos a whole society was wiped off the face of the earth, with the CIA playing a major role.

I shall concentrate on the third area, CIA police activities in South Vietnam, because I think that it is the most relevant today. We are not yet at the stage where we have organized groups in the United States involved in a liberation struggle. That is why the paramilitary and air war aspects are not directly relevant. But the question of CIA police activities for political control affects us all quite directly.

CIA Police System in Vietnam

I think the issue of the police system that the CIA initiated, created, planned, trained, implemented, and ran on a day-to-day basis in Vietnam is one of the most important matters of the post–World War II era. You see the tip of the iceberg when you talk about political prisoners in Thieu's South Vietnam. Not enough thinking has gone into the reason why there are so many political prisoners, why they are so badly treated, what the system is that generated all these political prisoners.

There are eight aspects of the police system that are entirely the creation of the CIA and the responsibility of the CIA. For although military personnel and AID personnel also were involved, the CIA was the controlling arm through William Colby, who was head of pacification in Vietnam and is now head of the CIA.

The first aspect was the building up (virtually the creating) of an entirely new police force. There were only about 16,000 policemen in South Vietnam at the time of Diem. By 1975 this number had grown to 122,000. The CIA armed that police force with guns, computers, and a vast telecommunications network linking all the police centers. A policeman in a very small village was able to punch into his computer or work through his radio to get information from Saigon. Strong emphasis was given to building up a corps of informers. I remember talking to a teacher in South Vietnam, a professor at a university, when I was there in 1973. I said, "What is the difference in the police system under Diem and under Thieu?" He said:

> Well, under Diem when I used to teach my classes, I assumed I had an informer, maybe one person who was watching me. But I wasn't really aware of it. Although they may have reported what I said, I never got any warning. Now, I have dozens of informers in my class. Most of them are young men who have student deferments and were told their student deferments would be taken away if they didn't become informers. As a result, most of them are guilt-stricken, and they come to me to talk about it.

Throughout Thieu's South Vietnam, through a very deliberate CIA policy, there are hundreds of thousands of part-time and full-time informers. There are people on every block, people in every home, informing on their friends and relatives in a very active effort to collect information to fit into a data-collection system.

Second, after the buildup of the police force, was the buildup of the prison system. Clearly, if you are going to have a police system, you will have to build a lot of prisons. Former AID Director John Hannah has admitted there are 552 in South Vietnam. Others say 1,000. The fact is that Vietnam is honeycombed with prison systems, interrogation centers, separate national police detention camps, district prisons, and small camps out in the middle of nowhere.

A third aspect was the setting up of separate paramilitary units controlled directly by the CIA as part of this police system. The CIA has units in South Vietnam who dress up like the Vietcong, go out, and commit atrocities, which can then be blamed on the Vietcong.

The fourth aspect is the mass surveillance program. The most notorious aspect of this program is the National Identification Card Project, which was set up as a separate operation by the Office of Public Safety. The Office of Public Safety was, in practice, under the control of the CIA. The National Identification Card Project involved the issuing of ID cards to every Vietnamese over the age of fifteen, ID cards that he or she would have to carry at all times. These ID cards were linked to a centralized computer system. In this way every fact, every piece of information that could be collected about an indivdiual was organized. Numerous people, anyone who might have the slightest political activity, would have a file. I shall never forget talking to a fifteen-year-old kid in Saigon who had been arrested because he was putting out a little magazine in his high school. He said that the first day they arrested him, he was amazed to discover that they had been keeping voluminous records of all of his activities since he was twelve, and he had not even been aware of it.

This National Identification Card Project is one example of the main point that I want to make: when you hear about political prisoners, when you hear about torture in South Vietnam, you often tend to say, "Well, torture is kind of an Oriental characteristic." (If you are on the Left, you say that it is "a right-wing Oriental characteristic.") The truth is that the United States is fully responsible for everything that has happened in Vietnam, including torture.

I would like to quote from a U.S. Office of Public Safety document called *The National Identity Registration Project*, dated April 1967. The quotation goes:

> the project envisions the registration of all Vietnamese, fifteen years of age and over, the issuings of i.d. cards and the establishment of a national identity record center in Saigon. The U.S. Public Safety Division provided the national police with a draft of a suitable decree. The police considered this and on March 17, 1967, the decree law was signed by General Thieu, Chief of State.

Time and again these programs were dreamed up by Americans and put into practice by Americans, with the Vietnamese government approving them at the end.

Under the aspect of mass surveillance I would like in addition to mention the "brown book." Every South Vietnamese family is required to have in their home a brown book showing their photographs and relevant information about who lives in and is sleeping in that home. We can see how this mass surveillance system is penetrating people's bedrooms, people's friendships, people's families.

The next aspect, and here we get to the heart of repression, is a program of mass detention without trial. The way this works came across to me very dramatically when I was in Saigon. I was suddenly awakened at about two o'clock one morning by a flashlight shining in my eyes through the window and a voice calling, "Open up, open up!" I opened the door, and two South Vietnamese policemen entered without apology or explanation and asked for my passport. One began looking under my bed and in my closet. Then they walked out. Then they went throughout the building all night, breaking into people's rooms, looking around, trying to find something, trying to find some reason to arrest someone.

Talking with Vietnamese after that experience, I found that this situation was typical throughout Thieu's South Vietnam. Every day and night policemen go throughout the hamlets and the city blocks breaking into people's homes. Vietnamese are not so lucky as American visitors, of course, and many of them are simply hauled off, not to be seen again by their families.

Why do the police do this kind of thing? It sounds rather brutal and capricious. It does not seem to make very much sense. We can get a feeling for why when we read the Kissinger papers and come across the State Department response. At one point they talk about report padding and say:

> report padding may have increased recently under the pressure of attempting to reach the quota set for the accelerated pacification program.

What is this quota? In the July 1969 *Vietnam Information Notes,* a State Department publication, we find: "The target for 1969 calls for the elimination of 1,800 VCI per month." William Colby's office set up quotas on the number of people to be arrested —and killed—each month. Policemen, afraid of not getting promoted or worse, were told by CIA advisers how many sweeps they would have to make each night and how many people they would have to arrest in the hopes of destroying the "Vietcong infrastructure." To them the "Vietcong infrastructure" is not just the members of the Provisional Revolutionary Government. To them the VCI are civilians: teachers, nurses, tax collectors— anyone working for the other side in a civilian capacity.

Another part of the mass detention program of the CIA in South Vietnam is the infamous "administrative detention." If you set up a system that will involve sending out hundreds of policemen every day to arrest people to fill a quota, the jails are going to be crowded all the time. That is precisely what happened in South Vietnam. There are figures that show that in 1969, 180,000 people were processed through the National Police Detention Centers alone. If you arrest all these people, what do you do with them?

If you have to give everyone a lawyer and a fair trial, you will not have sufficient evidence, that is clear. So what you do is dream up something like the notion of administrative detention. This procedure is very simple. It means that the police can arrest anyone they want, and the person's dossier will be submitted to something called the Provincial Security Council, which is made up of a policeman, a province chief (who is a military person), a local prosecutor, and so on. This Provincial Security Council is entitled to arrest anyone for "two years renewable."

Congressman McCloskey estimates that of the 10,000 people in the prisons he visited when he was in South Vietnam, 5,000 never had a trial. If anything, the percentage is probably higher. Most of the people sitting in prisons under this mass detention program of the CIA were simply swept up without evidence, without proof, without any chance to prove their innocence.

When they do get a trial, the situation is even worse. In Saigon I attended a trial at the Bach Dang navy yard. The day I was there, they were not prosecuting political prisoners, but the process was the same. Young men would stand up before three judges. All of the judges were military people. One of them was wearing dark sunglasses, which struck me as most unjudgelike behavior. The chief judge would scream at the defendant for a while, insisting that he validate this confession that had been tortured out of him. The other two judges never said a word the entire morning. After some back-and-forth between the chief judge and the prosecutor with the defendant present, a young man would stand up dressed in black lawyer's robes and a white wig and say something. The first time, I asked the fellow who was interpreting for me what had been said. He said, "He is asking for the mercy of the court." This kind of thing is what went on all morning. Each trial took about ten minutes, with the lawyer begging for the mercy of the court. After three hours the judges retired to their chambers for ten minutes, then they came out and read the sentences for the twenty people who had been tried that morning.

I shall just list here the last three programs carried out by the CIA under its police system. They were: deliberate assassinations of civilians; systematic torture (to get information and intimidate); and, finally, incarceration designed to break inmates (imprisonment involving lack of water, lack of food, beatings, deprivation techniques, and other such methods).

But the CIA is also a threat to *our* freedom. Originally designed to protect freedom, the CIA has now become a totalitarian organization using totalitarian means to pursue totalitarian goals. It is, in fact, the greatest single threat to the freedom of people around the world. The CIA is a very important issue, not only for other peoples of the world, but also for ourselves in this country. I see a period over the next ten years of economic decline in the United States, of increasing agitation for social justice, of the beginnings of movements and political parties on the Left.

There is no doubt in my mind that the major enemy these will be confronting at that point will not be the KGB or the Chinese or anybody else abroad. It will be the CIA. I have interviewed many CIA people and find the Vince Shields type much much more frightening than those like the agent who sent the head. I think that the CIA today is characterized by a technocratic mentality that has reduced human beings to mere objects to be manipulated. I personally do not find any way of communicating with CIA people, of discussing things with them, of trying to raise a moral question with them.

Unlike someone like the agent in northwest Laos who admits moral precepts and then goes on to claim that it is the communists who are violating these moral precepts, the CIA officials are value-free. Their only goal is the accumulation and protection of power. They'll support the Left (the liberal-type Left), they'll support the Right, and so on. In Chile they overthrew Allende because he was a Marxist, which was farther left than they could allow. In other places they will support a liberal-type regime if that seems to be the thing that will keep people down.

The level of debate about the CIA must be raised beyond the questions of what is proper congressional oversight, which covert activities should be abolished, how we can separate intelligence-gathering from covert activities, and so on. It seems to me that the time has come to say that the CIA as it now exists cannot be controlled by Congress; it can only be abolished by Congress. It seems to me that the time has come to say that there is no distinction between intelligence-gathering and covert activities if your goal is totalitarian control, if an organization has become one characterized by the use of totalitarian methods and totalitarian ends. It seems to me that the CIA must be understood as part of a larger system. It is a kind of enforcer, the police arm of a much larger system. Although it is perfectly clear that the president is the one responsible along with his national security adviser, it also seems clear that without the CIA neither the president nor the national security adviser would be the kind of threats they are today to all of us.

South Vietnam's Police and Prison System: The U.S. Connection

Fred Branfman

■ The following article discussing the police and prison system of South Vietnam before the fall of the Saigon regime was written for this volume to provide detailed background for the points made by Mr. Branfman (see preceding selection) in his talk at the Conference on the CIA and World Peace.

WATERGATE SURPRISED and stunned many Americans. To those of us who had closely followed the behavior of American leaders in Indochina, however, Watergate was less a revelation than a confirmation. Numberless incidents from the Gulf of Tonkin to the secret bombing of Laos and Cambodia had convinced us that the U.S. presidential branch habitually treated Congress with contempt, was willing to use illegal means to achieve hidden policies, would deceive the American people whenever it chose to do so. Watergate simply confirmed to us that if American citizens wish to preserve their own freedoms, they would do well to study more closely their leaders' actions abroad before such international behavior inevitably becomes applied here.

From this perspective one of the most disturbing aspects of mid-1970s America is the extent to which we have put our Vietnam experience out of our minds. It is, of course, natural that we would find thinking about what most Americans regard as an awesome mistake and ugly stain on the national conscience an unpleasant task. Although understandable, this national amnesia about Vietnam is not, however, necessarily useful. The Vietnam experience is rich in lessons extending far beyond the general question of presidential abuse of power. Our failure to learn these lessons from our Vietnam experience led to Watergate; it could, à la Santayana, doom us to repeat our Vietnam history again in many other ways.

One of the most pressing and dramatic aspects of our Vietnam experience, for example, is the role played by top American policy makers working under both Democratic and Republican administrations for over a decade in South Vietnam's police system. Most of us have seen this American involvement as primarily indirect, involving our funding of a South Vietnam police state. In the course of 1974, however, the Indochina Resource Center obtained a number of internal U.S. government documents that revealed that U.S. funding is the least important aspect of U.S. involvement. These documents, never before made public, along with extensive research into a wide variety of other official and nonofficial sources, show that U.S. officials *created* South Vietnam's police system, often against the desires of South Vietnamese officials themselves. This documentation has profound implications for our understanding of ourselves and our society, as well as for what goes on abroad.

As Americans, for example, we tend to react to reports of torture in such countries as Vietnam as regrettable, but an inevitable outgrowth of an "Oriental" propensity for torture that we as Americans, happily, abhor. A study of the practice of torture in South Vietnam, however, opens such assumptions to question.

Senator James Abourezk, for example, sent some of his aides to the International Police Academy (IPA) in Washington, D.C. The IPA, directed and financed by the U.S. Central Intelligence Agency through the Agency for International Development, trains top-ranking foreign police from around the world. After being given a tour of the IPA, during which they were assured that the IPA does not teach anything but normal methods of combating crime, Senator Abourezk's aides were shown through the IPA library. By accident, one of them noticed several theses prepared by IPA students. Looking through them, he discovered to his amazement that many of the theses dealt with torture.

On October 2, 1974, Senator Abourezk inserted notes taken by his aides on these theses into the *Congressional Record*, beginning page S. 18047. One of his aides, writing about a paper by Lam Van Huu, *rédacteur de police*, written in 1969, number f73–07, wrote this about policeman Huu's paper:

> This was the most disturbing of the five theses I read. It dealt entirely with torture. It was 14 pages long, 3½ pages were devoted to a history of torture, from the ancient Greeks to the present day, using entirely European examples. . . . Excerpts follow in translation: "What do we mean by 'force and threat'? Physical force—beating, slapping, execution . . . impose indirectly on the suspect physical suffering, such as denying food, not permitting sleep, forbidding going to the toilet."

Lam Van Huu was also quoted as having written under the topic "Favored tortures" the following:

> (a) Drugging: intravenous injection of pentothal or scopolamine making the subject lose his judgement. He is in a state almost without consciousness. He will respond docilely to questions which normally he would refuse to answer. (b) Hypnotism. (c) Polygraph or lie detector.

Abourezk's aide also quoted another South Vietnamese police student at the IPA, *rédacteur de police* Le Van An, as writing in 1971:

> Despite the fact that brutal interrogation is strongly criticized by moralists, its importance must not be denied if we want to have order and security in daily life.

This revelation that American instructors at the International Police Academy ask that their students write papers on torture is only one example of American encouragement of, and participation in, every aspect of South Vietnam's police system.

In the pages that follow, there are numerous examples of such direct American involvement in South Vietnam's police and prison system. These examples do not, of course, mean that America will become a police state, or that American policy makers are all torturers or jailers. This documentation does, however, throw into question some of our most cherished as-

sumptions about ourselves and our leaders. And Watergate
has taught us nothing if we have not learned that we ignore
such questions only at our own peril.

U.S. Financing of South Vietnam's
Police and Prison System

To establish American responsibility for South Vietnam's
police system, one need not go much further than noting that
only U.S. funding allows the government of South Vietnam
(GVN) to remain in power. In this fiscal year alone, for example, the United States spent $1.614 billion in South Vietnam.[1]
The GVN's budget is on the order of $800 million. U.S. funding
supplies some 85 percent of this budget, as well as virtually all
of its arms. The GVN's jailing of its political prisoners, therefore, is clearly possible only because of this overall U.S. subsidy.

To understand how the GVN's police and prison system is
an American creation, however, one must go on to other issues.
The first is the direct U.S. funding of the great expansion of this
system that took place in the 1960s.

South Vietnam's police force of the early 1960s bore little
resemblance to the GVN's National Police Command of the
mid-1970s. In 1961, for example, there were 16,757 police.[2] Few
had more than minimal training. Almost none were in rural
areas. Communications were almost nonexistent. Beginning in
1964, however, the United States began financing a rapid expansion in the police force. In the first year alone, the number
of police was increased from 19,711 in 1963 to 33,567 in 1964.[3]
The number was steadily increased thereafter, until its present
level of 122,000 police.[4]

Much of this funding was to build up a rural police force.
By 1971 the number of rural police had grown from almost
nothing to 11,000. In 1972 the number was more than tripled
to 35,000.[5] The United States also funded the construction of
rural police stations. An official U.S. newsletter dated February
28, 1972, for example, reported that

> By 1 October, 1972, 503 new rural police stations were con-
> structed or were under construction through the use of ex-
> cess U.S. military buildings.[6]

The focal point, however, was the cities. Urban police increased from some 15,000 in the early 1960s to more than 80,000 in 1973.

The United States financed everything from uniforms and arms, to training, to the provision of a sophisticated police telecommunications network for every village and hamlet. Between 1968 and 1971 alone, for example, official U.S. documents report that 93,663 police were trained in-country.[7] Agency for International Development (AID) Administrator Robert Nooter testified before Congress in 1971 that

> In 1965 a separate National Police Telecommunication System was established involving radio, telephone, telegraph and teletype. U.S. technicians helped design the system and AID paid for much of the equipment . . . the Village-Hamlet–Radio System [has] nearly 40,000 two-way radios in virtually all villages and hamlets.[8]

It is not known how much total funds the United States devoted toward transforming South Vietnam's police. The AID Office of Public Safety (OPS), with some 150 to 200 U.S. police advisers annually, is the one major police program on the record. It officially expended $193 million between fiscal years 1965 and 1973.[9]

The U.S. Central Intelligence Agency's police activities, however, are not accounted for officially. Thus, although it is known that the CIA had many U.S. and third-country nationals working with the Phoenix program and advising at interrogation centers, it is not known how much money it spent.[10] Total U.S. Department of Defense (DOD) police expenditures, both in terms of military personnel working with the police and provision of arms and communications equipment, are also not known. Finally, how much money was funneled to the police directly through piasters generated by the Food for Peace and Commodity Import Programs is also not available.

The U.S. also financed a considerable expansion in the prison system during the period. The U.S. government has admitted supplying $6.5 million to the forty-two major prisons run by the GVN Directorate of Corrections between 1967 and 1973. The biggest expansion of the prison system began in 1968. In 1967, for example, U.S. commodity and direct piaster budget support totaled $122,000. In 1963 it amounted to $908,000.[11]

This money was listed as including financing for the construction of new prisons at Phan Thiet, Dalat, Dinh Tuong, and Binh Thuan; for expansion and renovation at dozens of other prisons; for the purchase of dozens of electric generators, which political prisoners testify are routinely used for torture; for "operating supplies," which would presumably include such items as the Smith and Wesson handcuffs used to attach political prisoners to hospital beds; for the 1971 construction of "three 96-cell isolation units" at Con Son, called the "new tiger cages" by prisoners and built after the old ones were revealed in 1970.

The United States also funded the construction of a variety of other prison facilities in South Vietnam. In July 1971, for example, the former U.S. head of pacification, William Colby, testified to Congress that

> The Provincial Interrogation Centers were built by local Vietnamese contractors funded directly by the United States.[12]

These "Provincial Interrogation Centers" exist in addition to provincial prisons. Some of the worst tortures described by political prisoners have taken place in these facilities, which they call "torture chambers."

American financing of new prisons also extended to the "National Police Detention Centers" referred to in a 1972 summary of Office of Public Safety programs in South Vietnam. This summary reports that the United States built thirty-three such detention centers between 1967 and 1971. It says that the capacity of National Police Detention Centers was increased from 3,300 (estimated) in 1967 to 15,857 in February 1972.[13]

Direct U.S. funding of South Vietnam's police and prison system has continued well beyond the 1973 Paris Peace Agreement, despite Article 4, which stipulates that the United States will not "interfere in the internal affairs of South Vietnam." It has also continued despite a State Department pledge in early 1973 that "in keeping with the articles of the ceasefire agreement, AID has terminated its assistance to the National Police and to the Vietnamese Corrections System."[14]

On December 13, 1973, eleven months after the Paris Agreement, the U.S. Senate Committee on Appropriations reported that

> The existence of political prisoners in South Vietnam is beyond any reasonable dispute. Only the numbers are in

question. . . . The Committee is deeply troubled by the ac-
knowledgement that at least $12,513,000 is proposed as
assistance to the South Vietnam National Police. . . . The
Committee is further concerned that portions of these funds
were initially not made sufficiently clear, being listed under
other categories of the budget presentation.[15]

As long as the United States continues to support the GVN,
it will continue to support its police and prison system. The
GVN simply does not have the resources to pay, train, and
equip its 122,000-man police force, maintain its hundreds of
prisons and hundreds of thousands of political prisoners, and
support its army, which continues to round up political
prisoners in sweeps through villages. U.S. direct funding will
continue through untraceable CIA channels, DOD transfers
of equipment, and general budgetary support to the GVN Ministry of the Interior.

U.S. Creation and Direction of the GVN National Police Command

Official U.S. documents also reveal that U.S. officials have
been intimately involved with creation and day-to-day supervision of South Vietnam's expanding police force since at least
1963. These reports also reveal intimate familiarity with the
horrors of the GVN prison system, even as their authors deny
knowledge of the prisons in public. On October 1, 1963, for
example, Frank Walton, then head of the U.S. Operations
Mission Public Safety Division, prepared a report entitled "The
Rehabilitation System of Vietnam." The report was prepared
by a Public Safety official named Benson, who

> visited each of the 44 rehabilitation centers . . . several of
> them many times . . . [and] travelled over 14,000 kilometers.

The report stated that

> Of the almost thirty thousand prisoners . . . over seventy
> percent are the so-called "political" prisoners . . . [who] may
> be anything from a North Vietnamese soldier to an indi-
> vidual in disfavor with a local politician . . . less than three
> out of ten have had their "day in court" . . . some will spend
> the remainder of their lives in prison.

Walton later denied any knowledge of the tiger cages after
they were revealed by congressmen Anderson and Hawkins and
Don Luce in 1970. In this report submitted under Walton's
signature seven years earlier, however, it is stated that

> . . . "Reds" are sent to the Tiger Cages in Con Son I where
> . . . confinement may . . . include rice without salt and water
> [and] immobilization—the prisoner is bolted to the floor,
> handcuffed to a bar or rod, or legirons with the chain
> through an eyebolt, or around a bar or rod.[16]

Such 1963 studies of South Vietnam's police and prison
system formed the basis for the major restructuring that began
in 1964. In March 1964, for example, Walton submitted a
report entitled "National Police Plan for Vietnam." This report,
whose recommendations appear to have been followed almost
to the letter in succeeding years, clearly lays out U.S. priorities.
The report does not suggest any legal remedies for political
prisoners or amelioration of the treatment of prisoners on Con
Son or anywhere else. It does, however, note with approval
certain features of the British antiguerrilla program in Malaya:

> Key factors in making the resettlement villages effective
> were police surveillance, the control of ingress and egress,
> the carrying out of continual aggressive patrols by small
> units, and the establishment of fixed and mobile checkpoints
> for the search of persons and vehicles and seizure of con-
> traband.[17]

Walton went on to remark that

> While these regulations might be considered unduly harsh
> by some, it must be recognized that they were *emergency*
> regulations.[18]

After noting that similar "minimal" measures already tried
in South Vietnam "had already produced good results," the
report went on to make major recommendations. The first was
as follows:

> It should be recognized that the present force level of the
> National Police is not sufficiently high . . . it is imperative
> that this force be augmented as soon as possible.

Walton's year-by-year projections were generally followed. By
1966, for example, he recommended a force of 62,850. The
actual figure for that year was 59,999.[19] Walton's other main
recommendation was the creation of a

Civil law enforcement agency of Vietnam . . . conceived as a single organization consisting of . . .
1. a national police and gendarmerie force . . .
2. a rural police force . . . somewhat in the same manner as the Police Field Force in Malaya.
3. a marine police force . . .
4. rural police and marine police reserve forces . . .
5. a civil security telecommunication service . . .
6. such transport facilities . . . as these law enforcement agencies require.[20]

Official American documents in subsequent years reveal that Walton's Office of Public Safety proceeded to set up just such a "single organization" called the National Police Command.

An official U.S. summary of Public Safety programs in South Vietnam reveals that as of February 1972 the organizational chart of the Republic of Vietnam National Police Command (NPC) included "field police," "marine police," separate "police commands" for each of the four military regions and Saigon under the control of the NPC, a national "transportation/maintenance" section, and a "telecommunications" section.[21] The organization chart of the U.S. Office of Public Safety, included in this same summary, reveals that there were 188 U.S. OPS advisers as of February 1972. Some of their branches included: "detentions," "field police," "investigations," "marine police," "curriculum and publications," training for "field operations," and "telecommunication operations, plans and programs and technical services."[22] A perusal of Public Safety budget requests to Congress over the years, moreover, reveal that these OPS advisers were in day-to-day control and supervision of National Police Command activities.

The OPS June 1972 budget proposal, for example, requested funds from Congress to allow the U.S. Office of Public Safety to:

". . . continue deployment and redeployment of [GVN police] units to all districts, giving priority to those having the most Vietcong infrastructure."
". . . continue operational activity against VCI [Vietcong infrastructure]. . . ."
". . . expand patrol systems to major urban centers commencing in FY 1972. . . ."
". . . ensure a jail administration program in being and functioning in 552 facilities."

". . . design and centralize communications facilities during FY 72 and FY 73. . . ."

"In FY 72, introduce a body of statutes, decrees and regulations for the administration, operation, training and support of National Police. The statutes to be enacted by the end of FY 72."

"Expand the Marine Police Force to 2,500 men. . . . Have 118 river patrol boats and 20 interceptor boats in operation by the end of FY 74."

"Issue operational and technical instructions and regulations by mid FY 72."

develop "a systems analysis and computer programming capability. This is scheduled by mid FY 72, as an indigenous police data management organization for collecting, preparing and editing data for electronic data processing and providing systems analysis and computer programming services for the National Police Command."[23]

After the signing of the Paris Peace Agreement on January 27, 1973, the Office of Public Safety was officially disbanded. It had become clear, however, that the American-created police force could not function on its own. Both the complexities of logistics and coordination of operations for this 120,000-man force, as well as the increasing technical sophistication of its operations, demanded American advisers to hold it together. Perhaps it was for this reason that it was reported that Public Safety officials had been reassigned to other divisions of AID in South Vietnam and that an AID spokesman reported on November 28, 1973, that

AID has had no advisers to the Vietnamese National Police since . . . the Ceasefire Agreement. In addition to advisors, AID employs individuals who administer and oversee the use of U.S. furnished funds and commodities without advising. Such employees work in the functional areas of programming, comptroller, auditors, inspections and investigations, logistics, and similar functions. . . . During FY 74, the USAID has provided some technical advisory services to the Combined Telecommunications Directorate. These advisers have not been advising the National Police, but rather the CTD in general. Only one such adviser is planned beyond the end of FY 74.[24]

Perhaps this is also the reason why congressional sources inform us that they have been told privately that some 400 U.S. CIA personnel have remained in South Vietnam beyond the ceasefire.

Even if we are incorrect, however, and no U.S. personnel remain involved in any way in the operation of GVN police, these official U.S. documents clearly reveal that it is the United States that created the GVN's police and prison system.

The United States, therefore, bears far more than simple financial responsibility for South Vietnam's political prisoners. Indeed, given the dominant role played by U.S. officials in the activities of GVN police over the past decade, it could be argued that the U.S. carries the primary legal and ethical responsibility for their incarceration.

U.S. Programs: Phoenix and the National Identification Card Project

The primary American responsibility for South Vietnam's political prisoners, however, goes far beyond what has already been discussed. Beginning in 1968, U.S. officials unilaterally initiated, implemented, and directed two programs that led to some of the most massive and indiscriminate roundups of men, women, and children since the 1930s.

The first of these programs was called Phoenix in English, *Phuong Hoang* in Vietnamese.

Phoenix was originally designed to "neutralize," that is, assassinate or imprison, members of the civilian infrastructure of the National Liberation Front (NLF). Phoenix offices were set up from Saigon down to the district level. U.S. advisers were present at each level. The function of district and province Phoenix offices were to: (1) collate intelligence about the "Vietcong infrastructure"; (2) interrogate civilians picked up at random by military units carrying out sweeps through villages; (3) "neutralize" targeted members of the NLF. This third task was often carried out by CIA-led Vietnamese organized into Provincial Reconnaissance Units (PRU).

This original Phoenix concept was quickly diluted, for two main reasons: (1) pressure from the top to fill numerical quotas of persons to be neutralized; (2) difficulties at the bottom of identifying NLF civilian infrastructure, who were often indistinguishable from the general population, and the near-impossibility of proving anyone's membership in the NLF. The result was vastly to increase the numbers of innocent persons rounded up and imprisoned, indiscriminately murdered, and brutally tortured in an effort to "show results."

"National Security Study Memorandum #1," prepared for Henry Kissinger in January 1969, makes it clear that Phoenix was an American creation. The State Department reported to Kissinger that

> Although the program [Phoenix] was launched in December, 1967, Saigon-level Vietnamese cooperation was minimal until Thieu, after considerable American prodding, issued a presidential decree in July 1968 formally directing that the network be set up.[25]

The Military Assistance Command in Vietnam and the Joint Chiefs of Staff were even more explicit in their report to Mr. Kissinger:

> The Phoenix–Phuong Hoang program is looked upon by many Vietnamese as having been forced upon the GVN by the Americans. Further, the PRU program is clearly identified as an American program—supervised, controlled and financed by Americans.[26]

The U.S. military also offered a possible explanation of the Vietnamese reluctance to carry out Phoenix:

> There are ways that are accepted to kill your brother and there are other ways such as "breaking his rice bowl" which are not. Further, an attitude of "if I don't bother his home, he won't bother mine" is sometimes prevalent, particularly at the hamlet level. One of the reasons why it took the GVN so long to initiate the Phoenix–Phuong Hoang program was just that reason.[27]

William Colby, head of the Phoenix program, later testified before Congress in 1971 that Phoenix was an American responsibility:

> the Americans had a great deal to do with starting the program . . . we had a great deal to do in terms of developing the ideas, discussing the need, developing some of the pro-

cedures, and so forth . . . maybe more than half the initiative came from us originally.[28]

One of the principal tasks of high-level U.S. officials, led by Colby, was to establish quotas for the number of Vietnamese to be "neutralized" each month. The same State Department report mentioned above states that

> report-padding may have increased recently under the pressure of attempting to reach the quota set for the Accelerated Pacification Campaign.[29]

Vietnam Information Notes, published by the U.S. State Department in July 1969, reports that "The target for 1969 calls for the elimination of 1800 VCI per month."[30]

High-ranking American officials in South Vietnam clearly bear the sole responsibility for the practice of setting quotas of Vietnamese civilians to be murdered and jailed each month. The United States clearly set quotas in an attempt to force GVN officials into something they preferred not to undertake. The State Department report to Kissinger, for example, also stated that

> The Phoenix program . . . [has] served notice to the Province Chiefs that their performance will in large part be measured by Phoenix results.[31]

The Military Assistance Command went on to note in the same study that

> Until . . . Tet 1968, the GVN was reluctant to carry out a systematic program of "neutralization" . . . as negotiations progress . . . the pressures within families to reach accommodation will increase and, correspondingly, the effectiveness of the Phoenix–Phuong Hoang program could decrease.[32]

In an effort to make Phoenix as "effective" as possible, U.S. advisers working for the CIA, U.S. Army, and Office of Public Safety were placed out in the field to assess and direct operations. Their guidelines were similar to the Office of Public Safety request to Congress for funds to

> Increase National Police inspections . . . to ensure that US/ GVN policies are implemented down to the lowest level to help identify and counter activities of subversive organizational cadre . . . [and] ensure closer cooperation in . . . intel-

ligence . . . between regular police, special police, and Phuong
Hoang (Phoenix).[33]

A number of such U.S. personnel at the ground level have
testified that one of Phoenix's main results was the mass and
indiscriminate murder of Vietnamese civilians. K. Barton Osborn, a U.S. Phoenix agent, testified to Congress, for example,
that

> I never knew an individual to be detained as a VC suspect
> who ever lived through an interrogation in a year and a half,
> and that included quite a number of individuals. . . .[34]

Osborn also testified that quite often Phoenix resulted in the
killing of individuals on the spot rather than in the process of
having agents going to the trouble of jailing them:

> After all, it was a big problem that had to be dealt with ex-
> pediently. This was the mentality. . . . It became a sterile
> depersonalized murder program. . . . There was no cross-
> check; there was no investigation; there were no second
> opinions. . . . It was completely indiscriminate. . . .[35]

Official figures would seem to corroborate this testimony of
mass killing under Phoenix.

In a document entitled *Vietnam: Toward Peace and Prosperity*, published by the Saigon Ministry of Information, the
GVN states that

> The Phoenix programme was launched on August 1, 1968,
> in order to eradicate the communist infrastructure, with the
> following results; . . . Killed—40,994.[36]

This document draws a distinction between these 40,994 Phoenix victims and "Communists killed" by the police, the number
of which is put at 9,270. This latter figure presumably refers
to NLF military personnel, unlike the civilians killed under
Phoenix.[37] Colby himself testified before Congress that Phoenix
had resulted in the death of 20,587 persons as of May 1971.
This number, proportionate to population, would total over
200,000 Americans deliberately assassinated over a three-year
period, were Phoenix in practice in the United States.[38]

The Phoenix quota system also produced a vast upsurge in
mass arrests. As Michael Uhl, a Phoenix military intelligence
operative, testified before Congress: a Phoenix military intelligence team

measured its success . . . not only by its "body count" and "kill ratio" but by the number of CD's [civil detainees] it had captured. . . .[39]

Between 1968 and 1972 hundreds of thousands of Vietnamese civilians were rounded up by both U.S. and Vietnamese troops, then turned over to the Vietnamese police for "questioning." Such "interrogation" has been usually marked by brutal torture.

This process of placing a quota on civilian detainees led to mass and indiscriminate imprisonment, with many civilians automatically being listed as "VCI" ("Vietcong infrastructure") in order to meet pressures from above. As Uhl has also testified:

> All CD's, because of this command pressure . . . were listed as VCI. To my knowledge, not one of these people ever freely admitted to being a cadre member. And again, contrary to Colby's statement, most of our CD's were women and children. . . .[40]

The scope of this program of mass roundups, as conveyed in official documents, is astonishing. An official summary of the Public Safety program, for example, reports that

> Thirty-four screening and detention facilities [jails] were planned in 1957 for construction. By the end of 1971, 33 were completed. . . . The population of National Police detention facilities averages about 2,000, although an average of about 15,000 are processed through the jails each month.[41]

National Police Detention Centers, therefore, are here reported "processing through" *180,000 persons a year*. The detention centers, moreover, do not include those "processed through" interrogation centers, provincial and military jails, and dozens of unofficial lockups such as private villas. Once again, a comparison with the United States is in order. Were a similar policy in effect here, at least *1,800,000* Americans would have been sent to jail per year.

This yearly "processing" of hundreds of thousands, this detention of tens of thousands, inevitably led Phoenix to change judicial procedures as well. Clearly the existing judicial system of civil courts for criminal offenses and military courts for political offenses would not handle the vast upsurge in detainees. American involvement in so potentially embarrassing a program meant that some more streamlined set of courtroom procedures would have to be devised. Civilians rounded up by Americans could not be simply sent to jail without even the pretense of sentencing.

The U.S. government was already on record before Phoenix as being dissatisfied with the existing judicial system. The State Department, for example, reported to Dr. Kissinger in January 1969 that

> Perhaps as many as two-thirds of the prisoners arrested in South Vietnam are released within a year as a result of flaws in the GVN judicial system.[42]

Once again, the military was even more explicit in this report:

> OSD [Office of the Secretary of Defense] estimates that roughly 60 percent of the prisoners arrested in 1968 were released (Dec. 1968). Steps are underway to remedy these problems.[43]

As a result, the U.S. Phoenix program resuscitated the Security Committee as a means of jailing detainees without a trial. Security Committees operate at the province level and are made up almost entirely of military and police officials. Under the so-called "An Tri" law, they have been empowered to jail any South Vietnamese citizen for up to "two years, renewable." The Security Committee does not see or talk with the accused. Its decision is based entirely on the accused's dossier, prepared by the province police office. The accused has no opportunity to be represented by a lawyer, confront witnesses, present evidence, or even plead in his or her behalf.

As William Colby noted in the following exchange with Congressman Ogden Reid in 1971, this procedure leaves something to be desired from a judicial point of view:

REID: Do you consider the law which permits up to two years under the An Tri law is on all fours with the Geneva Convention?

COLBY: I think it is. . . . It is not what I would frankly prefer and . . . I would quite frankly say that he [the accused] does not have a hearing today. . . .

REID: Does he have any right to counsel?

COLBY: No, not under the present situation.

REID: Then is it not a kangaroo trial?

COLBY: It is an administrative proceeding, not a trial. . . . As I said, I do not think they meet the standards I would like to see applied to Americans today.[44]

Ray Meyer, second secretary of the U.S. Embassy in Saigon, repeated this description in an April 1973 letter to Senator Edward Kennedy, adding:

> An Tri detainees need not be accused of committing a specific criminal act.[45]

The reason behind the Phoenix reliance on this "administrative" jailing of political prisoners without a trial was made clear in the following exchange between Colby and Representative McCloskey:

McCLOSKEY: Let me try to quote from one of your Phoenix documents. The administrative detention applies to those against whom there is insufficient evidence to convict, isn't that right?

COLBY: Right.[46]

The quota system, moreover, was also used for sentencing. The Phoenix program decreed that at least 50 percent of those captured were to be sentenced. As Congressman Reid suggested in the following exchange with Colby, such a quota inevitably increased the number of persons imprisoned without evidence. Colby's answer is revealing of the mentality that governed the U.S. Phoenix program from top to bottom:

REID: If you set a quota, is not that almost automatically saying we are setting a quota irrespective of the facts . . . ?

COLBY: The reason for putting in the 50 percent sentencing was to put a greater pressure on officials to do a more professional job of capturing and interrogating and then sentencing. . . .[47]

The U.S. Phoenix program in Vietnam, then, assassinated
and jailed large numbers of Vietnamese civilians without evidence or judicial procedure. This fact was officially confirmed
in a startling admission made by Colby to Representative Reid
in Colby's July 1971 testimony before Congress. Colby had
earlier inserted into the record a chart showing that some 67,282
persons had been neutralized by "Phoenix operations against
VCI" between 1968 and 1971. Of these, 31 percent had been
killed, 26 percent had "rallied," and 43 percent had been captured or sentenced.[48]

Representative Reid and Colby later engaged in the following exchange:

REID: Mr. Ambassador, does CORDS or any other agency keep
a record about each individual whom Phoenix has neutralized?

COLBY: We have been working with the Vietnamese Government to set up a data processing system, which will put into a
single file, all of the people identified as VCI, and also give us a
set of followup reports on any of them that have been picked
up, where they stand in the processing, when they are convicted, how long they are convicted for, where they go to prison,
how long they stay there, whether they come out when they are
supposed to and so forth.

REID: When did this verification start?

COLBY: *In its full-blown operation, it is just about right now,
Mr. Congressman.* The full VCI listings we have had now for
about a year.

REID: Of the listings you have had for about a year, what degree
of accuracy did you find? . . .

COLBY: *I have never been highly satisfied with the accuracies
of our intelligence effort on the VCI.*[49]

Colby thus admitted in sworn testimony before the U.S. Congress, that despite the fact that the Phoenix program had killed

or rounded up *49,565 persons* in the past three years, *no records had been kept to indicate who these persons were, what offenses they had been accused of, what evidence had been presented against them, or what had happened to them.*

These facts would seem to corroborate that it was the United States government under the Phoenix program that indiscriminately rounded up a large portion of the political prisoners still jailed in South Vietnam in 1975. It is powerful confirmation of the contention that the vast majority of those in prison on political charges were not working for either party in the conflict and were jailed illegally.

The Phoenix program has continued beyond the January 27, 1973, Peace Agreement. AID Director John Hannah stated in a letter dated May 9, 1973, that

> Plan F–6 is an acceleration of the Phuong Hoang (Phoenix) operation which the GVN directed in view of the North Vietnamese invasion of 1972.[50]

On May 17, 1973, the French newspaper *Le Monde* published an official telegram dated April 5, 1973, from the National Phoenix Committee. Sent out to province-level Phoenix committees, this official order stated in part:

> Request the Provincial Security Committee to continue to make efforts to neutralize all troublemakers against the public order.[51]

Although the Phoenix program is the major American contribution to South Vietnam's political prisoner problem, another U.S. program also had an important influence. This program was the National Identification Card Project, which has issued ID cards to over 10 million Vietnamese.

The National Identification Card Project represents one of the most sophisticated attempts to control and keep tabs on large masses of people in recent history. All Vietnamese over the age of fifteen are required to carry these ID cards at all times on pain of arrest. Each ID card is in turn keyed to a computer containing well over 10 million bio-dossiers and sets of fingerprints. GVN officials regularly use the threat of confiscating citizens' ID cards as a means of forcing them to comply with orders. The GVN has carried out numerous arrests on the grounds of ID-card irregularities. Either confiscating the individual's ID card, claiming that it had been tampered with, or claiming that it identifies the bearer as either a "Communist" or other wanted person, has become one of the most widespread means by which police fulfill arrest quotas, secure bribes, or take personal vengeance.

A U.S. Office of Public Safety document, "National Identity Registration Project," dated April 1967, makes it clear that this project was American-initiated. It states, for example, that

> The project envisages the registration of all Vietnamese 15 years of age and over, the issuance of identification cards, and the establishment of a National Identity Record Center in Saigon. . . . *The Public Safety Division provided the National Police a draft of a suitable decree. The Police considered this and on March 17, 1967, the decree law was signed by General Thieu, chief of state.*[52]

After some nine million Vietnamese had been registered and issued ID cards, the nationwide computerized linkup went into effect in October 1971. As an official summary of U.S. Public Safety programs in South Vietnam notes,

> In October, 1971, the initial links of a nationwide teletype system were installed. During the first month, over 20 percent of the individuals checked were found to be wanted persons.[53]

This report also notes that

> As a result of cross checks between existing cards and biodata and the newly classified and filed individual fingerprint cards, over 300,000 offenders have been identified. These include 225,333 deserters, 2,053 subversive criminals, 36,725 draft evaders, 19,954 miscellaneous criminals, and 88,194 registration irregularities.[54]

American responsibility for the day-to-day operations of the National Identification Card Project were made clear in the June 1972 OPS budget request to Congress, which requested funds to:

> —ensure universal compliance with GVN policies applicable to the i.d. card program

And

> —establish a central records system containing 12 million individual biodata documents and 11.5 million dossiers

And

> —complete initial registration of Vietnamese 15 years of age and older by the close of CY 71.[55]

By February 28, 1973, the Public Safety Division reported that

> The national Police Command Identification Service accumulated more than 15 million sets of classified fingerprints and allied biographic and records data.[56]

This creation of a nationwide system designed to identify electronically and keep track of 15 million Vietnamese has also helped create much of South Vietnam's prison population. It is a significant aspect of the American responsibility for South Vietnam's police and prison system.

American Responsibility Officially Acknowledged—Then Ignored

The American responsibility for South Vietnam's political prisoners has been explicitly and implicitly acknowledged by American officials in a number of ways. The first has been in testimony before Congress. In July 1971, for example, William Colby acknowledged that U.S. officials were directly involved in Phoenix operations, in addition to the admission mentioned above that the U.S. was directly involved in setting up the Phoenix program.[57] After stating that 637 U.S. military personnel were directly involved in Phoenix, in addition to a "small number" of civilians—presumably CIA personnel—Colby engaged in the following exchange with Representative Moorhead:

MOORHEAD: Do U.S. personnel ever participate in arrests of VCI?

COLBY: They do not arrest, Mr. Chairman, but they do participate. . . .

MOORHEAD: Do they ever participate in those attempted arrests that result in killing?

COLBY: Yes, because sometimes that kind of an operation results in a fire fight and people get killed on both sides.[58]

Colby then went on to state that

> Frankly, I was never able to take the position that if something wrong went on over there, it could be sort of left to the Vienamese as to responsibility. I felt that our country and our Government are involved in the support of the overall effort there, that there is nothing that we can say we do not have some responsibility to improve, to do something about.[59]

The second acknowledgment of U.S. responsibility has been a response by the U.S. Ambassador to the UN in Geneva, Idar Rimestad, to the International Red Cross:

> With respect to South Vietnamese civilians captured by U.S. forces and transferred by them to the authorities of the Republic of Vietnam, the United States Government recognizes that it has a residual responsibility to work with the Government of the Republic of Vietnam to see that all such civilians are treated in accordance with the requirements of Article 3 of the [1949] Geneva convention.[60]

The Article 3 referred to in this letter reads as follows:

> Persons taking no active part in the hostilities, including members of armed forces who have laid down their arms . . . shall in all circumstances be treated humanely . . . shall remain prohibited at any time . . . cruel treatment and torture . . . humiliating and degrading treatment . . . the passing of sentences . . . without previous judgement pronounced by a regularly constituted court, affording all the judicial guarantees which are recognized as indispensable by civilized peoples. . . .

This official U.S. admission of responsibility for seeing that Article 3 was observed for civilians captured by U.S. forces carried with it broader implications. As the *New York Times* noted from Washington, D.C., on December 14, 1970:

> Because the civilians the United States detains end up in the same jails as those seized by the South Vietnamese, officials here maintain that the United States has in effect assumed "residual" responsibility for all of South Vietnam's jails. . . . This means that if there are allegations in the future similar

to recent charges that prisoners were being held in "tiger cages" at Con Son Prison, the United States has officially committed itself to taking action.

A third official acceptance of U.S. responsibility for political prisoners was the decision by American officials to sign the Paris Peace Agreement. Article 8b of the Peace Agreement's Protocol on Prisoners stipulates that

> All Vietnamese civilian personnel captured and detained in South Vietnam . . . shall be protected against all violence to life and person, in particular against murder . . . torture and cruel treatment, and outrages against personal dignity. The detaining parties shall not deny or delay their return for any reason. . . . They shall be given adequate food, clothing, shelter, and the medical attention required for their state of health. . . .

This provision related to members of either party to the conflict. In addition, Article 11 of the Agreement itself guaranteed full freedom for all South Vietnamese citizens, including:

> personal freedom, freedom of speech, freedom of the press, freedom of meeting, freedom of organization, freedom of *political activity*. . . . [Emphasis added.]

By signing the Paris Agreement, the U.S. clearly officially acknowledged its responsibility to help provide proper treatment for political prisoners, to work for the release of those now in prison, and, above all, to stop any further participation in new arrests for political reasons.

Since January 27, 1973, when the Agreement was signed, however, U.S. executive branch officials have not only failed to live up to these responsibilities, they have also, in fact, denied any special responsibility, beginning what can only be described as a monstrous attempt to rewrite history by denying any American role in the creation of South Vietnam's police and prison system. On January 16, 1974, for example, the U.S. ambassador to South Vietnam, Graham Martin, told a group of visiting peace activists that he was

> revolted at the thought that any American, as many of their "Peace Movement" colleagues had done, would circulate charges that any part of any American AID Mission would participate in any way in advocating, advising about, or fur-

nishing any equipment for, any measures that would be brutal, involve torture, or political repression of any kind.[61]

An official State Department bulletin that is sent out in response to citizen inquiries about the treatment of South Vietnamese political prisoners states that

> the United States is not directly involved in this matter except insofar as we are a signatory to the Agreement and are working to the extent possible to see that all of its provisions are implemented by both sides to the conflict. . . . Questions about the release of individual Vietnamese said to be imprisoned are internal matters. . . . Accordingly, inquiries about individual cases should appropriately be directed to these authorities.[62]

Don Luce, the Vietnamese-speaking American who helped two U.S. congressmen discover the original tiger cages in South Vietnam, has widely disseminated copies of a U.S. Navy contract directing that a new "isolation compound" be built on Con Son Island. The contract is to the American construction company RMK–BRJ, and is dated January 7, 1971—six months *after* the old tiger cages were revealed to the world. Written on official Department of Navy stationery, the contract is for "Project S 623/70, NOTICE TO PROCEED . . . Isolation Compound, Con Son."[63] On August 13, 1973, a young naval officer sent a copy of this contract to Rear Admiral Francis L. Garrett, chief of U.S. Navy chaplains. The officer requested that the matter "be included in the Chaplain Corps scope of pastoral concern and service to the U.S. Naval Community." On September 6, 1973, Rear Admiral Garrett replied in a letter that stated in part:

> It is my understanding that the isolation compound conforms to modern penal standards and that the funds used were Vietnamese funds and not Navy appropriated funds. . . . I trust the above comments will speak to your basic concerns. . . .[64]

On May 17, 1974, U.S. Secretary of State Henry Kissinger wrote Senator Edward Kennedy that

> The Department of State cannot agree with the . . . assertion that "the record is clear that political prisoners exist in South Viet-Nam.". . . As an outside power our ability to influence events in this sensitive area is clearly limited, but we will

continue to do what we reasonably can to secure the humane treatment and prompt release of prisoners of both sides . . . we would add that the extensive evidence available to us simply does not sustain the highly publicized charges that civilian prisoners are subjected to widespread systematic mistreatment in the jails of the Republic of Viet-Nam.[65]

According to the official version of history put out by the executive branch of the U.S. government, therefore, the United States has not been involved in setting up an inhumane police and prison system in South Vietnam, has no particular responsibility to help civilian detainees, has never built new isolation compounds on Con Son Island, and can, in any event, do little to help South Vietnam's political prisoners who, in any case, do not exist and are not being mistreated.

The CIA in Africa

Tony Monteiro

■ Tony Monteiro is executive secretary of the Anti-Imperialist Movement in Solidarity with African Liberation and is involved in a nationwide petition campaign calling for the expulsion of the Republic of South Africa from the United Nations. He was a delegate to the Sixth Pan-African Congress, held at Dar-es-Salaam, Tanzania, and has lectured at the University of Mogadishu in Somalia. He is author of a number of articles. For this volume Mr. Monteiro extended his presentation at the Conference on the CIA and World Peace to include further material on developmen⬛ the spring and summer of 1975.

THE CIA, as an instrument of United States foreign policy, is an integral part of United States imperialism's efforts to set back and destroy the global struggle for national liberation and world peace. Because of the inherently aggressive nature of United States foreign policy, I believe that a critical step toward world peace can be made by totally dismantling the CIA.

The present level of the African liberation struggle, which is now at its second stage, combines two sides of a unified historical process. Today there is a convergence of the process to attain political independence and to secure the rudiments of national sovereignty, on the one hand, with the process to advance the socioeconomic development of the newly freed nations. The forty-six independent nations of Africa are now constructing political and economic systems in accordance with their special national characteristics. For most nations the principal consideration is how to rupture the legacy of colonial domination, which is now taking the form of neocolonialism. Within this context, two fundamental paths of development exist—capitalist or noncapitalist development. To phrase the matter another way, the question is one of whether economic independence can be achieved within the context of the world capitalist market and division of labor or whether it is necessary totally to break away from the capitalist world economic order. In spite of the social, economic, and political variations on the African continent, there exists, however, a continental movement, manifested in the Organization of African Unity (OAU), which is a strategic center of the global struggle for peace and national liberation.

The mighty force of the liberated peoples and nations of Africa at this time meets the borders of the remaining vestiges of classical colonialism on the continent in the Republic of South Africa, Namibia (Southwest Africa), and Rhodesia. The collapse of Portuguese colonialism in southern Africa has qualitatively altered the struggle to liberate that region from colonialism. This fact has at the same time made the Republic of South Africa even more important strategically to imperialism's efforts to preserve a colonial base from which to control the vast mineral resources and immense labor force of southern Africa. The Republic of South Africa, the nerve center of imperialism on the African continent, therefore assumes the role of the last major defense of imperialism in Africa. The Republic of South Africa not only is a powerful industrial and financial base for the Western transnational corporations, but is also a special link to the aggressive policies of the Pentagon in both the southern Atlantic and the Indian Ocean.

The U.S. military buildup on the island of Diego Garcia, which is in the middle of the Indian Ocean, has been protested by many East African nations, including Tanzania and Somalia. The response of the Pentagon, however, is to accuse Somalia of being a missile base for the Soviet Union. This Cold War lie is geared at pressuring Somalia into reversing its anti-imperialist and independent foreign policy and at justifying the expansion of Diego Garcia as a military and telecommunications base. The $105 million appropriation for Diego Garcia is to build a naval base for the nuclear-powered Trident submarine, which can act as a special weapon operating in the Indian Ocean against the independent nations of Africa. The telecommunications center on Diego Garcia links the U.S. tracking stations at Asmara in Ethiopia with South Africa and the Philippines. The buildup on Diego Garcia is tied, moreover, to the process now taking place of integrating South Africa into the United States Strategic Air Command's South Atlantic operations as well as into U.S. Indian Ocean policy.

In talks held in May 1974 between Connie Mulder, South African minister of information, and Vice-President Gerald Ford, it was decided to integrate South Africa more fully into the Western military alliance, in particular into the North Atlantic Treaty Organization. The *Johannesburg Star* on August 10, 1974, stated: "It is clear that South Africa has closer links with Mr. Ford than [with] any previous American President." In June 1974 Admiral Hugo Biermann, commander of South Africa's armed forces, stated (clearly reflecting the discussions between Ford and Mulder) that "South Africa's Defense Force is prepared to meet any challenge that may emerge from Mozambique and Angola."

Moreover, in April 1974 the first-ever French-South African naval operations were held. (France remains the main weapons supplier to South Africa.) It has also been disclosed by the United Nations Apartheid Unit that in the first months of 1975 the North Atlantic Treaty Organization quickened the rate of shipments of weapons to South Africa. In June of 1975, when a resolution was presented in the United Nations Security Council calling for an arms embargo in response to South Africa's refusal to remove its military forces from Namibia and to decolonize that country, the United States, France, and Britain all cast vetoes of the resolution.

The United States government is also deeply involved in aiding South Africa in building a nuclear strike force. One indication of this fact was the announcement last spring that the U.S., while curtailing its sales of enriched uranium to its Western allies, would increase the sale of enriched uranium to South Africa. The militarization of South Africa and its elevation into a nuclear force on the African continent is inspired by the White House and the Pentagon and is part and parcel of the U.S. policy of neocolonial containment and rollback of the national liberation struggles in Africa. The transformation of the Republic of South Africa into a nuclear power runs counter to the main direction of the Organization of African Unity, which has time and again demanded that Africa remain a nuclear-free zone. The OAU by taking such a position clearly anticipated the present effort on the part of South Africa, the United States, and NATO.

What we are witnessing at this moment is the maturation of a policy begun in Richard Nixon's first term in office. This policy is best reflected in "National Security Memorandum #39," which was presented by Henry Kissinger to a December 9, 1969, meeting of the National Security Council. "Option Two" was apparently chosen from five possible alternatives presented in the memorandum. Its main thrust urged "preservation of the American economic, scientific and strategic interest in the White states and expanded opportunities for profitable trade and investment there." On September 28, 1974, the *Johannesburg Star* reported, confirming the Kissinger memorandum, that the Nixon administration had decided "to relax the isolation of the White Governments of Southern Africa and to ease both economic restrictions and the arms embargo on them."

Already in 1969, in violation of the arms embargo, the United States government had permitted the sale of engines and spare parts for Falcon jets to South Africa. In 1970 when the Tory government of Great Britain announced its plans to increase military sales to South Africa and to increase the frequency of British naval visits to the Simonstown naval base in that country, British Prime Minister Edward Heath, while on a state visit to the United States, announced the full approval of the Nixon administration for these actions. In 1971 the U.S. government extended $431 million in aid to the then Portuguese colonial government. This aid was deemed rent for the utilization of the Azores for military bases. In reality it was aid for the pursuance of the Salazar regime's colonial wars in southern Africa.

In recent years the Africa policy of the United States has reached a new level of aggressiveness. U.S. Ambassador John Scali's veto in the UN Security Council of the 1974 resolution to expel the racists of the Republic of South Africa from the United Nations and his subsequent attack upon the antiracist majority in the General Assembly as "tyrannical" demonstrated the fact that U.S. Africa policy is based upon collaboration with the apartheid regime of South Africa. The Ford administration's appointment of Daniel P. Moynihan to fill the UN post vacated by John Scali is U.S. imperialism's response to the antiracist majority in the General Assembly. Moynihan, an official apologist of racism in U.S. domestic policy (under the cover of "benign neglect") in general, and for the Nixon administration in particular, will execute the policy of racism in foreign policy at the United Nations.

In line with these developments was the appointment in March 1975 of Nathaniel Davis to the post of assistant secretary of state for African Affairs. Davis, it should be recalled, as U.S. ambassador to Chile, was the central figure in the Central Intelligence Agency, Pentagon, and National Security Council plans to overthrow the Popular Unity Government of Salvador Allende. His appointment was strongly protested by the Organization of African Unity as an attempt by the United States to intervene against the sovereignty of the African nations. Henry Kissinger responded that the protest of the African nations was an effort to dictate U.S. foreign policy. Though rejected by the OAU, Davis's nomination was greeted warmly by Prime Minister John Vorster of South Africa.

Deane Hinton, a specialist in economic intelligence, director of the Agency for International Development (AID) in Chile in 1969–1971, and a member of the National Security Council subcommittee on nationalization of U.S. companies abroad, has become U.S. ambassador to Zaïre (formerly the Congo). In May 1975 Hinton was kicked out of Zaïre, only months after his appointment, for his subversive and CIA activity, according to the government of Zaïre. Frederick Latrash, the AID official who helped bring down the Arbenz government in Guatemala in 1954, helped "destabilize" the Nkrumah government in Ghana in 1966, and served as political director of the U.S. Embassy in Chile in 1971, has been reassigned to Africa. William Bowdler, a member of the National Security Council known for his CIA activity in Latin America, has been appointed Ambassador to South Africa.

The activities of these new appointees on the African continent, all of whom have very striking and obvious backgrounds in CIA and other counterinsurgency activity, are supplemented by the activities of Frank Carlucci in Portugal to aid the right-wing and fascist forces in that country. Carlucci began his foreign service in 1956 in the post of economic officer in the U.S. Embassy in Johannesburg, South Africa. In 1960–1962 Carlucci

served in the newly independent Congo as political officer in the
U.S. Embassy in Leopoldville (now Kinshasa). This service was
during the period when the United States, in conjunction with
mercenaries from West Germany, France, South Africa, and
Belgium began operations against the anti-imperialist government of Patrice Lumumba that led to Lumumba's assassination
in 1961. During this same period, the CIA enlisted mercenaries
from around the world, including counterrevolutionaries who
were veterans of the invasion of Cuba at the Bay of Pigs, to
operate in the Congo. These activities led to the invasion of
Stanleyville in 1964 and the murders of thousands of Congolese
citizens and freedom fighters. In 1962 Carlucci received a Superior Service Award from the State Department for his work
in the Congo.

Since 1958, the year that the U.S. State Department created
the post of Assistant Secretary of State for African Affairs, the
entire apparatus of the State Department has been utilized
against the new nations of Africa and the liberation movements
in southern Africa. Though the CIA has played the critical role
vis-à-vis the execution of the policy of deterring progressive
developments in the new states, the United States Information Agency, the Peace Corps, and the cultural and military
attachés have also played a significant role against the new
states.

Moreover, the United States government used the leadership
of the AFL-CIO, headed by George Meany, in its subversion in
Africa. In the last thirty years AFL-CIO activities in Africa have
often been a cover for CIA activities against the popular and
trade union movements in the new states of Africa. In *Inside
the Company: CIA Diary* (New York: Stonehill, 1975) Philip
Agee indicates that a central policy of U.S. foreign policy in
Africa was to undermine the unity of the trade union movement. This policy took the form of splitting the working-class
movement in Africa. For a period the AFL-CIO and the CIA also
utilized the pro-West International Confederation of Free Trade
Unions. This policy also meant that the AFL-CIO could not
come out against apartheid in South Africa or the discrimina-
tion against South African black workers that denied them the
right to legitimate unions.

The record of CIA activity in Africa, its efforts to "destabilize"
progressive governments, its collaborative activity with United

States multinational corporations, its assassination activity, and so on date from the achievement of independence by Ghana in 1957. As noted above, in 1961 the CIA was involved in the brutal overthrow of the first independent government of the Congo. In the same year the CIA, aided by Moishe Tshombe and Joseph Mobutu, among others, including Belgian colonialists and South African, French, and West German mercenaries, set up the assassination of the outstanding freedom fighter Patrice Lumumba. In 1964 the CIA organized the invasion of the Congo by South African, Rhodesian, West German, and anti-Castro Cuban mercenaries. This invasion was a horrific action leading to the torture and slaughter of thousands of Congolese men, women, and children.

In 1966 the CIA, through the U.S. Embassy in Ghana, led and organized the overthrow of Kwame Nkrumah's government, leading eventually to the installation of the neocolonial government of Kofi Busia. In 1967–1969 the CIA organized mercenaries to aid the secessionists of Biafra in their effort to split the Nigerian Federal Republic. The overthrow of the progressive and anti-imperialist government of Modibo Keita of Mali in 1968 had the aid of the CIA as well. The assassination in 1973 of Amilcar Cabral, the extraordinary theorist and leader of the African Party for the Independence of Guinea and the Cape Verde Islands, was with the complete knowledge and support of the CIA. These facts indicate only the tip of the iceberg, the racist and imperialist role of the CIA against the African liberation struggle.

Guided by the Defense Department policy of militarizing the remaining colonial sector of southern Africa, the CIA operates within the new states and within the liberation movements to weaken them. A recent and very clear example of CIA activity to frustrate the independence of an African nation can be seen in Angola. It should be remembered that U.S. corporations are the largest importers of Angola's products, even more than Portugal itself. The United States is the largest importer of Angola's largest crop, coffee. Most important, however, are the growing investments in the oil-rich region of Cabinda. In 1974, 10 million tons of oil were extracted from the offshore shallows, bringing in $530 million. Angola is also rich in diamonds, phosphates, copper, zinc, and nickel.

Gulf Oil, whose payoffs to leaders of various countries to protect its corporate interests have been exposed, is no doubt deeply involved in the efforts to split Cabinda off from Angola and is probably financing the so-called Front for the Liberation of the Cabinda Enclave (FLEC). This policy would be logical because Cabinda is second only to Kuwait in terms of foreign oil production for Gulf. Because of the mineral riches of Angola, U.S. and European transnational corporations do not look favorably upon its achievement of full independence free of neocolonialism. The support that Western sources are giving to FLEC is indicative of efforts to dismantle Angola.

The United States government has for some time now been supporting the National Front for the Liberation of Angola (FNLA), which is based in Zaïre. FNLA has been attempting to impose a civil war upon the nation and to undermine its independence. Many sources report CIA activity in Angola dating from July 1974. The Algerian newspaper *Al-Moujahid* reported that small groups of Americans passing themselves off as businessmen and newsmen started coming to Angola at that time. The paper reports that among them was the CIA Deputy Director, General Vernon Walters. The Algerian paper claims that these persons had sought, with the help of domestic reactionaries in Angola, to discredit the Popular Movement for the Liberation of Angola (MPLA). The African press has also reported that the CIA has been supplying arms, money, and advisers for the FNLA. The FNLA also enjoys the support of South Africa. It has been reported that South Africans have been advising FNLA forces and are operating in southern Angola.

In essence, United States policy in Africa is a policy of neocolonial containment of the African liberation struggle. United States policy is geared to aborting the second stage of that struggle, to frustrating the efforts by the African peoples to transform their continent into a zone of peace, economic freedom, and social progress.

United Nations resolution 1514, which in 1960 established colonialism as incompatible with the UN Charter and the UN Declaration of Human Rights as well as with the struggle for world peace, establishes the inalienable unity between the struggle to complete decolonization in Africa and that to secure world peace. The OAU—through the Lusaka Manifesto of 1969, the Mogadishu Declaration of 1973, and the Dar-Es-Salaam Declaration of 1975—elaborates upon this resolution in conformity with the struggle to liberate southern Africa.

Africa must become a central focus of all peace forces. The liberation struggle in Africa is a point of intersection of the converging processes that make decolonization and peaceful coexistence irreversible. Irreversible victories over racism and colonialism are essential if détente and peaceful coexistence are to become irreversible. The preservation of apartheid colonialism in southern Africa, as the majority of states at the twenty-ninth UN General Assembly session pointed out, is incompatible with international peace and security.

The CIA in Portugal

John L. Hammond and Nicole Szulc

■ John L. Hammond is assistant professor of sociology
at Columbia University, a research associate of the
Center for Political Research, and a consultant for the
Center for National Security Studies. He has traveled
extensively and frequently in Portugal, researching
his interests in political sociology and social movements.

Nicole Szulc has worked as a researcher on repression in Latin America, as an assistant to journalist
Tad Szulc on articles and books on U.S. foreign policy
and national security matters, and as an associate at
the Center for National Security Studies. Presently
she lives in Lisbon as the correspondent for Spain and
Portugal for Pacific News Service.

The following article originated in a presentation
made jointly by Dr. Hammond and Ms. Szulc at the Conference on the CIA and World Peace that was later expanded to include events through October 1975 and
written in its present form by Dr. Hammond, who states:
"Events in Portugal continue to move rapidly, and we
are painfully aware that anything written on them will
soon be out of date. It is the basic analysis that
counts, however."

DEVELOPMENTS IN PORTUGAL demand our urgent attention. In
a relatively short period of time the country moved rapidly on
a path toward independence, democracy, and socialism, and
strong political forces are still working to defend these revolutionary advances. Yet Portugal's geographic position and its
international alignments make it very vulnerable to U.S. inter-

vention, which is actively trying to reverse the tide of progress. There is some chance, however, that progressive Americans can make a difference there, that our political activity can forestall intervention and allow Portugal to take its own course.

To understand the aims and methods of the intervention now occurring in Portugal, a brief summary of the Portuguese political context is necessary. During the year following the April 25, 1974, coup, the Portuguese Right suffered a series of consecutive defeats, which permitted the first steps toward socialism. The outside world—and Portugal itself—were surprised by the strength and rapid consolidation of the Left. The more decisive economic policies adopted beginning in March 1975 led to an escalation of the counterattack against the Left. But outside intervention has not used the now discredited Right as much as it has worked through political forces identified as the center of the political spectrum.

The bloodless coup of April 25, 1974, brought down the longest established fascist regime in the history of the world and the only remaining colonial empire. The forty-eight-year-old regime had denied freedom of the press and the right to organize or strike. Its system of oppression was based on a secret police (the PIDE) in such tight control that it maintained files on one out of every five Portuguese adults and subjected many of them to prison and torture. Keeping wage rates down by repression of worker militancy and welcoming the capital of multinational corporations, the regime had permitted Portugal to become almost a colony itself. At the same time it attempted to perpetuate its own colonial domination by pursuing unwinnable wars against the liberation forces of Angola, Guinea-Bissau and the Cape Verdes, and Mozambique.

The fascist government did not encourage mass mobilization, but attempted to keep the people depoliticized. The opposition, on the other hand, developed a network of clandestine organizations that carried out political and economic struggles and emerged aboveground in the form of the Democratic Electoral Commission (now the Portuguese Democratic Movement) to enjoy limited freedom during the manipulated periodic elections. This clandestine movement attracted a wide range of civilians, but the only well-organized group within it was the Communist Party. The lack of organization by other groups before the coup enabled the Communist Party to assume a visible and important role, particularly within the trade union movement, after April 25 and to support the more progressive officers in the political struggles of the months since.

While repression bred opposition at home, the colonial wars created a cohort of young officers who ultimately decided that the only way to end the wars that bled the country was to bring the government down. The Armed Forces Movement (AFM) organized itself around a program of decolonization, democratization, and antimonopolistic economic development. The AFM led the coup but turned over power to a coalition of senior officers (naming General Antonio de Spinola as president) and four civilian parties: the Communists, the Socialists, the social-democratic Popular Democratic Party (PPD), and the Portuguese Democratic Movement.

Within both the civilian and the military elements of this coalition, there was agreement on a minimal program but profound areas of disagreement over concrete policies. All agreed that the colonial wars must end. But some, led by Spinola and the monopoly interests in Africa, wanted to maintain access to the natural resources of the colonies by establishing a neocolonial federation. Others recognized that the liberation movements in the African colonies would end the wars only if they achieved complete independence for their countries.

Within the Portuguese economy some wanted to see the country more closely integrated with the advanced capitalist systems of Northern and Western Europe, while others wanted to embark on an independent socialist course.

In political terms some wanted to establish a tutelary democracy that would gradually build toward a bourgeois-liberal society on the Western European model, while others wanted to make a national-democratic revolution as the first step toward socialism.

These conflicts quickly produced several major crises. The first three crises were fomented by the Right, which was surprised and disturbed by the growing strength of the Left. In each the Right escalated its tactics. In each the Left won a decisive victory and consolidated its revolutionary gains.

The cabinet crisis of July 1974 arose when Spinola attempted to slow down decolonization and consolidate his power by calling for early presidential elections, while postponing the election of a constituent assembly. The Armed Forces Movement was able to install its leader, Vasco Gonçalves, as prime minister, reaffirm its commitment to hold elections for a constituent assembly, and force Spinola to accept the principle of independence for the colonies.

Spinola tried his hand again on September 28, 1974, by calling for a mass demonstration in Lisbon. According to some observers, the demonstration was to be the prelude to a military coup against the AFM. Masses of people, however, poured into the streets in Lisbon and in towns throughout the country to defend the revolution and demonstrated that the AFM held much greater support than Spinola. The AFM then forced Spinola's resignation, replacing him with President Francisco da Costa Gomes.

The most serious attempt to halt Portugal's progress was the unsuccessful coup attempt of March 11, 1975, in which rightist elements of the armed forces bombarded a progressive artillery regiment near Lisbon. Having failed at cabinet maneuvering in July and at mass mobilization in September, the Right now discovered that it could not reestablish itself by military coup either.

The March 11 attempt provided the opportunity for the most decisive moves against the traditional oligarchy: nationalization of the banks, insurance companies, and major monopoly industries, with first steps toward worker control in those sectors; expropriation of large estates and formation of agricultural cooperatives; creation of the military High Council of the Revolution; and the decision that the military would maintain a decisive role in Portugal's development for the next three to five years.

The new Portuguese government's strength despite repeated attacks was demonstrated by the fulfillment of its promise to hold elections for a constituent assembly within a year of the coup. On April 25, 1975, over 90 percent of Portugal's adult citizens went to the polls. The vote affirmed the AFM's socializing program. Although the Communists, under vitriolic attack from the right-wing clergy, did poorly, the right wing itself was soundly defeated, and the Socialist party won a plurality.

The Socialist Party was founded by Portuguese exiles in West Germany in 1973. Prior to April 1974 it was not organized or active in opposition within Portugal. The Communists, though, were solidly implanted among workers, landless peasants, and, to a lesser extent, students. Though on paper the Socialist Party professes a revolutionary socialist program, its left wing was defeated and withdrew from the party at its December 1974 congress. Those who remain in the party profess socialism but in practice have opposed many of the revolutionary advances. Electoral victory in 1975 was due in part to an American-style political campaign and in part to the AFM's discussions of the need for socialism, through which the word became current and was identified in many people's minds with the Socialist Party. Before the elections the party pledged to support the AFM's program and its continued sharing of power, but it has violated those pledges on many occasions.

After the elections things began to come apart. The Right, discredited and deprived of its economic base by decolonization and nationalization of industries, began to work through the parties with moderate reputations, the Socialists and the Popular Democrats. These parties began to use the constituent assembly as a forum for veiled attacks on the government's socializing program, focusing particularly on Radio Renascença and the newspaper *Republica.*

Republica had supported the Socialist Party, and Radio Renascença had belonged to the Catholic hierarchy. Both were taken over by their workers and transformed into organs supporting the revolution and the struggles for popular power in workplaces, neighborhoods, and military units. The workers of both news organs were falsely accused of being dominated by Communists, and a campaign to oust them began. In July 1975 the Socialists and the PPD quit the government and began fierce attacks on the left-wing military leadership. In August, during a two-week wave of anticommunist violence, conservative northerners attacked more than fifty headquarters of communists and other left-wing parties. The clashes left several dead.

The crisis that began in July continues as of October 1975. Vasco Gonçalves, the prime minister who led the revolutionary advances after March 11, was forced out. The sixth provisional government, more moderate than its predecessors, has been installed, but it has little effective authority. Its actions clearly show that attacks on the previous government over *Republica* and Radio Renascença were an entering wedge to reverse the progress toward socialism and economic equality. No effort has been made to return these news organs to their former owners, but the previous government's measures for agrarian reform and worker control have been impeded.

The political situation today is unstable. Workers in factories, on farms, and in barracks are mobilized to preserve their gains and move further toward national independence, while the "moderate" parties are eager to reestablish the dominance of their privileged constituencies. This is the situation in which the United States is intervening. U.S. intervention has contributed to instability and is continuing to support reactionary forces in a political struggle that could easily lead to tragedy.

The United States is intervening in Portuguese politics through a variety of means, covert and overt. Though we may focus on the CIA, it is important to recognize that the CIA does not act alone. When a country has been targeted as an enemy, it becomes the victim of a carefully orchestrated program of overt diplomacy; covert action; attacks in the U.S. press; and economic sabotage through international credit and commerce, foreign aid, and multinational corporations. Intervention also takes advantage of reactionary forces within the country. The CIA is not omnipotent and neither is the whole panoply of covert and overt activities. Any country will contain within it groups that oppose progressive regimes for reasons of economic interest or traditional ideology. Their actions become part of the program just mentioned, and they receive outside assistance.

Portugal has already been attacked by all these means. It has been forced out of the NATO nuclear planning council. The United States and the Common Market countries made many public statements about their willingness to provide economic aid to Portugal if they have guarantees against communist influence. With the formation of the less socialist sixth provisional government, they announced aid packages totaling about $275 million. Western European countries that have traditionally supplied foreign exchange have engaged in a systematic boycott, particularly of Portuguese wines and tourism. Many multinational corporations have closed their Portuguese subsidiaries rather than pay the new minimum wages, and their control over both supplies and markets makes it impossible for the subsidiaries to carry on independently. Finally, the preceding Portuguese governments were subjected to a systematic campaign of distortion and inaccuracy in the American press. Leaders of the centrist parties were built up, leftist leaders were denigrated, and worker militancy was unquestioningly, and usually inaccurately, described as communist-inspired.

It is in this context that allegations of covert U.S. intervention, not all of them well substantiated, must be evaluated. When public activities exhibit a pattern similar to that observed in previous full-scale interventions, and some CIA activities are documented, we can assume that many more operations are going on but are being successfully kept secret. The most eloquent testimony to the CIA presence in Portugal was presented to Representative Pike's committee investigating the intelligence agencies by Lieutenant General Samuel Wilson: "No comment." (He said he would be willing to testify in executive session.)

According to the testimony of its own officers, the CIA was caught by surprise by the April 25, 1974, coup. Lisbon, close to some excellent beaches, had been a retirement post for Agency officers, and its principal activity there had been training the PIDE in "modern methods of interrogation" (that is, electrical and psychological torture), as documents released after the coup demonstrate.

The Agency, however, quickly established a larger presence. Deputy Director Vernon Walters was in Portugal within a few months after the coup. His visit was publicly announced as a visit to an old friend (the former ambassador). Though the American Embassy subsequently acknowledged that he was there to assess political developments, the CIA has refused to comment on his trip.

Within a few months after the coup, there were some difficult strikes in subsidiaries of American corporations, especially ITT and Timex. It was reported at the time that the CIA was bankrolling the companies to drag the strikes out and contribute to the deterioration of the Portuguese economy.

The International Confederation of Free Trade Unions (ICFTU), long since unmasked as a CIA conduit, was quick to seek influence in the Portuguese trade union movement. Irving Brown, Paris representative of the AFL-CIO, and Michael Boggs, of the American Institute for Free Labor Development, were in Portugal for the first trade union congress after the coup. In the following months the ICFTU stepped up its activity with the formation of the Study Center for the Creation of New Trade Unions, intended to create competing unions that would under-

cut Communist influence. The Socialist Party first demonstrated
its antilabor policy in January when, with support from CIA-
influenced international labor organizations, it unsuccessfully
opposed the law that mandated the creation of a unified trade
union federation. The Armed Forces Movement supported the
law in the belief that it would prevent diversionary divisions
within the working class and allow the federation to be a unified
representative of the interests of labor.

All of these developments, except the creation of the Study
Center and the dispute over the trade union law, occurred well
before the present U.S. ambassador, Frank Carlucci, testified
under oath at his confirmation hearings on November 26, 1974,
that he knew for certain that the CIA was not engaging in covert
activity in Portugal. For nearly a year after the coup, intervention was, in fact, merely warming up. It was only after the right-
wing coup attempt on March 11, 1975, and the acceleration of
the revolutionary process that the CIA decided to act in full
force.

After March 11 right-wing officers responsible for the coup
attempt fled the country, and a "Portuguese Liberation Army"
(ELP) appeared in Spain. It appears that the CIA offered ex-
ploratory financial support and arms to the ELP, which is still
active, claiming responsibility for some bombings in Lisbon and
making excursions across the border from its Spanish base to
destroy some strategic targets, including a radio beacon.

There are also persistent rumors that the CIA is financing
the Movement for the Reorganization of the Party of the Prole-
tariat (MRPP), a self-styled Maoist organization, whose strategy
has gone through several phases, including attacks on right-
wing parties and the American Embassy and an alliance with
the Socialist Party to take over trade unions. Though the rumors
of CIA support are not well substantiated, it is true that the
MRPP, alone among Portuguese parties, finances a daily paper,
despite a small constituency largely restricted to middle-class
radical students.

Most CIA money and other assistance, however, has gone
to groups at the center of the political spectrum, most notably
the Socialist Party. Since its creation at the height of the Cold
War, the CIA has maintained close contacts with European
socialist and social-democratic parties and labor unions, financing them and offering technical assistance to strengthen them

against Communist parties and unions. Because the Agency's freedom of action has been limited by domestic protest, its support to the Portuguese Socialist Party has been indirect. In many cases it has used these old associates (especially the Belgian Socialist Party and the West German Social Democratic Party [SPD]) as intermediaries.

Official sources have revealed to the *New York Times* (as reported in its September 25, 1975, issue) that the CIA has been funneling "several million dollars a month" to the Socialist Party through these means. The most important chain for laundering CIA money runs through the German SPD, the SPD-supported Friedrich Ebert Foundation, and the Portuguese Antonio Sergio Foundation. Because the CIA is avowedly using its influence to strengthen democratic forces against what it regards as the antidemocratic, unscrupulous Communists, it is ironic that its support includes small arms being smuggled to the Socialists through two Western European trade unions.

Paulo Francis, a Brazilian journalist reporting from Washington, has learned from congressional sources that the CIA contributed $10 million to the campaign to oust Prime Minister Vasco Gonçalves. His report has not specified the way in which the money was spent, but a major part of the campaign was the two-week wave of violent attacks against Communist Party and other leftist headquarters in the north of Portugal, which had clear earmarks of a well-organized and well-financed campaign. The majority of the attackers undoubtedly participated spontaneously and without pay. The north is saturated with Catholicism and small property-holding, two bulwarks of traditionalism among peasants almost everywhere. The attacks were, however, organized by groups who traveled from one town to another. On market days when the towns were full of people, anticommunist rallies incited them to attack the available targets.

There are three further fronts on which the CIA is seeking to stay the tide of progress in Portugal: the church, the military, and the Azorean autonomy movement. The church, a bulwark of traditionalism and a mainstay of the former fascist regime, plays an extremely reactionary political role in Portugal today. Philip Agee, author of *Inside the Company: CIA Diary* (New York: Stonehill, 1975), has reported that the church is now receiving CIA funds to support its campaign. Because of its loss of control over Radio Renascença, it has opposed the worker control movement. In at least one archdiocese (Braga) it actively provoked anticommunist violence. The archbishop himself contributed by addressing a rally that resulted in a bloody clash.

Since 1950 over 3,000 Portuguese military personnel have studied at advanced training institutions in the United States. American military personnel stationed at the United States Embassy maintain contact with many of these men, hoping to stimulate divisions within the Portuguese military. Particularly since men in enlisted ranks began openly demonstrating their leftist sympathies in September 1975, some officers who formerly supported the revolution enthusiastically have begun to feel superseded and to call for more discipline within the ranks.

The strategic Azores Islands in the mid-Atlantic have been a burning issue between Portugal and the United States, which used its airbase there to refuel planes supplying Israel during the October 1973 war. Because there are nearly twice as many Azoreans in the United States as in the Azores, it has been relatively easy to funnel support through them to an increasingly insistent movement for Azorean autonomy and alliance with the United States.

Finally, events in Portugal are heavily contingent on developments in two other areas of the world where the CIA is active: Spain and Angola. At a time when Franco is suffering international repudiation, the United States is avidly pursuing renewal of its military agreements with Spain. The American military installations provide significant support for a regime whose deposition would free Portugal from a pressing threat of outside military intervention (and free Spain from an oppressive dictatorship).

CIA financing of the neocolonialist National Front for the Liberation of Angola (FNLA) has been a major factor in the outbreak of civil war there. Angola remains the last major test of Portugal's decolonization policy, which has met outstanding success in Guinea-Bissau and the Cape Verdes, Mozambique, and several smaller territories. Moreover, conservative white settlers returning from Angola to Portugal to escape the ravages of civil war threaten to become an important factor in internal Portuguese politics. Most of them feel that their exploitative privileges in Angola were not protected by the new government, and some are now being recruited for a new military security force. Much of the aid Portugal is receiving from the United States supports the airlift from Angola. While one cannot challenge the humanitarian necessity of removing the refugees from a dangerous situation, it has probably not escaped American attention that their return to Portugal can only contribute to domestic political instability. And American intervention in Angola also bears a large responsibility for creating the very turmoil from which the refugees are escaping.

The U.S. press has created a smokescreen around all this covert activity. For many months, the press reported blithe denials of intervention by Ford, Kissinger, and other government officials. Those denials were usually accompanied by twinges of regret: "Isn't it too bad that the CIA is under so much domestic attack that we don't dare use it now that we really need it?" This theme has been repeated in editorials and opinion columns, in some cases even after the same papers had evidence that intervention was in fact occurring.

What is the basis of U.S. interest in Portugal that, in the eyes of policy makers, warrants intervention? Direct economic interests are relatively small. The United States accounted for less than 10 percent of foreign investment in Portugal and of Portuguese foreign trade in 1973. Protection of the Azores base is more important. The major concern, however, appear to be the symbolic significance that the establishment of an anti-American government on the western flank of the Mediterranean would have. The "Southern European domino theory" predicts that Portugal might influence Spain, Italy, Greece, and even France and lead to the collapse of the Western alliance. The lives of 50,000 Americans and hundreds of thousands of Indochinese were sacrificed in an unsuccessful defense of American hegemony in Southeast Asia. Is a similar adventure under way in Southwest Europe?

With or without major military intervention, this conception of U.S. "interests" can only be defended by depriving the Portuguese people of their right to self-determination. The national independence and the transition to socialism for which the vast majority of the Portuguese people thought they were voting in the elections of April 1975 have already been threatened by U.S. intervention in a mockery of the "democratic process" that Washington rhetoric claims it is defending there. When the real interests being pursued are so at variance not only with the

wishes of the Portuguese people but also with the publicly expressed goals of the United States, the only possible result is
gross contradictions. These contradictions become evident if we
analyze the elements of the CIA's operations and try to infer an
overall strategy from them. It appears that the CIA envisions
three objectives. Some of its actions are directed toward one
objective, some toward another, but the three are mutually in-
consistent.

A first objective that might be assumed from our knowledge
of the CIA's covert activities is the establishment of a sta-
ble, moderately progressive social democracy. The efforts to
strengthen the Socialist Party and to sow divisions within the labor movement might be designed to contribute to this end, the
most benevolent possible objective that can be attributed to the
CIA. To establish such a regime will, however, clearly take more
than political intervention. Many believe that the social conditions for social democracy (appropriate levels of education and
political consensus, for example) simply do not exist in Portugal. Even if they do, the economy is not strong enough for such
a transformation without massive infusions of foreign capital,
which are unlikely to be forthcoming in the present world economic crisis.

A second objective, in which intervention has clearly had
some success, is destabilization. There is a problem with destabilization, however. Once unleashed against an "enemy" regime,
it is likely to remain to afflict a friendly regime unless that regime can rapidly establish its authority by force. Clearly the
sixth provisional government has not been able to establish such
authority and is plagued by the very instability the CIA encouraged to bring down the fifth. If it is true that the CIA has
financed the MRPP, the ELP, and the church, it may have unleashed forces it cannot control.

A third possible objective is simply to ensure the existence
of a reliable ally. We learned in Chile that the easiest way to
install an ally brings with it immense human suffering and the
destruction of a whole people's aspirations. Given the weak-
nesses of the present Portuguese government, a similar repressive "solution" is not out of the question.

But "Portugal will not be the Chile of Europe," in the words
of a slogan frequently chanted at Portuguese rallies. There are
several reasons why a right-wing repressive government cannot

be established in Portugal as easily as it was in Chile. First, the people have just emerged from forty-eight years of fascism and will not permit it to return without a fight. Secondly, the right has little political organization of its own. Even the Socialists and their allies are unlikely to contribute—at least not deliberately—to such an outcome. Finally, and most crucially, the Portuguese armed forces are highly divided, and some significant sectors, especially at the enlisted-man level, are leftist and prepared to defend the revolution.

Any effort to install a right-wing regime will therefore be met with strong resistance. It could plunge the country into a bitter civil war, one which might quickly involve other countries.

The present—and predictably increasing—activities of the CIA in Portugal constitute a major threat to world peace. It is our duty to use whatever means we have to put an end to those activities and eliminate that threat.

Spies with and without Daggers

Kirkpatrick Sale

Kirkpatrick Sale has been a writer and editor for twenty years, contributing to such publications as the New York Times Magazine, Ramparts, WIN, Commonweal, The Nation, and the New York Review of Books. He is also the author of Power Shift: the Rise of the Southern Rim and Its Challenge to the Eastern Establishment and SDS: the Rise and Development of the Students for a Democratic Society.

It seems particularly fitting that a conference on the CIA should take place at Yale University, which is, after all, the spiritual—and to a considerable degree the actual—fountainhead of the Central Intelligence Agency. Easily a quarter of the top officers of the CIA since its inception have been Yale men, including such famous people as Cord Meyer, number two man in the Clandestine Services Department; Richard Bissell, the agent who ran the Bay of Pigs operation; and James Angleton, the former head of the Counterintelligence Division. Dozens of Yale men are prominent in the corporations and foundations that the CIA uses to do its dirty work and channel its funds. And some of the agency's most hardened operatives have even served on the boards of and in the very offices of the university.

By mentioning all this—and it is just the tip of the iceberg —I don't mean to be uncharitable to the institution that is housing this conference. I do think it wise, however, especially in a discussion of domestic spy activities, to remember that institu-

148

tions of *all* kinds have worked—and continue to work—hand in hand with the CIA, and that people don't have to wear cloaks and carry daggers to be spies.

Before going on to examine three specific areas of CIA activity on the domestic front, I would like to make one broad point, which is necessary to keep in mind throughout. That point is the fact that the CIA has been mixed up in domestic spying activity every single day since its inception. The revelations by the *New York Times* about 10,000 files on civilians, or about this or that proprietary front, uncover only one small corner of what's under the rug. In just a few days of casual research, I have managed to come up with easily more than fifty instances, involving hundreds of institutions and corporations and thousands of people, in which the CIA has operated in clandestine, often illegal, ways within the borders of the United States. We must remember that when one of these instances gets "exposed" by prominent papers like the *New York Times* and there is a resulting flap in the Congress and the media, this situation is a reflection much more upon the state of the nation at that particular time than it is upon the CIA. The CIA is *always* doing these things. Public attention just depends upon when the powers that be are going to decide to be shocked about it all.

We all must know, somewhere underneath our civics lessons, that the CIA has to have domestic operations. It has to have (and it does have) agents to interview prospective employees; to keep tabs on the 15,000 or so CIA employees in this country; to supply background reports and security checks on firms and individuals with which it does secret business; to isolate and "debrief," as they say, American citizens who return from travel abroad to sensitive areas; to keep a watch on foreign officials stationed in this country; to locate and work with academic specialists on foreign countries; and so on. Moreover, it has to have (and it does have) an elaborate filing system to keep track of employees, prospective employees, past employees, travelers, and other helpful American citizens—a total of about 35,000 names in all. It has to have (and it does have) a network of field offices around the country—at least thirty-six of them to which it owns up—in most major cities and at certain key points where it figures there is a lot of contact with useful foreigners— for example, New York, Los Angeles, New Orleans, and Miami.

All right, then, so we all know subliminally that the infrastructure, the machinery, is there. We also know—or at least it is made public with alarming regularity—that this machinery is used for spying on, manipulating, pressuring, and invading the privacy of American citizens.

To wit: as early as 1954, various politicians, including Senator Mike Mansfield, raised public questions about the CIA's using two agents to trail Owen Lattimore across the country at a time when Lattimore was accused by Joe McCarthy of being disloyal. This surveillance, an operation that would normally be an FBI job, was illegally performed by the CIA.

In 1961 it was revealed that the CIA had used dozens of bases in Florida, Louisiana, and other points throughout the South to train American citizens—not just regular agents—and Cuban émigrés living in this country to run guns, stage raids, and prepare for the Bay of Pigs attack on Cuba. It was also revealed that the operation involved extensive surveillance of Americans and the establishment of a dozen dummy fronts—Zenith Corporation and Gibraltar Steamship Lines in Miami, Southern Air Transport, and so on—on American soil.

In 1966 *Ramparts* magazine revealed that the CIA was using Michigan State University to train and provide cover for "police" —actually torture—operations in South Vietnam. Subsequent disclosures proved that such universities as MIT, Harvard, Columbia, Miami, and California were being used, with the willing participation of various university officials, to help the CIA not only in its "white" intelligence operations but also in its "black" covert operations as well.

Then in 1967 the storm broke around the National Student Association, which was shown to have been a CIA front for manipulating American students into the CIA's Cold War line. Then it was found out that a whole range of American institutions—foundations (at least fifty of them), labor groups, church groups, book publishers, magazines, civic organizations, God knows what—was being used by the CIA for its various nefarious purposes, all in secret, with much of the activity involved illegal.

In 1971, despite all the attempts by the CIA to disguise its covers and to use all the sophisticated methods of "cut-outs" and whatnot, it was revealed that the CIA was training police forces in at least a dozen cities across the land. It turned out that the CIA had been doing so at least since 1967, a clear violation of its charter prohibiting it from having police powers.

Finally in 1972 and 1973, with Watergate and all its attendant revelations, we learned that the CIA had participated in and been a leader of the negotiations setting up the Huston Plan for domestic spying and a variety of illegal activities including wiretapping, bugging, burglary, and mail surveillance—a plan that was never rescinded and whose operations were in fact carried out. We learned that the CIA had participated in the burglary of Daniel Ellsberg's psychiatrist's office, in the interrogation of Dita Beard, in the planned burglary of Hank Greenspun's safe in Las Vegas, and in surveillance for the Republican Convention in Miami. We learned that the CIA had participated in and supplied equipment and cover for the actual Watergate burglaries, with all of the burglars subsequently caught having direct links to the CIA and at least one being on the payroll.

All those revelations in ten years, and yet people are still surprised and shocked and the *New York Times* thinks it is important enough for a big headline and an all-out campaign when it is found out that the CIA has a file on 10,000 American dissenters and was part of the government operation of repression against the Left in the 1960s and 1970s. *Of course* they had files, *of course* they spied—with whatever legal excuse, with whatever internal justification, the CIA operates just as it wants to in the domestic area.

There is no place for shock and surprise, for offended innocence. We knew all along, or we should have known, just what kind of an outfit the CIA was and what it was capable of. Outrage and anger, yes—there is plenty of room for that, for no agency of this government, nor a score of them, should be allowed to do the sort of things the CIA has done. But let us not be innocent and surprised and shocked any longer to discover that these things are going on. They have gone on, they are going on, and they will continue to go on.

Let me turn now to the three specific areas of the CIA's domestic involvement I want to examine more closely. I want to examine these areas because I think that they reveal dramatically the three essential functions of the CIA on the home front. The first is the sheer survival function, the task of self-protection, of bureaucratic hegemony. The best example of this function is the CIA role in the assassination of John Kennedy in 1963. The second is the repressive function, the task of being a political police, a part of the whole machinery of state repression. The best indication of this function was the CIA's part in the disruption and repression of the New Left in the 1960s and 1970s. The third is the corporate function, the task of meshing with and protecting the interests of major American businesses, especially of the multinational corporations. The most interesting example of this function is the apparent collusion of the CIA and the empire of Howard Hughes.

I

First, to take the Kennedy assassination. The CIA top echelons may have had a number of reasons for either tempering or doing away with John Kennedy, for his policies toward Vietnam, the Soviet Union, East Germany, and Cuba were all running counter to those put forward by the CIA. It seems to me more probable, however, that the overriding reason was survival— survival of the careers of the CIA men, of the Agency as they felt it should be. Remember that in 1963 the CIA was in the throes of sweeping changes. It had been disgraced following the Bay of Pigs fiasco, when Kennedy had vowed that he would establish much greater White House control over its operations. It was being reorganized according to a Kennedy plan that was to have abolished its so-called Research Division and limited its covert activities. It had been brought on the carpet by Kennedy over the affair of Frederick Barghoorn—a Yale professor, incidentally—in which Kennedy had promised Khrushchev that Barghoorn was not a spy, only to discover later that there were indications that Barghoorn was in fact being used by the CIA. It had been brought on the carpet when Kennedy learned that the Agency had lied to him about its Southeast Asia operations, particularly its role in the drug-running in the Golden Triangle of Southeast Asia.

The CIA was threatened by Kennedy's new dovish stance on Vietnam, symbolized by the October 2 announcement of the phased withdrawal of U.S. troops there. Its Cuban operations in the wake of the Bay of Pigs were also being curtailed by the President, who ordered the arrests of Cuban trainees at CIA-operated camps on at least four separate occasions in 1963. The Agency had even been threatened outright by Kennedy, who had said not long before that fateful trip to Dallas that he was going "to splinter the CIA in a thousand pieces and scatter it to the winds."

Such was the danger to the Agency in November 1963. By December 1963 everything had changed. The withdrawal program in Vietnam was halted and escalation begun. All dovish noises in Southeast Asia were silenced and CIA operations there expanded, including new U–2 overflights of Chinese territory (the Chinese claim to have shot down nineteen U–2 planes between 1964 and 1969) and new border raids into China from Laos. The CIA was permitted to reactivate two bases in Florida and stage continued raids on Cuba from 1963 right through 1968. It was even allowed to contract with General Dynamics for a special high-speed boat to be used for Cuban raids. The CIA reorganization schemes were abruptly halted, only minor changes being allowed to take effect, and the Agency was returned to the good graces of the White House, now occupied by a hawkish Texan.

All this is not to say that the CIA did in fact engineer Kennedy's assassination. However, operating on the old Latin principle of *cui bono?*—"to whose advantage?"—we can deduce that the CIA stood to benefit a great deal from the removal of Kennedy at that particular time. There are other hints and clues of the CIA's involvement in the affairs of Dallas that November. Anyone interested can read the excellent research put out by the assassination buffs on these matters. There is evidence for the conclusion that Dallas may have been an instance of the CIA operating on domestic soil, in service to its survival function.

II

The second instance of domestic involvement is the CIA's role in the disruption of the New Left. This disruption was the fulfillment of the CIA's political function in the national machinery.

It should be emphasized that the CIA was only one of many groups active in the repression of left activities in the 1960s and 1970s. That, however, does not mean that its role was insignificant. We know that it had enough money and interest to finance the National Student Association at some $150,000 a year for twenty years. It seems clear that it was also financing other student groups during the 1960s, possibly including Young Americans for Freedom, the right-wing group founded by former CIA man William F. Buckley. (In his column of March 8, 1975, Buckley acknowledged the truth of revelations that he had worked with E. Howard Hunt in the Mexico City CIA station in the early 1950s and been his friend since then.)

We also know that the CIA was active in New York radical circles. According to Seymour Hersh of the *New York Times*, one CIA agent there infiltrated and spied on the New Left from 1967 to 1971, and he was only one of twenty-five agents in the city working under the CIA's Domestic Operations Division and engaged in wiretapping, bugging, surveillance, disruption, infiltration, provocation, and assembling files on the student Left. According to this particular agent, the CIA was only one of many agencies so engaged but was more important than the others because "we had the manpower and the money."

We also know that the CIA:

—was used for at least forty "psychological assessments" of antiwar leaders all across the country, assessments presumably based on information obtained by domestic surveillance;

—followed and spied on many Americans with only faintly leftist connections who went overseas to countries regarded as suspicious—for example, Algeria, Cuba, Egypt, the Soviet Union, Tanzania, Vietnam, Yugoslavia;

—sent agents to infiltrate overseas organizations where Americans might make contacts, particularly guerrilla training camps in Algeria and the Middle East, where it claimed blacks were being prepared for urban guerrilla warfare;

—organized, trained, and paid for its own goon squads to beat up war protesters in New York, Washington, and presumably other cities, and to attack Left movement bookstores and coffeehouses in at least Los Angeles and Columbia, South Carolina, as confirmed by the police of those cities.

From this evidence and other admissions by the CIA in the course of the Rockefeller Commission and congressional investigations, it is possible to assert flatly that the CIA was used for at least a decade to spy on and try to destroy the American Left and that this one task was the day-in, day-out concern of at least several hundred CIA people in cities right across the country.

No one should ever forget that the CIA has a political role to play within the borders of this country. At the very minimum it tries to conserve the system-as-is, to suppress movements for change. At the maximum it tries to subvert those legal forms of dissent that it regards as threatening.

III

The third and last example of the CIA at work domestically concerns its function as a partner of and promoter for American corporations.

The CIA has always had an intimate relationship with American business, of course, because in practically every way they are working the same side of the street. But with the growth of multinational corporations in the last decade and the CIA's decision following the National Student Association exposures to go deeper undercover, the relation has grown much cozier and the mutual interests much larger. The multinationals, for their part, with divisions in all kinds of uncertain foreign countries and resources in all kinds of insecure places, like to have the CIA around arranging convenient coups or propping up unpopular dictatorships. The CIA, wanting to use legitimate organizations with worldwide interests as its cover, likes to have the multinationals through which to work.

This identity of interest has reached a pinnacle with what seems to be a clear interlock between the CIA and the Howard Hughes interests, some of which we learned about with the exposure in early 1975 of the $350 million *Glomar Explorer* caper. In my view this incident represents the out-and-out merger of the CIA and a single corporation. I believe that there is evidence

to indicate that the Howard Hughes corporate empire has not
only been used but taken over by the CIA.

On Thanksgiving Day 1970 there was a coup within the
Hughes corporate structure. Robert Maheu was kicked out of
Hughes headquarters in Las Vegas by a couple of sharpies from
the East, and Howard Hughes himself was removed from the
country and ended up in the Bahamas. Right at that time several interesting things began to happen. (1) A new security
police for the Hughes organization moved in and took control
of all Hughes's gambling casinos and other property. The police
force, known as Intertel, was begun by a variety of people with
intelligence experience in Washington and is loaded with former
CIA people. (2) A new public relations–political lobby organization was designated by the Hughes empire for its Washington
arm-twisting and payoffs. This work was taken away from Larry
O'Brien, the Democratic bigwig, and given over to Mullen and
Co., reputedly a longtime CIA front. (One of Mullen's vice-
presidents was E. Howard Hunt, who went there after "retiring"
from the CIA.) (3) A new venture was begun by the Hughes
corporation. It signed a contract with the CIA to build a super-
secret ship to scoop up a Soviet submarine from the Pacific
Ocean bottom. For the next four years dozens of its top officials
and several of its corporations were working hand in glove with
the CIA. (4) New officers came into control of the Hughes Aircraft division, causing the upper ranks of the company, according to *Time*, to become "studded with former ranking military
and CIA officers." (5) The CIA opened its office in, of all places,
Las Vegas, Nevada, the seat of the Hughes empire. Not very
many foreign agents there, one would have thought, and a far
cry from the places you would expect American spies to operate.
That office is now said to be one of the biggest offices, perhaps
the biggest, outside of the headquarters in Langley, Virginia.

This apparent takeover of a single corporation may be an
unusual move for the CIA. But the advantages are overwhelming. The CIA gets a privately held company, without public
accountability or interference, with a reputation for and machinery to allow elaborate secrecy. It gets a huge gambling network, useful for laundering and dispersing money around the
world, and at the same time valuable for its reputed contacts
to the world of organized crime, which has always served the
CIA as a useful ally. It gets a major defense contractor—ranking

number nine at last count—with information from, and contacts with, the upper levels of the military establishment, certainly including the intelligence part of that establishment, and a contractor that can provide cover for the development and building of almost any kind of weaponry or espionage gadget the Agency would want. It gets a business that is already established around the world, with offices in several key overseas locations, such as Southeast Asia and the Caribbean. According to a report by the Los Angeles police, these overseas offices have in fact been used by CIA agents for payments and cover. And it gets a complex of divisions involved in a wide variety of affairs—a medical institute in Florida, for example, an ocean-mining company, and a domestic airline looking to expand overseas. The last of these could be an obvious replacement for such CIA airlines as Southern Air Transport and Air Asia. In short, the CIA gets the perfect corporate machinery for its multifarious operations.

If the CIA has taken over one large corporation, as I think is possible, then how many others, perhaps smaller and less likely to be noticed, might it already have taken over? At this moment just how many American corporations are being used at home and abroad to carry out the CIA's nefarious schemes? Five hundred agents, CIA Director Colby admitted, use corporate covers. Forty journalists, he admitted, have been in the service of the CIA. Literally scores of American corporations have been set up for CIA operations. More than seventy businesses have supported one single CIA front operation, the AFL-CIO's American Institute for Free Labor Development. Why not might another score or so have been taken over outright?

These, then, I see as the three most revealing functions of the CIA, the three that are necessary to isolate for a clear idea of the way the Agency operates: its survival function, its repressive function, and its corporate function. There may be others, of course, but I think it is important to see at least these three, for then *nothing* that the CIA does will seem mysterious. Then, too, we can fit the little pieces of the puzzle together whenever we read this or that about the CIA. Do we hear that a man trained in the CIA was in charge of the Los Angeles police investigation into the killing of Robert Kennedy? Well, then, we can see this fact merely as an example of its survival

function. Do we read that the CIA funds the UCLA Behavior
Modification Institute or that the CIA has been reading citizens'
mail ever since 1953? Merely the CIA's repressive function at
work. Do we learn that a company called Interarmco has made
major sales of American-made arms to the Middle East? Well,
that's a CIA company, by all accounts, tightening security along
the oil pipelines, performing the corporate function.

One last point. To understand the CIA's behaving in these
ways is not to excuse it or justify it or, of course, approve it.
There should be no doubt as to where I stand with regard to
the CIA, nor, I should think, where any right-minded person
stands. The CIA should, quite simply and directly, be abolished.
Its functions for the American empire at home and abroad are
only odious and malevolent and should be done away with
forthwith. If by the least chance there is a valuable function
that the CIA performs—say, perhaps, the monitoring of satellites to determine which countries in the world are likely to be
starving next year—this function could easily be taken over by
the State Department.

Simply enough: the CIA should never have been created.
Now that we have a chance, it should be speedily demolished.
It is offensive, immoral, obscene, irrelevant, and unnecessary.
Its "white" operations are useless and distorted. Its "black"
operations are stupid and dangerous. What we must all press
for, now that the question has come up again, is the total elimination of this agency and the return to a more reasonable and
orderly form of international and domestic behavior.

Not that this one stroke, even if we could accomplish it,
would automatically cleanse the American system or eliminate
the multitude of threats to individual freedom represented by
the American government. Far from it. There would still be
dozens of other agencies operating in ways both obvious and
subtle to diminish our strengths and our freedoms, to undermine the rights that we are taught from the textbooks belong
to us inalienably. But it would be a start, an important start,
and worth working for.

Considering the offensiveness of the CIA in every sphere,
and particularly its subversion of American religious, political,
and educational institutions, one can say that at the very least
the elimination of the CIA would strike a blow for God, for
country, and even for Yale.

The CIA at Home

John D. Marks

■ A biographical sketch of John D. Marks precedes the first of his presentations at the Conference on the CIA and World Peace printed in this volume.

THE CIA HAS BEEN GETTING a bad name lately. In some ways that is just not fair, especially as regards domestic surveillance. The CIA got into trouble when the *New York Times* in its December 21, 1974, issue reported that the Agency had kept files on 10,000 domestic dissidents. Although the number of files the CIA kept was actually larger than the *Times* figure, consider for comparison the case of the Bureau of Special Services of the New York City Police Department. This intelligence division, or "red squad," kept about 1 million files. In virtually every other city of over 50,000 population in this country, there was—and is—a similar red squad for surveillance of private citizens. In Baltimore there has been a major scandal over the revelation that members of Congress and local politicians, as well as civil rights and antiwar leaders, were under police surveillance. In Houston a member of Congress was surveilled. In Chicago community leaders as well as politicians were followed. I am willing to bet that in any city where there is a good investigative reporter, the same type of scandal can be turned up.

FBI conduct has been quite scandalous also. In addition to keeping files on tens of thousands of Americans, it ran a special counterintelligence program, or COINTELPRO in FBI language, to disrupt the antiwar and civil rights movements. There was a charming case in 1970 out at Arizona State University, where a professor named Morris Starsky was up for tenure. Every member of his tenure committee received an anonymous letter

159

sent by the FBI but signed a "concerned ASU alumnus" listing all sorts of scurrilous charges against him. The committee turned him down, and he lost his job.

There was another case down in Mississippi in 1969. A civil rights leader named Muhammad Kenyatta received an anonymous letter from the FBI that purported to come from something called the Tougaloo College Defense Fund. The letter threatened Kenyatta and warned him to stay away from the Tougaloo campus. Shortly thereafter he left the state of Mississippi. I do not recall ever seeing Efrem Zimbalist, Jr., on the TV show *The FBI* ever writing anonymous letters that caused people to move away or get fired from their jobs. Yet in actuality the FBI was doing quite a bit of this sort of thing.

So when we talk about the CIA and domestic operations, let's keep the real issue in perspective. The CIA was carrying on extensive operations in this country, operations forbidden by the National Security Act's section banning it from any domestic "police, subpoena, law-enforcement powers or internal security functions." Much of what the CIA was doing in this country, therefore, was illegal. Much more illegal surveillance was, however, conducted by local police, the FBI, and other federal agencies than by the CIA.

On the whole, the CIA would probably prefer to operate overseas—to "destabilize" governments in Chile, to put the president of Costa Rica on its payroll, to organize a "secret" war in Laos. But though the CIA has been extremely active around the world, much of its clandestine support structure is located right here in the United States.

One of the things that offends me the most is the CIA's literary efforts—its domestic book publishing efforts. Books have appeared regularly in this country that have been subsidized and financed by the good old Central Intelligence Agency. In 1967 Praeger Publishers admitted to having published "fifteen or sixteen" books for the CIA. Perhaps the CIA's most famous publication was a book called *The Penkovskiy Papers* (New York: Doubleday, 1965), which went to the top of the bestsellers in 1965. It was supposed to be the journal of a Soviet spy who worked for the CIA.

The fastest way to become an ex-spy is to keep a journal. Oleg Penkovskiy did not write *The Penkovskiy Papers*. What Penkovskiy did was to make secret reports to various Western intelligence agencies during the early 1960s. After he was arrested and executed by the Soviet Union, the CIA wanted to reap a propaganda windfall from this success. And so the CIA arranged for the publication of a book that included both material actually sent in by Penkovskiy and material in the category of "disinformation." Disinformation is false propaganda, with truths and half-truths mixed in.

The Penkovskiy Papers was a fraud. In fact, Penkovskiy's whole role in the damn thing was a fraud. Penkovskiy originally had volunteered to spy for the CIA in the 1950s. He was turned down cold on the grounds he seemed to be a Soviet deception agent. As a colonel in Soviet military intelligence, he seemed to the CIA to be too good to be true. Then the British recruited Penkovskiy. They made him a spy and subsequently went to the CIA and offered to share his reports. But to get in on the action, the CIA had to pay the British by providing satellite photographs that involved the most sensitive intelligence techniques. In effect, the CIA had to pay blackmail to British intelligence in order to get access to the man it had previously turned down. And Penkovskiy is supposedly one of the CIA's greatest triumphs. The essential point, however, was that the CIA was propagandizing the American people with the publication of *The Penkovskiy Papers*.

A similar CIA publishing effort occurred in 1953 when the MIT Center for International Studies put out a book called *Dynamics of Soviet Society*. There were two versions of that book. One was classified, and the CIA put it to its own internal use. One was unclassified and made available to the general public with no indication of CIA involvement. Walt Rostow, among others, participated in the writing of that book. Victor Marchetti and I discuss these two books and other CIA literary productions in our own book, *The CIA and the Cult of Intelligence* (New York: Knopf, 1974).

American universities are infiltrated by the CIA in another way. Currently on over a hundred campuses, there are CIA "spotters," whose secret job for the agency is to identify and help recruit foreign students to be spies. It is easier for the CIA to hire these students on campus here than in their home country because the local police are friendly and because American operatives can just fit into the crowd. The CIA's professors are looking for bright students, especially from Third World countries, who have a good chance of rising quickly—perhaps with some help from the CIA—into positions of power back home. Foreign students—and indeed, all foreign visitors—are a regular target of the CIA's domestic operatives.

Other professors do no recruiting but carry out secret research contracts for the CIA. These can be close to legitimate academic research, for example, a study of the Soviet economy or Chinese population growth. The problem with this type of research is that the results are usually classified and the CIA's involvement is kept a secret through dummy contracts supposedly signed by other government agencies. Often professors do technical and scientific research, which can vary from developing new secret writing devices or secret weapons, to developing a better lens for a satellite camera. Again this classified work is hidden under the cover of a contract to another federal government agency, not the CIA. Another way that a professor can work for the CIA is by contracting his or her services to a CIA proprietary, or false-front company.

These companies seem to be private enterprises but in fact are CIA-owned and under CIA control. The CIA has several hundred of these proprietary companies operating in the United States and overseas. The most famous ones are the CIA airlines: Air America, which was deeply and openly involved in the Vietnam War, and others, such as Southern Air Transport in Miami and Intermountain Aviation in Tucson, which the CIA recently sold off to friendly buyers. These companies are quite profitable because the way to build up cover in an airline is to charter the planes out on the commercial market. Thus, the CIA operates one of the largest charter businesses in the world. The Agency has chartered its planes to other government agencies as well as to private individuals. For instance, in 1972 a CIA proprietary, Southern Air Transport, received a $2 million contract from the Agency for International Development to fly relief supplies to Bangladesh. The possibilities for conflicts of interest and inside deals when one government agency is seeking a contract from another are enormous.

I have talked with a former vice-president of one of the CIA airlines who told me that in the early 1950s the CIA had seventeen airlines operating in the United States. One function of these airlines was to fly American GIs from the East Coast to the West Coast. Any domestic carrier could have had those contracts. Lack of equipment was no obstacle because all the planes needed was provided by the Air Force. The only reason I can think of for giving these contracts to the CIA was to shift funds over to the secret agency. In this and many other cases the CIA was literally earning a profit from another part of the government.

The point I am making is that the CIA itself has been a profit-making business. Its revenues from its companies have been as high as $200 million a year. As Victor Marchetti and I wrote in *The CIA and the Cult of Intelligence* (p. 60): "An agency holding company, the Pacific Corporation, including Air America and Air Asia, alone accounts for almost 20,000 people, more than the entire workforce of the parent CIA." In 1974 the Pacific Corporation declared revenues of about $50 million.

I can conceive of a time when Congress might even cut the CIA appropriation and the CIA would say: "Well, that's O.K., we'll just increase our profits." Remember, the Constitution says that only the Congress shall appropriate funds; it says nothing about government agencies raising their own funds on the private market. I think that, as the CIA scandal unfurls further, an area of major concern is going to be the Agency's financial dealings. The CIA has been investing in the stock market and otherwise engaging in all sorts of dubious financial processes.

For example, Southern Air Transport was for years the CIA's air-intervention arm in Latin America. In 1973 the CIA decided that it wanted to sell the line because its cover had been blown. The company was to be sold to its president, Stanley Williams, the man who had run it for the CIA for years. By definition, this kind of thing is an inside deal. The *Miami Herald* in an article about this deal pointed out that Stanley Williams paid $2.1 million to buy Southern Air Transport at a time when the line had assets of over $4 million.

Taylor Branch and I discovered another interesting kind of CIA proprietary (see *Harper's Weekly*, January 24, 1975). It was a police training school called International Police Services Inc., located just off Dupont Circle in Washington, D.C. The CIA used it to train foreign policemen in everything from laboratory techniques to bugging and surveillance methods. INPOLSE, as the CIA called it, trained thousands of foreign policemen, who supposedly had come to the United States for private instruction.

There has been extensive criticism in the last few years of

the International Police Academy, which was run by the Agency for International Development. AID has been charged with fronting for the CIA. That charge is perfectly true. The CIA was instrumental in the setting up of the International Police Academy. Yet during all the time IPA was under attack, there was another CIA school, INPOLSE, just about as big located fifteen blocks away that was carrying on the same kind of training, but even more secretly. That's why the CIA sets up its private companies. The proprietaries provide another degree of cover, another layering away from the real source.

I discovered another one of these companies and wrote about it in *Rolling Stone* of July 18, 1974. Psychological Assessment Associates on Connecticut Avenue in Washington, D.C., was a company that was doing psychological research in a field called "indirect assessment." Indirect assessment is the art of making judgments or testing people who do not know that they are being tested. It obviously has importance in the espionage world, where you do not want to tell people that they are being tested as you are recruiting them for spying and trying to decide whether they are telling the truth. Psychological Assessment Associates was looking for correlations between certain kinds of behavior patterns and whether a person was telling the truth or whether a person had vulnerabilities. By observing a person's physical behavior, the CIA hoped to learn if he would be vulnerable to women, or men, or drugs, or alcohol, or whatever. The application of this kind of thing for espionage work is obvious. Many college professors contracted with Psychological Assessment Associates. Although most of them knew that they were dealing with the CIA, they did not have to tell their colleagues or their students. They could say that their work was for a private company.

My overall point is that the CIA does an awful lot in this country—and a lot that's awful.

Domestic Political Intelligence

Frank Donner

■ Frank Donner is an attorney specializing in labor law and civil liberties. He serves as general counsel of the United Electrical, Radio and Machine Workers of America. He has also served as an attorney for the National Labor Relations Board, the CIO, and the United Steelworkers of America. He has lectured at over a dozen colleges and universities and is the author of over thirty articles and reviews and a book, The Un-Americans. His legal practice has seen him involved in a number of notable cases, and he is currently preparing a series of studies for the American Civil Liberties Union Foundation on surveillance of political activities and associations in the United States.

POLITICAL INTELLIGENCE has three components: the first is data collection, or operations; the second is the intelligence product, or the files; and the third is a body of assumptions, or the philosophy of intelligence. In a developed intelligence system these three components fuse into an instrument of political control, a mode of governance. Even before we reach this final stage of development, the operational practices are institutionalized into a control apparatus that outruns the forms of law.

Domestic political intelligence has two historic sources. The first is the military. Every domestic political intelligence system is rooted in military practice. For example, in Britain MI–5 (Military Intelligence) is a domestic intelligence operation but bears the imprint of its military origin. The second model for domestic political intelligence is diplomacy or statecraft—the relationship of nations to other nations. What is important to bear in mind here is that while domestic political intelligence is targeted against our own nationals and citizens, it nevertheless assumes that they are enemies, to be neutralized by any means necessary. In short, domestic intelligence retains the hostile assumptions of the milieu in which it is rooted. Domestic intelligence is thus a gross anomaly in a free society governed by constitutional norms. Why extend constitutional protections to an enemy?

I am talking about a system that is unrelated to law enforcement but for which law enforcement frequently serves as a cover. Intelligence breeds other deceptions as well. Like every stigmatized calling, intelligence has developed a pervasive cosmetic rhetoric, a way of disguising what it really is and how it functions. You may recall, for example, that White House master plumber E. Howard Hunt did not speak of "casing" Daniel Ellsberg's psychiatrist's office, but of making a "judgment visit." The vocabulary of intelligence is saturated with a pseudoprofessional jargon that, as I have suggested, is intended to cosmetize, and even ennoble, what is really involved.

One of the most important terms in this intelligence lexicon is "mission." A "mission," which on its face bears the imprint of its military origin, is a means used by intelligence agencies of redefining and ideologizing their functions. That is, it is a term that gives some superordinate, nation-saving role to the intelligence agency. On a more lowly level, one speaks not of an informer but of a "source" or an "asset." Even the word "intelligence" has a kind of awe-inspiring resonance that is quite remote from the reality.

Two other functional aspects of intelligence must be mentioned. Intelligence is typically secret and, in this country at any rate, usually an executive function. It is a means of promoting the power of the executive, defending the executive against attacks from critics, and, at the same time, concealing itself.

Now let me turn to the assumptions, the political theory of intelligence. It hardly needs to be said—anybody who reads the newspapers would recognize it—that intelligence is a resource of conservative politics. There are no progressive, liberal intelligence agents or functionaries—at least there are none who have survived in the intelligence agencies. Second, we must note that the basic commitment, the mission if you will, of American intelligence is to win the "long twilight struggle" against communism for supremacy. Intelligence is a projection of what I have called "the politics of deferred reckoning," the conviction of the inevitability of an apocalyptic showdown with the bad guys. For the present, we have to know who they are and must record their doings and watch them. The origins of this notion of a final struggle, which has so strongly influenced both our politics and our culture, are rooted in the American response to the Russian Revolution. Since the 1920s the fear of a Bolshevik-style bloody revolution has deeply gripped the American imagination.

Intelligence has a powerful negative bias. That is, it sees subversive targets everywhere. This trait is not only an occupational characteristic of intelligence people but also a political necessity. In order to justify its existence in a democratic society, intelligence must exaggerate the power, the intentions, and the number of the enemy. This exaggeration is, of course, the source of the constant, ever increasing funding for intelligence.

Next, an important part of this body of assumptions is the notion of foreign instigation or control, the belief that social unrest and protest are instigated by some foreign principal and are the product of some plot hatched abroad. You may recall that one of President Nixon's earliest assignments to the CIA was to ferret out the foreign instigation of the antiwar movement. He was enormously disappointed to learn that the CIA could find no such foreign sponsorship. His disappointment became understandable enough when we read in a transcript of a White House conversation the suggestion by H. R. Haldeman: "Wouldn't it be a good idea to label all this peace stuff as part of a foreign plot?"

Now I come to another aspect of intelligence. Intelligence individuates social protest. The great scare-figure in the intelligence world is the agitator, the sinister fellow who comes into an otherwise contented scene and disrupts. This notion that protest has no social dimension but is simply the product of subversive plotters is a very deeply held assumption of intelligence.

Finally we note the intelligence assumption that no matter how innocent an act may seem or how justified a demonstration may appear to be, it may ultimately turn out to be part of a sinister jigsaw puzzle of which you have seen only an innocuous part. So it is that everything is grist for the intelligence mill, however innocent it may appear on the surface.

Now I would like to talk about intelligence institutions. In addition to local police intelligence units there are some twenty federal institutions that are most prominent in what is called (again one of those beguiling terms) the "intelligence community," institutions bound together by common assumptions and engaged in some form of liaison relationship. That is, some of these agencies have more operational capability than others; some of them have better files than others; and they trade off whenever they can in order to achieve their missions. Again, it must be emphasized that the agencies that are linked in an intelligence community perform intelligence functions for purposes unrelated to law enforcement. Most of them are executive agencies, with one important exception: the congressional antisubversive committees. These panels use a lawmaking (rather than a law enforcement) cover or justification for intelligence activities.

Because American intelligence posits a sinister foreign threat, it perceives itself as a purely defensive response. Foreign intelligence agents and functionaries are quite amused at the readiness of our intelligence agencies to justify their tactics as defensive. The notion of innocence and righteousness compromised and befouled by outsiders is widespread in our culture but nowhere so clearly expressed as in spy work. All we are trying to do is defend our sacred institutions from the threat of the machinations of foreign spies; our intelligence is merely defensive counterintelligence, while theirs is aggressive and evil. Hence the claim that the KGB is simply convulsed with glee over investigations of the CIA because their traditional enemies are in disarray, etc., etc. There is, of course, a huge irony in all this. The CIA's intervention in the political life of other countries has made it the "foreign spy," the sinister outsider, par excellence.

There is another characteristic of American intelligence agencies that commands attention. Almost every one of our intelligence agencies has invented or abused its powers. Probably the clearest examples of this deception are the congressional antisubversive committees, which for years have used their power for intelligence purposes, while claiming that they were merely exercising a legislative function. The grand jury practices of the Nixon years, the CIA's domestic operations, the IRS, have all converted powers that were granted for other purposes into intelligence functions. In the case of the CIA we must go further: the agency has deliberately defied a ban on domestic political intelligence activity.

But the best example of this abuse remains the FBI. For over three decades the FBI has been engaging without any legitimate authority in political surveillance unrelated to law enforcement. I used to be a voice crying in the wilderness about this abuse, but more recently the questionable authority of the Bureau has become a congressional concern. The FBI traditionally justified its power to engage in people-watching, that is, surveillance unrelated to law enforcement, on the basis of a memorandum that was sent on September 6, 1939, to the Attorney General by President Roosevelt, in which FDR said, in effect, "Look, we are on the brink of a war; we have to worry about sabotage; we have to worry about spies; and so I would like you to set up an intelligence capability as a protection against these contingencies."

Long after World War II ended, through the Cold War and the McCarthy era, this letter of Roosevelt's was torn from its context and used as an authority for political surveillance. Americans are very responsive to claims of violated rights. But they are reluctant to confront questions of abuse of power. A claimed usurpation of power threatens their faith in the American experience and in the ability of our institutions to resist the subversions of the Old World. But here is a gross usurpation of power that can no longer be evaded. It was not until L. Patrick Gray was nominated as FBI director in the spring of 1973 that this issue was finally flushed out.

The reason why Gray's nomination became an avenue for this kind of exploration was that Congress had passed a law requiring Senate approval for the post of FBI director. In the course of the Gray confirmation hearings and subsequently in the Clarence Kelley confirmation hearings, congressional committees established beyond a shadow of a doubt that the Bureau had no authority to engage in political surveillance unrelated to law enforcement.

Included in the documents submitted to a congressional

committee by former Attorney General Elliot Richardson in the spring of 1974 is a memorandum addressed by him to the FBI that states: "I have your memorandum of August 7, 1973, which recommends the issuance of an Executive order, concerning the authority of the FBI to conduct domestic intelligence operations." In other words, FBI Director Kelley had written a letter to the Attorney General saying, in effect, "Please, get me an Executive order authorizing me to engage in the kind of thing that the Bureau has been doing for over thirty years." To continue the quotation from the document by Richardson to the FBI:

> Your memorandum indicates that the proposed order is designed to accomplish several objectives: (1) to establish that the FBI has been instructed to engage in domestic intelligence operations; (2) to supplement the statutory authority of the FBI by delegating any constitutional power that the President may have in this area; and (3) to direct the Attorney General to establish guidelines for domestic intelligence.

This request for peacetime intelligence authority was submitted some thirty years too late. Why did we tolerate this kind of usurpation of power for three decades? After reviewing that experience, how can we smugly sit back and say, "It can't happen here?" What repressive forces were at work in this society that silenced the cry that the emperor wore no clothes? I don't know the answers to these questions, but I leave you to ponder them.

I do not want you to think that just because the Bureau itself questioned its authority to engage in political intelligence that it ended political surveillance. Oh no. The Bureau continues as before as a political intelligence agency, but now with an improvised law enforcement justification.

This conversion unifies and explains all intelligence practices. The Bureau is now saying, in effect, "All those people whom we were watching before because they were revolutionaries, radicals, activists, liberals, dissenters, etc., we are continuing to watch because they might in some time in the future commit subversion or treason. It is quite true that sedition laws have not been enforced for almost a generation now, but who knows? You can't be too careful when the life of a nation is at stake." And so again, an illegality breeds deception, here a triple deception: the deception (1) that you are engaged in law enforcement, (2) that the people you are surveilling are really threatening to violate some law, even though all that they are doing is exercising a right protected by the Constitution, and, finally, (3) that our security is so fragile that unless these people are wiretapped and infiltrated we may be faced with a serious threat to our national safety.

Another price we pay for living in a democracy (it is getting to be very expensive, you will notice) is the need to create in the popular mind a fear that our national security is continuously endangered. We Americans are programmed for fear. For example, we permit ourselves to be terrified by advertisements that if we do not use the right antifreeze our cars will not function, or if we fail to use the right toothpaste, our social life will suffer. We create anxieties and convert them into consumption. In the same way we convert fear into repression. And so every intelligence agency must at some point become a ministry of propaganda. It has to revive and freshen the fears that nourish the very life of the agency.

The classic example is, of course, Hoover's FBI. Hoover would regularly insist that the Reds were getting stronger and stronger. But he couldn't say that they had actually obtained their goal—not only because it would obviously defy the reality, but also because it would indicate that the FBI wasn't doing a very good job. And so he would say something like, "Oh, they're worse than ever. Sure they've lost their membership, but now they're down to their hard, bloodthirsty core." The trick was to keep alive and renew the mass fear of Communism, but at the same time to reassure the frightened citizenry that the Bureau had the subversives well in hand. This dual strategy worked: not only did Hoover become a culture hero, but he also never failed to get as much money as he asked for from Congress.

We have been victims, then, of deliberate, institutionalized manipulation and propaganda for a very long time. Intelligence is supposed—in theory, anyway—to be an aid to policy making and decision making. By acquiring as many facts as are available, the executive is supposed to be able to make the right decisions. It is bad intelligence practice to entrust to the collector of the data the responsibility for evaluating or interpreting the data. But Hoover's operation was not in support of some legitimate government function; it was not reviewed by higher authority nor was the intelligence product used for decision making. It was, almost from the beginning and remains to this day, an end in itself.

Now we come to operations. American intelligence operations do not aid in decision making. Moreover, the FBI's intelligence activity is not confined to passive intelligence operations. All intelligence operations in this country tend to become aggressive. The Bureau has been engaged in this kind of guerrilla warfare against its targets for a very long time. The most obvious example of this form of aggressive intelligence are the "counterintelligence" (COINTELPRO) programs, which were formally launched in the 1950s and the 1960s. But even before that time, harassment of targets was routine in the Bureau's political intelligence operations. Finally, to enlarge on an earlier observation, we should note the term "counterintelligence program," which assumes that the targets have engaged in spying and sabotage and that these programs were a defensive response.

I want to speak very briefly about files. Intelligence files are immortal and indestructible. Attorney General Harlan Fiske Stone went to J. Edgar Hoover in 1924 and said, in effect: "I want you to cut out all of this political intelligence work and only investigate when there is probable cause that a crime has been committed." But he, in effect, also said to Hoover: "Unfortunately we can't eliminate our files. That will require an act of Congress." And so we have forests of files, the living and the dead, the fathers and the sons, the grandchildren, their friends and their friends' friends too.

We have learned from European intelligence systems (although we have ignored this truth in our own national life) that every intelligence program ultimately becomes an instrument of blackmail. Fouché, Napoleon's famous minister of police, knew about all his enemies because his enemies' mistresses were in his pay. Hoover knew about his critics in Congress because he had something on *them,* or so they feared. He knew about his allies and he had their support because he had something on *them.* And he knew about the enemies of his allies because he had something on *them.* In this way Hoover built up a system of blackmail that effectively silenced criticism and ensured his power against all challenge. So we have gone the whole route. We have reproduced in our time, in the past fifty years, the very experience that we are quick to denounce in the repressive autocracies of the nineteenth century.

I am doubtful about the possibility that Congress will do anything about this intelligence structure. Intelligence agencies survive through what I call the "Barbarossa syndrome." When things get bad they retire to the cave and wait for conditions to improve. Then they emerge and continue their business at the old stand.

Surveillance
and Mind Control

Blanche Wiesen Cook

■ Blanche Wiesen Cook is a writer, editor, and teacher. Associate professor of history at John Jay College of Criminal Justice of the City University of New York, she is senior editor of the Garland Library on War and Peace, a 360-volume reprint series. She is coeditor of Past Imperfect (2 vols., 1973) and author of Toward the Great Change: Crystal and Max Eastman on Feminism, Antimilitarism, and Revolution. As a journalist, her columns have appeared in many newspapers. She is currently working on a book on Presidents Eisenhower and Nixon. Dr. Cook incorporated information on several developments occurring after April 1975 in the following article based on her presentation at the Conference on the CIA and World Peace. Shortly before this book went to press, she made the following comment:

My analysis was presented at a time of great national crisis. Our murderous "destabilization" of Chile had followed ten years of tragedy in Indochina. Horrors seemed endless. Most of the Watergate conspirators had yet to be imprisoned; the Senate's assassination hearings had yet to be held; and the CIA's various psychological and chemical experiments had yet to be revealed. It was felt then that we might finally be crossing the line into a technologically grotesque garrison state.

Concerted public effort, the eternal vigilance so necessary to safeguard civil liberty and human dignity, now seems to have triumphed temporarily. If so, it is important to know that

while some of the surveillance programs described below have been suspended, and others
scuttled entirely, all of the technology con
tinues to work, most of it is still in use, and
much of it continues to be exported throughout
the world. Moreover, psychosurgery has now been
given the government's stamp of approval. Ex-
perimental psychosurgery has been designated a
psychological "therapy."

While our crisis no longer seems quite so
immediate, it has by no means passed entirely.
The threat of a garrison state will continue,
changing always in content and tone, until the
people of this planet are politically free and
economically secure.

CONTRARY TO ACCEPTED MYTH, the victory of the Allies at the
close of World War II did not ensure a victory of democracy
over fascism. Rather, the elements of the modern military state
erected by the fascists were dismantled by the victors and trans-
ported home. What the prescient political scientist Harold D.
Lasswell described in 1941 as the movement "toward a world
of garrison states" began to develop in the United States over
the next three decades.

By 1975 specialists on violence had introduced weapons to
control an entirely militarized society. Lasswell pointed out that
the fascist rulers of Europe had not integrated their military
systems with modern technology. They merely used some of
technology's "specific elements." The American military state,
however, has fully integrated the most advanced technological
apparatus. True to Lasswell's vision, "the military men who
dominate a modern technical society will be very different from
the officers of history and tradition."[1]

Today we are in a struggle against time and technology to
retain the sanctity of our minds and the independence of our
thoughts against the onslaught of mind-control devices. Although opposition to the employment of these devices remains
strong and the struggle to preserve and increase the liberties
that we claim as our tradition remains hopeful, the minds of
many have already been numbed by the electronic media. The

minds of others have already been altered by sophisticated advances in electronics, chemistry, and medicine, notably psychosurgery. Since 1965 wherever there has been public protest and resistance to it, the government has been forced to curtail its ongoing mind-control program. But in the absence of economic security and social justice, domestic tranquility depends on brutality and propaganda.

As Lasswell says, the "enormous importance of symbolic manipulation in modern society" is a fundamental key to social control. We like to think that we are free. Our technological structures, however, may be conveniently used to alter our perceptions of our individual needs, to intensify materialism, to encompass counterproductive violence, thereby assisting the managerial class to impose value priorities: "From the earliest years youth will be trained to subdue—to disavow, to struggle against—any specific opposition to the ruling code of collective exactions." As a result, the modern garrison state will appear "far less rigid than the military states of antiquity."[2]

One of the features of the contemporary garrison state is an inability to distinguish between the state's civilian and military functions. Political spokesmen entertain us while colorless bureaucrats run the wiretaps, the banks, the wars, the heroin traffic. These bureaucrats juggle public opinion and sensibilities by alternately expanding and contracting social services.

In order to ensure a civilized ruling elite able to cope with all eventualities while appearing entirely benign, the contemporary garrison state is administered by several bureaucracies. These structures camouflage the identity of the corporate owners who give the orders. At the head of these bureaucracies is the CIA. When things get rough, domestically or internationally, the CIA can always be called upon to lower its profile.

Recent revelations have focused attention on the CIA and its past activities. Too rarely have we noticed how the CIA fits into the larger game plan. Too rarely have we even noticed that there are game plans in operation in the United States. Too rarely have we investigated the research and development programs that are funded for future use by the CIA and all the government's military and paramilitary agencies. Unless we begin to see these connections, the unseen managers of our society will extend their computerized network until they achieve total control.

Computer technology has enabled machines to replace people and laws. We no longer have a system of checks and balances. We have a system of military espionage and total surveillance. Surveillance operations are conducted by the FBI, the IRS, the U.S. Civil Service, state and local "red squads," a variety of bank, credit, and insurance operations, the Air Force and Marine intelligence units, state National Guard commands, the Continental Army Intelligence Command, the Immigration and Naturalization Service, the Secret Service, the Army's Counterintelligence Analysis Branch [CIAB], and several other surveillance operations located in the Justice Department. There are also private organizations, such as one in the Midwest, which boasts in its advertising that it has complete, computerized files on every known American dissident and all 160 million of their friends, relatives and fellow travelers.

These organizations employ informers, *agents provocateurs*, twenty-four–hour infrared lens closed-circuit TV cameras attached to telephone poles on the streets of America's cities, sensors and other electronic gadgetry developed for the military in Indochina. As former Attorney General, now Supreme Court Justice, William Rehnquist told Senator Sam Ervin during hearings on military espionage and federal data banks in 1971: the government has the "right to collect whatever information it wants on anybody."

And collect it does. The Army, for example, has collected information on 25 million people considered "un-American" because they wrote their congressperson, signed petitions, or marched in demonstrations. The Army's espionage program cost Americans over $3 billion. This money paid for Army agents to infiltrate such organizations as the Young Adults Project in Colorado Springs. Established by local church groups, the Young Democrats, and a ski club in order to operate a recreation center for emotionally disturbed young people, the Young Adults Project was entirely nonpolitical. It was infiltrated because one of its founders had attended antiwar demonstrations and had once been a member of Students for a Democratic Society. There is, however, no evidence that Army agents were ever so thorough as the FBI agents who once investigated a "mental hospital patient who asserted his claim to the throne of Spain." Mostly, Army agents attended demonstrations and clipped newspaper accounts of demonstrations. At one peace rally there were 119 persons present, 67 of them demonstrators and 52 of them agents. The agents had orders to tape speeches, but the five military helicopters continually overhead prevented that.[3]

The Army has compiled organizational files, personality files, and mug books. It has published a two-volume compendium and a six-volume "black list." The CIAB has records on over 760,000 organizations and events. The Army has some of the best pictures taken in the past decade. Their videotape unit (which appears at demonstrations as Midwest Audiovisual News) is so adept at infiltration that it claims to its credit the only interview Abbie Hoffman granted to TV during the 1968 Democratic National Convention in Chicago.[4]

Arthur R. Miller, University of Michigan Law School professor and author of *The Assault on Privacy: Computers, Data Banks, and Dossiers* (Ann Arbor: University of Michigan Press, 1971), testified before the Ervin committee that

> Whether he knows it or not, whenever an American travels on a commercial airline, reserves a room at one of the national hotel chains, rents a car, he is likely to leave distinctive electronic tracks in the memory of a computer that can tell a great deal about his activities, his movements, his habits and associations.
>
> Unfortunately, few people seem to appreciate the fact that modern technology is capable of monitoring, centralizing, and evaluating these electronic entries, no matter how numerous they may be, making credible the fear that many Americans have of a womb-to-tomb dossier on each of us.[5]

These dossiers are instantly available to all municipal, state, and federal agencies. For many years Congress opposed the establishment of a National Data Bank. Unwilling to adhere to the democratic commitment of our national legislature, the FBI erected the National Crime Information Center in Washington. The Center includes files on people who attended NAACP meetings, antiwar meetings, many other kinds of meetings, and all known criminals and arrested persons. According to Miller, it also includes "soft, spongy, hearsay, unevaluated, perhaps malicious or inaccurate data."[6] NCIC's computerized files are available from 5,000 remote-access terminals located throughout the U.S. and are shared by all levels of law enforcement, banking, and insurance agencies.

In addition to data banks computerized by the FBI, CIA,

CIAB, and IRS, the Department of Housing and Urban Development keeps an "adverse information file"; the National Science Foundation has its own data bank on scientists; the Customs Bureau has a data bank on "malcontents" and "activists"; the Department of State has its own "Report Lookout Service"; and the National Driver Registration Service keeps its own files on 2.6 million Americans for as yet unclear purposes.

Just as torture is not employed merely to cause pain, but to repress dissent, to frighten people of conscience into silence, so too we are faced with a system that uses totalitarian surveillance to inspire fear and encourage political acquiescence. The goal is a realm of lethargic and silent people willing to labor for the greater gains of the ruling class.

According to Ralph Stein, formerly with CIAB, the domestic surveillance of civilians began "long before the riots." During the 1960s CIAB published its first document, *The Civil Disturbance Estimate.* Mindful of the history of labor organizing during the 1930s and 1940s, it estimated the future of labor unrest. Gradually, Army Counterintelligence Analysis established an "all-encompassing" program to monitor "civilian organizations and personalities who . . . might be linked to civil disturbances, . . . or who were engaged in the politics of dissent."[7] Ultimately, the activities of the following groups were monitored intensively. Stein recited them to the Ervin committee from memory:

Right wing: American Nazi Party (later National Socialist White People's Party), National Renaissance Party, Ku Klux Klan, United Klans of America, John Birch Society, The Minutemen, numerous anti-Semitic and lunatic fringe groups.

Left wing and antiwar: Workers World Party, Communist Party, Communist Party—Marxist-Leninist, Socialist Workers Party, Progressive Labor Party, Students for a Democratic Society, Southern Students Organizing Committee, Spartacist League, Young Socialist Alliance, National Mobilization Committee to End the War in Vietnam, SANE, Fifth Avenue Vietnam Peace Parade Committee, Business Executives Move to End the War in Vietnam, Clergy and Laymen Concerned About the War, National Lawyers Guild, Emergency Civil Liberties Committee, The Resistance, The Revolutionary Contingent, Yiddisher

Kultur Farband, National Conference for New Politics, Women's Strike for Peace, Women's International League for Peace and Freedom, Peace and Freedom Party, Urban League, Youth International Party.

Racial: Congress of Racial Equality, National Association for the Advancement of Colored People, Student Non-Violent Coordinating Committee, Revolutionary Action Movement, Southern Christian Leadership Conference, and many local groups.

Dossiers were collected on individuals who acted on behalf of their moral and political convictions. These included both public personalities as well as fundamentally nonpolitical individuals who attended random meetings. Information entered was generally unevaluated and included material forwarded by the FBI, CIA, and state and local red squads. It was "filed, coded, microfilmed and retained." It included information relating to sexual habits, personal preferences, finances, family relationships, and partisan political activities.[8]

The records of CIAB are uneven. They depend on the quality of the local agents. New York City's 108th Military Intelligence Group, for example, has one of the most thorough files of all. According to Stein, it is "an absolutely massive collection." Most of it was compiled by a black woman agent reputedly

well-connected with black militants. She took it upon herself, without official authorization, but with the tacit approval of her superior [Captain Alfred Diaz], to not only spend her day putting together a large file on campus dissident groups in New York City but she also went out at night, into Harlem, Bedford Stuyvesant, Brownsville, and reported the next morning on black activities.[9]

The value of CIAB reports correspond to the intelligence and integrity of the agents. An example of that value was noted by Stein when he explained who ran the "racial desk" at CIAB. This officer

had no background or training in racial problems, and yet each morning he briefed Under Secretary McGiffert on the black mood in America. He had very strong rightwing opinions and opinions about black people which most of us considered to be outright racism.[10]

These briefings, which generally included detailed police lists of stolen cars, continued until McGiffert ordered them stopped.

The fear of black people—for example, the state's almost phobic preoccupation with every move made by Martin Luther King and his associates—has been too often dismissed as harmless ignorance. The intensity of this preoccupation is fully revealed in the Army's instructions to its agents to report every fifteen minutes, via a hotline to Fort Holabird, Maryland, the conversations and movements of the mourners at Martin Luther King's funeral.

A month later, on May 9, 1968, when Coretta King spoke during the Poor People's Campaign in Atlanta, an Army agent called his field officer to report that "her husband had had a dream and now this dream was going to come true." The captain ordered the agent "to go back and find out what dream she was referring to."[11]

Total surveillance, fear, and unlimited ignorance are not the sum of this mammoth military operation. We are talking about political repression and violence. What does it mean to have Army agents spy on delegates on the floor of the Republican National Convention in Miami "with really ambiguous orders just to circulate"? What does it mean to tap every phone Martin Luther King could conceivably use, to shadow his every move, to have every available officer of the 111th Military Intelligence Group in Memphis assigned to peer into his motel room, along with scores of state and federal agents from other departments, and then to have them stand idly by as an assassin moved among them to fire a fatal shot and flee? What does it mean when we have no reason to doubt Philadelphia Mayor Frank Rizzo who boasted in 1971 when he was police chief: "We know everything about the troublemakers. And we know who comes into the town, we know who's going to leave it, when they're going to leave it." Clearly this surveillance system serves the needs of the garrison state. Protective and fidgety, the garrison state cannot tolerate such discussions as Martin Luther King was creating about the connections between racism and class divisions at home and imperialism abroad.

The general efficiency of our surveillance system made it possible to shelve a program submitted to President Nixon in August 1971 to wire every house, car, and boat in America. The plan included a blueprint for a government-operated propaganda system via a TV network that would have linked every state, city, and home. One channel would have been devoted entirely to children's programs. Another program considered unnecessary called for the psychological testing of all school children between six and eight to see if they were potentially criminal. Extensive treatment and camps were to be set up for the potentially hard-core six-year-olds. Because grants from the Law Enforcement Assistance Administration had already enabled states to computerize the records of schoolchildren for easy storage in the FBI's National Crime Information Center data bank if the child looked potentially difficult, this testing service was considered redundant.[12]

While no self-respecting garrison state would stop short at surveillance, the secretive nature of our rulers has generally enabled them to hide their coarser works. But they are not subtle, and the all-pervasive nature of modern technology promotes leakage. People are still required to monitor the tapes. In the final analysis it will be the people who will determine the limits of technology's reach. As more and more information seeps out into the realm, more and more choices will become available to the concerned citizen. Where we shall go from here is not at all clear. Once we have catalogued the garrison state's priorities that have been already funded or projected, we shall have a better understanding of future options.

To begin with, our garrison state has 3,300 military bases around the planet. These troops that encircle the globe to preserve America's imperial reign are trained in a variety of tactics to fetter the minds and consciences of its inhabitants. Torture training is the primary ancillary to total surveillance. This training used to occur at the International Police Academy in Washington. At the Academy police agents from over thirty nations enrolled in the Public Safety Program received extensive training in electronic and psychological torture. The methods taught there incorporated the newest electronic and engineering discoveries. Research on even more refined methods of torture was underway when the training program was first curtailed and then suspended as a result of public disclosure and opposition.

While almost no money has been invested to control the noise pollution that is driving residents of urban comunities into neurotic conditions, money has been invested to explore the use of noise as a weapon. Dr. Giovanni Straneo of Italy has demonstrated that noise alters the heart beat, thickens the blood, increases the stomach's flow of acid, and constricts the blood flow in peripheral vessels. Because noises we do not hear affect us the most, the infrasonic range has been used to alter the natural rhythm of the brain. Vladimir Gavreau of France has developed an "acoustic laser" that provokes "very emotional" reactions. Ordinary noise for sonar torture is also considered effective. Grotesque sound and light shows have been developed that reduce people to nervous wrecks. Pictures of a victim's family are alternated with pictures of approaching high-speed trains as piercing screams assail the viewer. Researchers have also found that the protracted use of intense noise prevents deep sleep and eventually causes "delusions, hallucinations, and homicidal tendencies."[13]

Since World War II, medical practitioners have been empowered with extraordinary control over people's minds and bodies. Insistent on their own inviolability, and the public's ignorance, a group of physicians and psychiatrists have carried on violent and repressive experiments with impunity. Clothed in the mystique of the medical profession, these experiments are considered hallmarks of scientific progress. In actuality they serve the garrison state.

In 1971 the Medical Committee for Human Rights, a group of concerned physicians, attorneys, and citizens, indicted the California Department of Corrections for "torture by doctors." Their charges against the Department ranged from the use of noxious chemotherapy drugs to the administration of psychosurgery to troublesome inmates and homosexuals.[14]

Behavior modification, chemotherapy, and psychosurgery provide the rulers of the modern garrison state with all that is necessary to entrap the free spirit and conquer the human mind. According to Professor James V. McConnell of the University of Michigan's Department of Mental Health Research, the "day has come when we can combine sensory deprivation with drugs, hypnosis and astute manipulation of reward and punishment to gain almost absolute control over an individual's behavior." For McConnell the function of behavior modification is clear:

> We should reshape our society, so that we all would be trained from birth to want to do what society wants us to do. We have the techniques now to do it. . . . The techniques of behavioral control make even the hydrogen bomb look like

a child's toy. . . . Today's behavioral psychologists are the
architects and engineers of the Brave New World.[15]

Social control is essential to an orderly garrison state, and in
psychosurgery modern medical technology has provided the ul-
timate in social control. Santa Monica, California, neurosurgeon
M. Hunter Brown sees "a bright future for operation on criminals, especially those who are young and intelligent." Not only
is Dr. Brown eager to transform criminals into "responsible and
well-adjusted citizens," he is anxious to free the state of the
economic burden of its youthful offenders. "Each violent young
criminal," Brown observes, "incarcerated from 20 years to life
costs taxpayers perhaps $100,000." For only $6,000 society can
simply burn out his or her brain. Even more economical, Dr.
Brown observed, would be a program that would enable doctors
to identify and operate on potentially violent people before they
commit a crime.[16]

An impetus for psychosurgery occurred during the street
and prison riots of the 1960s. One of America's most enterprising
psychosurgeons, Mississippi's Dr. O. J. Andy, contended that
those "involved in any uprising such as Watts and Detroit could
have abnormal brains." Massachusetts' Dr. William H. Sweet
agreed. He observed that "the proponents of urban disorder seem
to be people who are most likely to suffer from organic brain
disease." Sweet and his associate Dr. Vernon H. Mark contend
that violent behavior results from brain disease, particularly
"focal lesions." At a symposium on psychosurgery sponsored by
the Boston University Center for Law and Health Sciences, Vernon H. Mark vigorously denied that there was a racist compo-
nent to his work. Brain disease was not "characteristic mainly
of black people," he asserted, but when violence "occurs in the
ghetto . . . it may be more visible."[17]

The psychosurgeons' refusal to deal with societal, parental,
psychological, developmental, and nutritional issues has isolated them from their colleagues and engendered social and political criticism. Their projects have, nevertheless, been funded
at various times by: the Boston Mayor's Office from a state
grant under the "Safe Streets Act" ($50,000), the Law Enforce-
ment Assistance Agency ($100,000), the National Institute of
Mental Health ($500,000), the National Institute for Neurologi-
cal Diseases and Stroke ($1 million), and (to expand the Boston

program and establish new ones in Houston and Los Angeles) the National Institute of Health ($1 million). The Department of Justice also agreed to institute test procedures to screen "habitually violent male penitentiary inmates for brain damage."

A concerted assault against psychosurgery by such people as psychiatrist Peter Breggin, who considers psychosurgery "an abortion of the brain" used "to repress and vegetabilize the helpless," and Dr. Willard Gaylin of the prestigious Hastings Institute caused the Law Enforcement Assistance Agency to hire outside consultants to check on the Boston City Hospital's violence clinic. They reported that the clinic's program contributed "little or nothing" to our knowledge or understanding of the relationship between violence and the brain. All the evidence so far indicates that although brain surgery can destroy a functioning brain, it cures nothing and may cause violent schizophrenic-like psychoses.

These findings have not stopped the faceless rulers of the contemporary garrison state. In fact they have performed "sedative neurosurgery" on children. Congressman Cornelius Gallagher of New Jersey held hearings in September 1970 on the issue of behavior modification drugs administered to over 25,000 grammar school children throughout the United States, despite the fact that there was nothing wrong with them "in the medical sense." Gallagher's hearings caused this program to be suspended, only to be followed by reports that doctors were performing psychosurgery on hyperactive children.

One of the most controversial of such programs was administered by Dr. O. J. Andy, director of neurosurgery at the University of Mississippi. Andy has only one psychologist on his staff, Marion Jurko. Together they identified and operated on children beginning at age five with "deviant behavioral problems," such as "aggression" and "emotional instability," whether or not there was something "neurologically wrong." Their stated goal was to reduce hyperactivity "to levels manageable by parents." Public protest has forced the temporary suspension of Andy's operations.[18]

These operations free parents and society from the responsibility for their children's problems. Once children have been lobotomized, nobody has to consider the fact that children reflect the environment they find themselves in. Psychosurgery reinforces society's escape syndrome. It is the victim's fault.

Neither the family nor violent social institutions are to blame
for what happens in the lives of angry, upset children. And besides, lobotomized children ensure an orderly society.

Even more appropriate for an orderly society is electrical
stimulation of the brain (ESB). ESB represents the most sophisticated advance in medical technology. This new technology
has enabled Dr. Robert G. Heath, chairman of the Department
of Psychiatry and Neurology at Tulane University in New Orleans and a former president of the Society for Biological Psychiatry, to implant more electrodes into the human brain than
anyone else in the world. With 125 implantations he has been
able to turn the brain "into a human pin-cushion" and his patients into his puppets. Heath's patients carry around "electrical
self-stimulators," traveling-companion transistorized packets
generally connected to their brain's "pleasure centers." Heath
believes that all untoward behavior can be replaced by "positive
pleasure feelings" through psychosurgery. To prove his case, he
has generously wired his patients up for sensations that he describes as "better than sex."[19]

Dr. José Delgado, the most prominent ESB researcher, is
very clear about its uses. Using such progressive rhetoric as the
"need to reorganize man's social relations" and eliminate hate,
anger, and aggressiveness, Delgado calls for a "cerebral victory"
for humanity. Until he returned to his native Spain, Delgado
worked at Yale University with research support from the Office
of Naval Research and the Air Force.

Delgado has been able to stop a charging bull in its tracks
through remote-control radio stimulation of an electrode in its
brain. With microminiaturized instruments wireless radio commands stimulate the brain to provoke or inhibit spontaneous
activities and bodily functions. Delgado observes that the "technology for non-sensory communication between brain and computer" is "at our fingertips." He believes in fact that "peace and
war—at least in monkey colonies—are within the control of the
scientist." With ESB we can ensure a happy society. Even raven-
ously hungry rats, Delgado pointed out, given the "choice of
food, water, sex or ESB, choose only to stimulate themselves."
"Truly," he concludes, "heaven and hell are within the brain."

To achieve the physical control of the human brain in society's interest, Delgado urged the government to invest a billion

dollars. That would enable him and his associates to explore such questions as whether we can

> induce a robotlike performance in animals and men by pushing buttons of a cerebral radio stimulator? Could drives, desires, thoughts be placed under the artificial command of electronics? Can personality be influenced by ESB? Can the mind be physically controlled?

In Delgado's electronically manipulated society scant attention is paid to individual freedom, personal integrity, or human dignity. Delgado argues:

> The loss of personal self-determination is one of the problems of civilized life which must be carefully confronted if we are to reach reasonable compromises.

Because science and technology have enabled us to create a truly contented psychocivilized state, why would people object to society's demand that they

> take a pill or submit to an electric shock for the socially protective purpose of making us more docile, infertile, better workers or happier?

After all, Delgado observed, people have already consented to mass immunization against, for example, yellow fever.[20]

One writer who interviewed Delgado extensively came away with a vision of the psychologist's version of the perfected garrison state. As she saw it, it would be an electroligarchy commanded by a small elite with untouched brains. They would have total authority over the computers that would program the Electrons, who would have a few electrodes placed "here and there" to make them happy and keep them creative. In the middle the Positrons would have sufficient electrodes to ensure a lifetime of contented white-collar work. Most of the people would be converted to Neutrons, self-stimulating robotized workers capable of performing the vilest tasks "all day long and loving every minute of it."[21]

Imagine a society in which computerized remote-control manipulations trigger or inhibit, as Delgado has demonstrated they can, fear, anxiety, apathy, depression, disorientation, and rage: a society in which we can be controlled like puppets by Teflon-tipped wires plugged into our brains.

The war in Indochina has hastened the development of electronic control devices. Telemetry, or long-distance remote-control measurement of a given phenomenon, was originally used to study the migration of birds. The demands of violent repression shifted its uses to the electronic battlefield. Spillover into our domestic life was inevitable. The faceless rulers of our garrison state have ordered the technocrats to declare war on all our precepts. As one San Francisco-based penologist has assured us: "Before long, parolees in this country will be wired up like the Ho Chi Minh trail and controlled like smart bombs."[22]

Electronic manipulation of the brain, spearheaded by Delgado, has stimulated such people as Doctors Gerald Smith (University of Utah), and Burton Ingraham and Ralph Schwitzgebel (Harvard) to contemplate twenty-four–hour surveillance and electrical intervention "to influence and control selected behavior." Their tracking devices, called telemeters, are to be permanently implanted in the brain. Attached to a computer that registers body functions, a telemeter could, for example, direct shocks to a parolee whose respiration and adrenalin flow as he walked around a store indicated that he contemplated shoplifting. The shock would cause him "to forget or abandon" his purpose. The good doctors indicate that alcoholics and other addicts could be similarly wired up. According to Dr. Gerald Smith, telemetry has "tremendous humanitarian value." Although he recognizes that "the lowest priority is the individual offender," he insists that "people will have to get over their 1984 fear that Big Brother is watching."[23]

That is not very likely. People are protective of their privacy and concerned about human freedom and personal integrity. Although much secret research and many ongoing programs have yet to be revealed, there is evidence that the American people are not resigned to inhabiting an image of the future projected from the frozen depths of a moral void. There is evidence that the American people will not be content to live forever in a garrison state.

Organizations to resist the spread of mind-control technology in prisons, mental hospitals, and schools emerged with the earliest evidence of its application. Citizen committees, medical authorities, and civil libertarians spanning the entire political spectrum have united to struggle against the threatened domination of America's hearts and minds. The temporary suspensions of certain aversion therapy programs in prisons, of O. J. Andy's operations at the University of Mississippi, and of the International Police Academy training project in Washington, D.C., all attest to the value of public protest and the need for continued vigilance.

Stripped of their moral authority, barren of virtue and divided among themselves, those currently in power have become isolated despots surrounded by hostile subjects. Threatened and fearful, they cling to their privileges with tactical nuclear weapons and Teflon-tipped electrodes. It is all they have left. But it is not enough.

Even their propaganda is faltering. It is becoming increasingly difficult to persuade the American people that the current state of our society is inevitable, that our violent technology is all part of our planetary progress: just political wisdom mixed with Yankee knowhow. More and more Americans are beginning to recognize what historian Warren Susman saw in 1963 when he said that Americans must

> face what now exists: A corporate state in serious economic trouble. Politically, it is plainly and simply a dictatorship. This is as complete a dictatorship as ever existed in history. . . . Hitler had no more power than John F. Kennedy.[24]

Until we begin to manage technology in the interests of human beings and on behalf of dignity, freedom, physical comfort, and spiritual development, we shall live in a garrison state. It will be a garrison state in which we are reduced to Social Security numbers. It will be a state marked by poverty, fear, and insecurity. It will be a state ordered by faceless corporate owners whose purposes are served by the excesses of the CIA and all its ancillary military and paramilitary counterparts.

We now inhabit a society that resembles the children's game, Stone Witch. The Stone Witch tries to tag all the players, freezing them into stone. Those not yet tagged are mobile and free, and they alone can free the frozen players. As the players run continually from the Stone Witch, there is much chaos and protest. Just as it looks as if all are to be frozen, a free player releases several others. The Stone Witch rarely wins.[25]

Domestic Political Assassinations

Jo Pomerance

■ Jo Pomerance is co-chairperson of the Task Force
for the Nuclear Test Ban. She has been a member of the
board of directors of the United Nations Association
of the United States, a consultant to the chairman of
the Senate Subcommittee on Arms Control and International Organization, and a member of the Arms Control
and Disarmament Committee of the National Citizens
Commission for International Cooperation Year. She
has held other posts in various peace organizations,
and lectures and writes.

IN THEIR BOOK *The Invisible Government* (New York: Random House, 1964) David Wise and Thomas Ross define the defense intelligence community in the United States today as the government the public does not read about, "the hidden machinery that carries out the policies of the United States in the Cold War." Seen in this context, the program of intelligence activities can be defined as an adjunct of the military. Indeed, the expenses for many of the intelligence agencies, including the CIA, are hidden in the defense budget.

The CIA was designed primarily as a weapon to combat the challenge to United States power presumably posed by the new order upon which Soviet communism was building an empire. Instead of meeting ideas with alternative ones, however, the CIA fights communism with a variety of clandestine methods, generally of a military nature, often designed to unseat radical or merely progressive governments. Even assassinations are considered a legitimate tool. *Time* magazine in its March 17, 1975, issue, for example, described CIA involvement in death plots against Cuba's Castro, the Dominican Republic's Trujillo, and Haiti's Duvalier. One of these plots was successful. How many more were there?

Increasingly the question is being asked: Did these conspiracies extend into the United States? When a U.S. president is assassinated, when a leading contender for the presidency is assassinated, when an attempt is made to assassinate another presidential candidate—all within one decade—suspicion of a plot or plots to disrupt the nation's democratic system seem unavoidable.

When the official intelligence reports on these events denying the existence of a plot leave a large element of the American people unsatisfied, and when new evidence contradicting the official verdicts continues to be uncovered, doubts as to the cerdibility of the government investigations increase. Because there is now an almost constant stream of information concerning the illegal and clandestine role of the CIA and other similar agencies in the domestic life of the American republic during the 1960s, the possibility emerges that the assassinations themselves will become legitimate subjects for congressional inquiry into the activities of U.S. intelligence agencies.

An unthinkable thought to hint that our own intelligence agencies might somehow be involved in the tragic events of the past dozen years? But how much that was heretofore unthinkable has now been revealed through the Watergate investigations? The possibility that there could be complicity in assassination on the part of official agencies of government causes traditional America to react with horror. But it is a thought not at all incredible in Europe, for instance, where conspiracy theories about the assassinations are widely accepted. There the general public, long accustomed to the skullduggery of palace politics, recognizes that when a leader or potential leader of a nation is assassinated, it is as likely as not that one of his own secret agents is involved.

We in the United States like to think we are different—a freer and purer breed of people, untainted by such unholy machinations. Past history largely justified this happy faith in ourselves. But this is not the past. It is the present, a new and different age of vast powers increasingly concentrated in ever fewer hands, an age corrupted by industrial and military elites. It is an age, in other words, that since World War II has witnessed the development in this country of an invisible government, more akin to the authoritarian regimes of older nations than to the frontier democracy of our own past.

Since the Watergate scandals, public awareness of these new dimensions of American political life has increased markedly. There is growing suspicion that somehow a cabal was involved in the assassination of President Kennedy. President Ford was questioned at a press conference about the rising criticism of the Warren Report. In his response, the president emphasized that the verdict of the Warren Commission that Oswald was the lone assassin—a verdict he had personally supported as a member of the Commission—was nevertheless not an unconditional one. "It was very carefully phrased," the president said, quoting the Commission's conclusion: "The Warren Commission has no evidence of another assassin." In other words, Mr. Ford was saying, if evidence of a conspiracy existed, the Commission had not seen it.

Apparently, however, the American public had seen it. By 1969 more than 75 percent of Americans, according to the polls, refused to believe the conclusions of the Warren Report. Evidently they preferred the explanations of independent researchers such as Thomas Buchanan, Jim Garrison, and Mark Lane, who claimed that the monstrous tragedy of President Kennedy's murder was the work of a conspiracy. Moreover, the public seemed to realize that because the Commission had based its conclusion on information assembled by the CIA and the FBI, its verdict exonerating these agencies from any responsibility was not necessarily reliable.

It is not only the general public that disagrees with President Ford about the Warren Commission verdict. Other officials connected with the Report have disagreed as well. Of the seven members of the Commission, two, Senator Richard Russell and Representative Hale Boggs, subsequently dissented from the Commission's verdict that the murder was the act of a single individual. They publicly expressed doubts that Lee Harvey Oswald planned the President's assassination alone. Just before his death in January 1973, President Lyndon Johnson, in an interview later published in the July 1973 *Atlantic Monthly*, speculated that the murder in Dallas had been part of a conspiracy undertaken in retaliation for the failure of a CIA-backed attempt on the life of Fidel Castro. It has also been reported that both Police Chief Jesse Curry and District Attorney Henry Wade of Dallas have been added to the list of dissenters.

Similar questions have now been raised about the assasination of Senator Robert Kennedy. Some new data, publicized by former Congressman Allard Lowenstein, seem to contradict the official verdict that this murder was the work of another lone assassin. Grant Cooper, originally Sirhan Sirhan's chief counsel, found this evidence of a plot so convincing, he was forced to recant his previous position that Sirhan alone was responsible. In addition, various revelations about the circumstances behind the wounding of Governor Wallace have led the governor to announce publicly his suspicions of a conspiracy.

What are the theories that attempt to explain the motivation for these events? For a clue some critics, citing the close relationship of the CIA to the Defense Department, go back to the warnings of former President Eisenhower in his farewell address when he cautioned that if the "unwarranted influence . . . by the military-industrial complex" was permitted to grow unchecked, this nation would be embarked on a vast armaments program piled on already existing arms programs ad infinitum, all leading to a kind of warfare-state philosophy whereby essential domestic programs for the general good of the public would be impaired. Expenses for a constantly accelerating defense program could lead to a breakdown of our fiscal and monetary well-being. The growing power of the militarists could lead to involvement in war. It could threaten our civil liberties.

Because United States foreign policy became increasingly militaristic after the death of President Kennedy, critics of the official version of the assassinations, such as Dr. Peter Scott and Vincent Salandria, argue that the persistence of this hard-line policy over the last decade gives further weight to the theory that the assassinations were the result of a right-wing plot.

This theory holds that in the summer of 1963, according to reports by Senator Mansfield and others, President Kennedy unmistakably signaled his decision to end the Cold War. He won Senate ratification of the historic treaty to ban atomic testing aboveground and subsequently delivered a series of moving speeches proclaiming the necessity for East-West accommodation. On October 2, 1963, after a meeting of the National Security Council, Secretary of Defense Robert McNamara and General Maxwell Taylor, chairman of the Joint Chiefs of Staff, announced to the press the president's intention to withdraw 1,000 men from Vietnam before the end of 1963 and to bring home all American soldiers by 1965. And troop withdrawals were in fact begun.

On November 22, 1963, the president was dead.

With Lyndon Johnson's accession to the presidency, the Kennedy policy on Vietnam was suddenly reversed, as Tom Wicker shows so well in his book *J.F.K. and L.B.J.* (New York: Morrow, 1968). The slogan "Johnson's war," coined to describe that "contrived" conflict, is endorsed as accurate by Robert Sherrill in his book on LBJ, *The Accidental President* (New York: Grossman, 1967). Kennedy had consistently argued that the war in Southeast Asia was the responsibility of the Vietnamese. On the day of Kennedy's funeral, however, President Johnson informed Henry Cabot Lodge, ambassador to South Vietnam, that he was not going to see "Southeast Asia go the way China went." That decision inevitably involved major U.S. forces in the longest and one of the bloodiest wars in the nation's history.

For the next decade, moreover, as the Cold War was renewed, the United States discouraged initiatives to resume discussions on an East-West agreement to ban all nuclear weapons' tests. This measure, which the nuclear powers had pledged to negotiate in the 1963 Partial Test Ban Treaty, could have slowed, if not halted, the arms race.

The brutal death of a young president evidently about to embark on a relaxation of the Cold War and withdrawal from the mire of Southeast Asia and whose removal was followed by a resumption of the Cold War, an accelerated arms race, and maximum intervention in Southeast Asia; the murder of his younger brother, a leading candidate for the presidency, who presumably would have continued his brother's program for an East-West détente; and the attempted murder of another candidate, whose disability ensured the election of a hard-line president: reportedly, in all of these cases there were unexplained linkages through our intelligence agencies to a wider network.

Were these accidental occurrences, or were they the outcome of a conspiracy?

A thorough investigation is called for by the Congress. The urgency mounts with the approach of a new presidential term. As former CIA agent Victor Marchetti has said in conversation: "This is the crunch. If we can't get to the truth about past CIA activities now, when there is renewed concern and several official investigations are underway, all hope of reform will be lost."

The Anatomy
of Assassination

L. Fletcher Prouty

■ L. Fletcher Prouty retired from the United States Air Force with the rank of colonel. During the last nine years of his Air Force career, he was the military officer responsible for the support of the clandestine operations of the CIA. In that capacity he was assigned to Headquarters Air Force, the Office of the Joint Chiefs of Staff, and the Office of the Secretary of Defense and traveled throughout the world on various CIA-related projects. He has also been vice-president of the General Aircraft Corporation and of several banks. Presently he is a writer, editor, and lecturer. His book The Secret Team was published in 1973.

ASSASSINATION is big business. In fact, assassination is the business of big business and of the CIA and of any other power center that can pay for the "hit" and control the assured getaway. Rare is the individual "nut" who even gets a chance to shoot a chief of state or other big figure. The CIA brags that its operations in Iran in 1953 led to the pro-Western alignment of that important country. It takes credit for what it calls the "perfect job" in Guatemala. Both were achieved by assassination. In the Dominican Republic, Trujillo was removed by assassination. In Vietnam, Ngo Dinh Diem was removed by assassination. In both countries the hand of the CIA was evident. But what is this assassination business? How does it really work? How is it set up?

In all but a handful of countries around the world, power

196

simply rests in the hands of those who have it until someone else is strong enough to take it away. There is little or no provision for change. The strongman stays in power until he dies or is removed by a coup d'état, which often means by assassination. King Faisal of Saudi Arabia, for all of his wealth and seeming power, died from an assassin's bullet on March 25, 1974. King Faisal, protected by an elite guard trained by a private contractor selected by the United States Department of Defense, could not, or would not, be saved. For all his apparent power it is evident that his lifeline was extremely fragile and that any planned attack could reach him. Or was the attack planned, in connivance with others in power, for the purpose of reaching him?

To say Faisal could not or would not be saved is to make a phony pitch. What happened in Saudi Arabia was that the king's elite guard was broken. But, just as De Gaulle was saved to die in bed, *any* ruler can live *if* the wall around him remains intact. Even in the deepest and darkest days of World War II, there were thousands of people who would have liked to have had a shot at De Gaulle. I remember that after the Cairo Conference Churchill was recovering from a bout of influenza in Marrakesh, Morocco, and De Gaulle came to visit him several times. You can't imagine the security precautions that were taken there to keep the good general alive.

As another example, I was in Lima, Peru, in March 1964 when De Gaulle came and captivated that country. Hundreds of thousands of Peruvians filled the Plaza de Armas to such an extent that they were pressing against the surrounding walls and trampling the trees. Yet De Gaulle, a very tall man, walked among those hundreds of thousands of Peruvians that night in that huge arena with searchlights on him, and no one took a shot at him. The reason was that in the six months before he went to Peru, the people whose business it was to keep De Gaulle alive, the "gorillas," if you remember that term of endearment, had thoroughly worked over the city of Lima, had combed every list of people in that city who might be anti-Gaullist, had provided them with resort hotels a long way off, and had made sure that when the general came to town he would stay alive.

What, then, are the actual mechanics of an assassination? (In the business, the assassin—the professional secret murderer—is, in fact, called a "mechanic.") How is an assassination made? If the CIA is involved, how does the CIA lay it on? The reality is much different from the usual picture. There is not some young character—an Oswald, a Ray, a Sirhan, or a Bremer —who broods over things for months, who writes a queer diary, who sends away for a mail-order gun and then draws attention to himself by all manner of strange activities. These are the characteristics of the "patsy" and the cover story. The real assassination scenario is quite different.

Foreign assassinations, and to a degree domestic murders of that kind, are set in motion not so much by a definite plan to kill the intended victim as by a sinister plan to remove or relax the protective organization that is absolutely essential to keep the victim/leader alive. If the CIA lets it be known, ever so secretly, that it is displeased with a certain ruler and that it would not raise a finger against a new regime, you may be sure that some cabal will move against that ruler.

This happens because there are two dominant human reactions to such information. First, such news encourages a dormant and aspiring cabal into action. Second, such news begins to scare the hell out of the existing elite corps. Most palace guards are hated. Most have been oppressive and domineering. Therefore when they learn that their USA/CIA support is being removed or lessened, they think of "old number one" first. They begin to head for exile, for the Riviera and their Swiss bank accounts. This situation depletes the ranks of the cadre that is most essential to the existence of the ruler concerned. His regime is automatically weakened where it hurts him most and threatened by the cabal that can harm him most. Thus the entirely passive "displeasure" of the USA/CIA kills or at least removes from power by taking no more action than that of a glacier: it doesn't appear to move, but it does. And the same applies to domestic assassinations. Consider, for example, the following scenario.

The autopsy was routine: suicide. A high government official, recently promoted, was found alone in his house, dead and with his own rifle beside him. A single bullet had been fired upward from his mouth, shattering his head, blowing the back of it completely off. There were no signs of any violence. A poorly typed note to his wife and son lay on the table near him.

The hastily scribbled signature was his own. Open and shut: suicide.

Murder is the violent and unlawful killing of one human being by another. Assassination is murder, but the motivation and sometimes the method is different. Historically assassination is the murder of the enemies of a religious sect as a sacred religious duty. The assassin is a professional secret murderer who kills for someone else or for a greater cause. In many cases today the religion called "anticommunism" is such a greater cause. The above "suicide" was not a suicide. And it was not simply a murder. It was an assassination.

The government official had been promoted into a higher job. Shortly after taking office he had found in the files of his predecessor papers that indicated beyond doubt that many unlawful things had been done, that huge payoffs had been made, that cases had been judged on the basis of favoritism and bribery and not on the basis of justice and good practice. A major industry had suffered grievously because of these unlawful acts and an earlier administration had accepted this corruption as part of its technique for staying in power.

The new official, long in the department and habitually fair and honest, was deeply troubled. He broke the news to his superiors. He was stunned when they told him to keep his mouth shut. They said that they would take care of things. Although he was a man who had never been known to drink and who had never been drunk before, the official now began to drink heavily. When he was drunk, he began to talk. He became extremely tense. His family scarcely knew him anymore. Right at a time when everyone was congratulating him on his well-earned promotion, he seemed to be going to pieces completely. His old friends could not understand it.

Meanwhile he worked long hours. He went through every one of those cover-up files. With his vast experience he was able to reconstruct what had happened, even though some papers were missing and others had been put in the files to confuse any chance review. He prepared a complete report and had just about concluded it. Much of his work was done late at night in his own home. His wife had gone, saying she was going to visit some old friends for a few days. (Actually she was desperately looking for help and guidance.) His son was at college.

The phone call to his home one evening was calm and official sounding: "This is the police. Have you heard from your son recently? In the last few hours? Well, something has happened." The policeman would like to come right over to talk about it. "Good, be there in a few minutes." The policeman would be in plainclothes and would drive an unmarked car. "Yes, he will have identification: Fairfax County Police. See you soon."

The car pulled up quietly. There was a quick knock on the door. The policeman entered, showed his identification, and was invited to sit down. At the split second when the official turned to usher the "policeman" into the house, he was hit a sharp blow on the back of the head. He suffered a massive concussion and was dead. The "policeman" went to a closet where he knew a rifle was kept. (The house had been well cased.)

The rest was simple. The killer hoisted the body up on the barrel of the rifle with the business end in the victim's mouth. One shot blew the top of the head off. All evidence of the first blow was now gone. The visitor had already typed the "suicide note" on the official's own home typewriter. The official's signature had been lifted from another paper signed with a ballpoint pen.

In moments the "policeman" was on his way. The unmarked car was left in back of the Forrestal Building, where it had been taken from a pool of cars. The assassin took a taxi to Washington National Airport. He shuttled on the last flight to LaGuardia and took the bus to JFK. He had already made arrangements for a series of flights that would eventually take him to Athens. Less than twenty-four hours later he was on the beach south of that city among old friends and acquaintances in the modern world's equivalent of the Assassin Sect. He was one of those faceless, professional, multinational "mechanics." He made good money, and he was convinced that he was doing an essential job for the power center that he believed would save the world from communism.

This scenario is, in most particulars, true. The government official was ruled a suicide, and the case did look like too many others. Too simple, too professional. Unless, however, someone in power chooses to set the wheels of justice in motion, nothing will be done. Outsiders, individuals who lack those powers that are vested in government, ostensibly "for the good of every citizen," can do little to prove that this "suicide" was murder. One must have the power of subpoena and the right to cross-examine to get to the heart of the matter. So we will have to say that the above is a scenario. But it is also a lesson.

Not long ago it was revealed that the CIA had been issued a number of identification kits in the name of the Fairfax County, Virginia, police department. This fact does not necessarily mean that the CIA planned to use those identities for the purpose of assassination. It is not clear just what the CIA did plan to do with those documents. What is clear is that they *were* used. When police IDs are used clandestinely by others for no matter what cause, our whole system breaks down. When the CIA uses, or permits the use of, police IDs, it is perpetrating a most serious crime against society.

Some years ago the CIA did have wigs, voice-changing devices, and other items but did not have them for the purpose of using them against Daniel Ellsberg's psychiatrist. They did not plan to use them for that purpose at all, or so they say. But that is not the point. The point is that the CIA did let someone else use its highly specialized equipment. And that someone else, E. Howard Hunt, did plan to use that material for the purpose of casing and later breaking into Dr. Fielding's office.

The CIA has all of those things just mentioned and many more, and it has spent a generation training people, thousands of people, in how to use such special items. Some of these people, working perhaps for others and for other purposes and interests, use these items to carry out burglaries, assassinations, and all sorts of unlawful activities—with or without the blessing of the CIA.

We are now finally beginning to hear much about the CIA and the subject of assassinations, both domestic and foreign. The CIA has been linked to the assassinations in 1963 of Ngo Dinh Diem, then the president of South Vietnam, and his brother Nhu. It is not important to decide whether or not the CIA did plan and participate in these assassinations. What is important is the fact that so many things that have come up about those murders confirm the presence of the CIA in and around the murders. One thing is especially interesting.

The Diems were killed in October 1963. During the summer of 1971 Charles Colson and E. Howard Hunt, among others,

were interested in seeing what could be done to forge and alter
official State Department messages in order to make it appear
that President John F. Kennedy had been closely and directly
implicated in those assassinations. This is a very important
point. If the White House wanted so badly to implicate a dead
president in that plot, it must have known then that President
Kennedy was not implicated in those murders and that records
in such repositories as those of the State Department proved
that he was not.

The timing of this "dirty tricks" project—that is, the forging
of those documents so that they would implicate Kennedy—is
interesting. It had been only a few months before that the *New
York Times* had published the Pentagon Papers. The *Times* version of the Papers, alleged to have come from the Pentagon, contained a somewhat detailed and mixed-up version of just what
had happened during the late summer of 1963 just before the
Diems were killed. Anyone reading the Papers carefully would
discover that the CIA had been very close to the plan and that
the CIA had had men on the scene.

Nowhere in the Pentagon Papers, however, is there any message or directive that states in so many words, "The Diems will
be assassinated." Lacking this explicit document many students
and researchers will conclude anyhow that the CIA was mixed
up in the affair, and researchers will not conclude that Kennedy
ordered the murders. Keep in mind that in 1963 E. Howard
Hunt was an active agent of the CIA and was at that very time
deeply involved with the former director of Central Intelligence,
Allen W. Dulles—a man whom Kennedy had fired—in writing
Dulles's most important book, *The Craft of Intelligence* (New
York: Harper & Row, 1963). In other words, Hunt was, on
many counts, at the center of things.

When the White House directed Hunt to forge State Department records in order to make it appear positively that JFK had
directed the assassination of the Diems, the White House knew
what it was doing, the CIA knew what it was doing, and Hunt
most certainly knew what he was doing. They were all doing
what we have long accused the Soviets of doing—some top-level
historical revisionism. But they goofed.

Even if they had gotten away with what they were trying to
do, and even if they had made it appear that true records con-

tained positive evidence that JFK had ordered the killing of the Diems, it would not have stood up. That is not how political assassinations are done. The whole clue to a real assassination is that it is the murder of an enemy of the sect (and this can mean many things today) as a sacred religious duty. In other words, no one has to direct an assassination—it happens. The active role is played secretly by permitting it to happen. This may be a new idea, but think it over a while and it will come out. Let's look more closely at the case of the Diems.

When Diem assumed power in South Vietnam in 1954, his country had no antecedent. It was simply a piece of real estate that lay south of the seventeenth parallel. When you take over a piece of real estate like that and begin to rule, where is your power? Who are your police, your army, your generals, your sergeants? Ed Lansdale, probably one of the best agents the CIA ever set in motion, flew over from the Philippines, where he had created Ramon Magsaysay as president, and brought his team with him to Saigon. Diem's leadership and power were, in effect, created from the beginning with covert U.S. assistance and an "elite guard" of secret police trained by the precursors of the Green Berets. And he owed his position to two clever maneuvers. One was the rapid placement of a good secret police. The second was the purchase of a mercenary army.

But by the summer of 1963 (a summer that we should write about and research a lot more because it was a very important period), the Diem regime had been in full control of South Vietnam for ten years, and things were going from bad to worse. It was a summer of great discontent and opposition to the Diems not only in Vietnam but also in Washington. It was, for example, the summer of the Buddhist uprisings and the deaths of many Buddhists who set themselves on fire with gasoline.

By August of 1963 memoranda were being circulated in the highest offices of the U.S. government. (At that time I was working in the office of the Joint Chiefs of Staff.) These papers were so secret that they were unmarked, with no classification, and hand-carried from "need-to-know" person to "need-to-know" person. If papers are really that secret, you don't put "top secret" stamps on them, or "eyes only" stamps on them, or registered numbers on them. You don't put anything on them. These memos frankly stated such things as "We've had enough of

Diem. What are we going to do about him?" and "We must find
a way to get rid of the Diems." Once that kind of idea has
started circulating, it won't be long until bullets are flying.

These memos led to a series of inquiries from the CIA in
Washington to Saigon for the purpose of assessing the opposition to Diem, what its strength might be, and whether or not
any of the prospective leaders might be better—from the point
of view of the United States—than the Diems were then.

The CIA, which had put Diem into the palace and had
worked for more than a decade to create a "father of his
country" image for him, was severely split over the problem of
what to do about him. One camp wanted to keep him and go
along with his further demands. Another group was ready to let
him go and to start over again with someone else. In the wings
it seemed that General Duong Van Minh, a Buddhist himself,
might be the best bet to follow the Diems. Others favored the
quieter and perhaps more trustworthy General Nguyen Khanh.
These were the two favorites in Washington. There were many
more in Saigon. Thus the groundwork for an assassination
begins.

Word gets out that the United States "may" withdraw its support of the Diems. This information plays into the hands of
every cabal in the wings. It also does something even more
important. As soon as this word begins to take shape, the people most affected are those who have been using every means at
their disposal to keep the Diems in power and to benefit from
the Diem regime while it is in power. In other words, the Diems'
secret police, their elite guard, and all of their inner circle began
to realize that their day was over and that they had better make
plans to move and to move fast. They had been oppressive. They
had been murderers. They had stolen hundreds of millions of
dollars. They had ruined many people in Vietnam. Without the
support of the United States, the CIA, and the Diems, the inner
elite were dead. Once the word began to filter around Saigon,
that city so filled with intrigue, everyone began to think of
evening the score against the hated and oppressive Diem machine. Death was in the air. As the elite began to fade away,
the Diems' strength was dissipated rapidly.

Yet in Washington, removed from that harsh reality, it
seemed only the better part of logic and good statesmanship to
study the situation from every angle. As August gave way to

September, the President vacillated, the State Department did little, and the CIA kept firing out messages to its agents on all sides to see what must be done. Gradually a plan began to take shape. Madame Nhu, who had ridiculed the Buddhist victims by saying that if they wanted to "barbecue" themselves it was none of her business, suddenly realized that it might be a good time for her to take a long trip to Europe and the United States. This was phase one. The next step would be to get the Diems out of the country following her. Plans were made for them to attend an important meeting in Europe. Formal invitations went out to them, and a special plane was arranged to take them to Europe.

As the date approached for their expected departure the CIA instructed its agents to work closer and closer to the leaders of prospective new regimes in the hope that one or the other would rise and be wholly acceptable as the new government. This situation hastened the disintegration of the Diems' elite guard. Then for reasons that have never been clear, after the Diems had gone as far as the airport, they all of a sudden turned, stepped back into their car, and sped back to the palace. They must not have understood the rules of the game. It was necessary that they leave. If they did not leave, they were dead.

They returned to a palace as empty as a ghost town. Naturally all of their guard had fled to save their own lives. There wasn't a guard there. There wasn't a friend there. There wasn't a doorman. There wasn't anybody there. The Diems sat behind their desks for a couple of minutes. Then they finally realized what was afoot and headed for a tunnel. In a short time they were dead.

The actual killing was a simple thing, "for the good of the cause." The USA and the CIA could wash their hands of it. They had had nothing to do with it. Like all assassinations, it had just happened. Nobody in Washington had said, "Shoot Diem." You don't do an assassination that way. The way people are assassinated is by taking away the power that has been created to keep them there. The deadly passive role of the CIA had permitted the termination of another ruler.

This is the assassination scenario, and it works in almost all cases, even when there is no elaborate plan. It would have seemed that the White House, and especially an old pro such as E. Howard Hunt, would have known that it happened that way and that changing the records would only have implicated them deeper than they already were by the summer of 1971.

Today there are a flood of charges about assassinations. Of course the CIA has been involved. The CIA has made it its business to get close to the elite guards of a great many of the Third World countries. As long as the leader of any of those countries plays the game, like King Hussein of Jordan and the Shah of Iran, all goes well. But if one of those leaders get out of line or if some cabal begins to grow in power and to offer what might seem like a better deal, as in the Diem case, the power of the United States will be withdrawn and—without doubt—"the king is dead."

We in America are not realists when it comes to understanding the fragility of government of the Third World powers. Many of them have armed forces no larger than and no more effective than a good-size military band. Many have an elite guard only large enough to provide round-the-clock, seven-days-a-week surveillance, and not much more. The most trusted of the guard are put in control of the ammunition supplies. Every time ammunition is issued for training purposes, a very close count is kept of rounds expended. No matter how wealthy the ruler may be, or how much wealth his country may possess in valuable raw materials, such as oil, wealth will not assure security. His money may tend more to threaten his life than to keep him alive. Eternal vigilance is his only protection.

These puny sovereigns must appeal to some greater power for their protection. For many years the United States, usually through the CIA, has provided the training—and this means everything—for the elite guards. When you train that guard, when you arm them, when you teach them to jump from an airplane at Fort Benning, when you give them all kinds of weapons training at Fort Bragg, when you bring them to Camp Perry, Virginia, where there is a nice little resort, then that guard knows how to keep a man alive—as long as that guard agrees to keep that man alive.

Without his elite guard King Hussein would have been dead or deposed years ago. His guard is highly trained by the CIA, even to the point of paratroop training laid on by a clandestine military assistance program provided under CIA operational control by the U.S. Air Force and the U.S. Army. The Shah leads Iran at the pleasure of the CIA's number one man in the world today, Richard Helms, who is called "Ambassador." As long as the guard in Iran can keep the Shah alive, he'll be our man there. And as long as the Shah is our man, he probably will remain alive.

This all sounds very normal and healthy: "What else would you do? Have the communists take over? Have some rebels kill him?" As a result a whole array of Third World rulers from Greece to Korea, in Latin America and in Africa, owe their role as chiefs of state, and in most cases their very lives, to the United States, the CIA, and, most recently, private U.S. corporations hired to train, and thereby control, the elite guards.

This is how it begins. Then comes the escalation. An elite guard is a small organization by most standards. As the ruler realizes his vulnerability, like the Diems and Haile Selassie of Ethiopia, he begins to look beyond the guard. He discusses an increase in the size of his meager and unskilled army with his "trainers," the CIA. They are quick to point out that he should have a larger army and that they can get him a military assistance program from the United States provided that he pledges undying loyalty.

Now the program begins to pay off. The vultures of industry move in. A modest military assistance program, of say $50 million, is begun. Of course, the entire $50 million is spent in the United States for U.S.-made equipment. An old rule in the military assistance program is that whenever a certain amount of aid has been provided, that amount will be multiplied by a factor of ten for the cost of spare parts before the equipment wears out. Here is where the manufacturing companies make a real killing. In providing spare parts they are not bound to the same pricing levels as with the original material.

Then the next factor arises. If the ruler of country A has been given a $50 million program, each of his neighbors will plead for similar programs for self-defense. And so it goes. Since World War II the military assistance racket has been a trillion-dollar business. Control of so much money and power rules the world. Meanwhile trade missions from the United States begin to work over the country to see what natural resources can be acquired and for what price. The CIA works with many selected U.S. manufacturers to portion out various franchises for products such as Coca-Cola and Singer sewing machines. Through this device selected families in the host country are put on the road to becoming millionaires and to becoming powers in their own country. Thus power centers are created, and at times one is played against the other. If the CIA swings from one to another, or if it just recognizes the existence of another power, it makes a minor decision to stand back, to relax its hold on the elite guard. Then the whole thing explodes. Unless the ruler is a hardheaded pragmatist and leaves post-haste, there will be another assassination, and so on and so on.

Since World War II there have been hundreds of coup d'états, a common euphemism for assassination. The list will grow for as long as the United States chooses to do its diplomatic work clandestinely. Why else does Henry Kissinger "shuttle" from country to country in the Middle East? (He had left there just the day before Faisal was assassinated.) If his relationship with each of those many countries is an undercover relation-ship, then he cannot meet with them publicly and in a group. If this country really wanted to achieve peace in the Middle East, one of the best and most reliable ways to do that would be to call all concerned countries to a single conference table and then let it all hang out. Historically peace is achieved at a peace conference and not on a multiple bilateral basis.

Practitioners of the profession of assassination by the re-moval of power reach the point where they see that technique as one fit for the removal of any opposition anywhere. Thus it was that President Kennedy was killed—not by some lone gun-man, not by some limited conspiracy, but by the breakdown of the very system that should have functioned to make an assas-sination impossible. Once insiders knew that he would not be protected, it was easy to pick the day and the place. In fact, those responsible for luring him to that place on that day were not even in on the plan itself.

The President went to Texas innocuously enough to dedicate a hospital facility at Brooks Air Force Base in San Antonio. That simple event brought him to the state. It was not too difficult then to get him to stop at Fort Worth "to mend political fences" and accept the plaudits and the backslaps and the promises of votes from the millionaires and the billionaires at General Dy-namics who had just brought off the tremendous $6.5 billion contract for the TFX, a plane that hasn't flown very well even yet. And, of course, no good politician would go to Fort Worth and skip Dallas. All the conspirators had to do after that was to let the right "mechanics" know that the President would be there, when he would be there, what time he would be there and, most importantly, that the usual precautions would not have been made and that escape would be facilitated.

This is the greatest single key to that assassination: Who had the power to call off or drastically reduce the usual security precautions that always are in effect—by law—whenever a President travels? The answer to this question is more important to me than a genealogy of Lee Harvey Oswald or the people on the grassy knoll.

Who said, "Let's go to Dallas. You've been to Fort Worth. Now you've got to go to Dallas." I understand that Kenny O'Donnell feels real bad about it. I understand that Bobby Kennedy said from time to time that he wished he had put his foot down. Jerry Bruno, the greatest advance man in politics, went to Dallas, but did he pick the route? What happened to the Secret Service between San Antonio and Forth Worth and Dealey Plaza in Dallas? How did it happen that there was a six-story building with a lot of empty floors on the President's route, and they neither wired nor sealed the doors as their manual says they will? How did it happen that they did not have anybody on the roof of that building with high-powered guns and radios as their manual says they will? How did it happen that they did not have a man in Dealey Plaza to look at roofs and windows as their manual says they will? How did it happen that they brought the President's car down to crawling speed instead of the usual 44 miles per hour as it went around a corner? Castro did not kill Kennedy, nor did the CIA. The power source that arranged that murder was on the inside. It had the power to reduce normal security, permit the choice of a hazardous route, and cover up the crime for years.

But no single individual makes an assassination. There must be a cause. There must be a "sect." Then the "professional secret murderer" moves in and eliminates the enemy of the sect "as a sacred religious duty" (though the killer is also well paid). We live in an era in which many people, many very sincere people, are convinced that there is a greater-than-life duty upon them to destroy all "Communists" no matter how they define that term. This almost sacred "anticommunist" fervor can be used to kill and to kill easily.

The climate is right, and assassination is a big business today at home and abroad. We need to understand its workings.

Was the CIA Involved in Dallas?

Mark Lane

■ Mark Lane is an attorney, lecturer, author of <u>Rush
to Judgment</u>, <u>Executive Action</u> (with Donald Freed),
and other books, filmmaker, former member of the New
York State legislature, founder of the Wounded Knee
Legal Defense|Offense Committee, and the only critic
of the Warren Commission Report who both conducted an
investigation into the JFK assassination and testified before the Commission. He is professor of law at
Catholic University and director of the Citizens Commission of Inquiry based in Washington, D.C. That
group has demanded release of all classified documents regarding the death of President Kennedy, is
analyzing the already available documents, and will
report to committees of Congress regarding the role
of the FBI, CIA, and other federal police organizations in covering up facts about the assassination.

PERHAPS YOU RECALL that day. It was in September of 1964.
The members of the Warren Commission, six of them, formed
a semicircle. In the middle were the chairman, Chief Justice
Earl Warren, and the President of the United States, Lyndon
Johnson, who had appointed the Commission to perform its
task. Earl Warren held the massive documents in his hand. It
was a tape-recorded, filmed event. People and reporters from all
over the world were watching it. Earl Warren handed the Report to Lyndon Johnson, and Lyndon Johnson held it. He was
absolutely silent for about thirty seconds. It was very embarras-

sing with the film going through the camera, the tape going through recorders, and Johnson not saying anything. Finally an aide said: "Won't you say something, Mr. President?" And Lyndon Johnson said: "Well, eehh, it's very heavy." History may record this comment as the finest short analysis of the Warren Commission Report.

When the Warren Report was released the *New York Times* referred to it as "the most authoritative document, the greatest investigation of a crime in the annals of civilization." It is true that the Federal Bureau of Investigation conducted some 25,000 interviews and the Secret Service some 1,550 interviews. The Central Intelligence Agency, the Dallas police, and the Dallas sheriffs, all poured their information into the Warren Commission. Some of this information was published in the one-volume report. More of it was published in the twenty-six volumes of evidence. And some of it has been locked away in the files of the CIA, the FBI, the Secret Service, the Department of State, the Treasury Department, and other agencies.

When the shots were fired in Dealey Plaza, Dallas, on November 22, 1963, many people were there. Yet in its massive investigation the Warren Commission failed to question 95 percent of the witnesses to the assassination of President John F. Kennedy. They also were supposed to find out who killed Officer J. D. Tippit. They said Oswald did that, but they failed to question the majority of the important witnesses to the murder of Officer Tippit. They were supposed to find out something about the murder of Lee Harvey Oswald by Jack Ruby. Before I say anything else harsh about the Warren Commission, let me say that not every conclusion issued by it was invalid. There was one accurate conclusion, their finding that Ruby killed Oswald. As you may recall, that event took place on network television, and it would have been difficult to deny. They were supposed to find out how it happened, however, and they failed to question 95 percent of the witnesses to the murder of Lee Harvey Oswald by Jack Ruby. They failed to ask a single relevant question of Jack Ruby himself.

How did they fill up the twenty-six volumes and the tens of thousands of documents filed since? Volume 18 is an example: It published, in full, the dental chart showing the condition of Jack Ruby's mother's teeth in the year 1938. I suggested to the Commission that the chart would not have been relevant unless it had been charged that Ruby bit Oswald to death, but I guess the FBI was too busy doing other things to investigate relevant matters.

Let's go back to 1960, three years before the assassination of John Kennedy, and to a book written by Robert Kennedy, who had shortly before that time been counsel to a Senate committee investigating the role of the Mafia in the United States and its effort to take over certain trade unions. Let's go back to page 84 of *The Enemy Within* (New York: Harper & Brothers, 1960):

> By 1949, with the help of Brennan and others, Jimmy Hoffa had consolidated his position in the Michigan Teamsters; but outside his home state he was still largely unknown. For him, the key to the entire Midwest was Chicago. He needed a powerful ally there—and he found his man in Paul Dorfman. Dorfman, our testimony showed, was a big operator— a major figure in the Chicago underworld who also knew his way around in certain labor and political circles.
>
> A slight man with thinning red hair and an almost benign manner, Dorfman took over as head of the Chicago Waste Handlers Union in 1939 after its founder and secretary-treasurer and counsel was murdered. . . .

Robert Kennedy goes on to talk about Dorfman's tie-ins with Al Capone and Longie Zwillman. He traces, in 1960, the power of the Mafia in the trade union movement in Chicago from the murder that occurred in 1939. This was the murder of Leon Cooke, counsel for the Chicago Waste Handlers Union. He was killed by John Martin, the president of that union.

This information was given to the Warren Commission. One of their six panels dealt with Jack Ruby's background. One question given to the commission was: Was Jack Ruby involved in the murder of Leon Cooke? Is that an interesting question? Bobby Kennedy had spoken of it three years before his brother's assassination. In the FBI report published quite solemnly as Exhibit 1235 of the Commission's twenty-six volumes we read: "An extensive search of the records of Chicago police department, did not reflect any reference to John Martin, Jack Ruby, or Jack Rubinstein as he was then known, or to the murder of Leon Cook [sic]."

Evidently the crime never took place. We find reference to it, however, in the major headline story on the front page of the December 9, 1939, issue of the *Chicago Daily Tribune:*

"Attorney Shot, Union Row." The article under this headline tells the whole story, how it happened, how Leon Cooke was shot, and how he died. He was shot by John Martin. One turns to the jump page. Here we have pictures of two individuals the Chicago police and the *Chicago Daily Tribune* considered to be the two most relevant persons involved. The caption reads: "Leon R. Cooke, left, lawyer and former secretary of the Junk Handlers Union was shot while in his union offices, and Jack Rubinstein, present secretary, who was seized for questioning." But the Warren Commission never heard about these facts because the FBI couldn't find any references to the story. I think the Commission relied upon the wrong agency to crack the case for them.

I am now going to give a brief analysis of what took place in Dealey Plaza in Dallas, Texas, on November 22, 1963. The presidential limousine moved northward, got in front of the Texas Book Depository building, then made a very sharp turn and slowed down. It almost stopped when it made that turn. It then started to speed up. The Commission's conclusion: No credible evidence even suggested that any shots came from anywhere other than the sixth floor of the Book Depository building where, it held, Lee Harvey Oswald was located.

Let's look at some of the evidence. Two-thirds of the witnesses in Dealey Plaza said that the shots came from behind a wooden fence high up on a grassy knoll in front of the presidential limousine. Every single employee of the Union Terminal Railroad who was on the railroad bridge in front of the limousine and was questioned in effect said: "I heard the shots, I looked in the direction where the shots came from, and I saw puffs of white smoke come from behind the trees, behind the wooden fence and dissipate into the air." This version was told to the Warren Commission counsel by S. M. Holland, senior supervisor of the Union Terminal Railroad. The lawyers seemed very disconcerted. Holland said: "You don't have to believe me if you don't like. Ask any of the other boys. A whole lot of us were up there and we all saw the same thing." That was sufficient warning for the Commission. They didn't call one of the other witnesses on the railroad bridge.

When the president was shot, he was brought to Parkland Hospital, where the doctors examined the wounds that he had suffered. They first of all examined the wound in the president's throat. Every doctor at Parkland Hospital who examined that wound, who talked to the media that day, said that it was a small, neat wound of entrance. The president had been shot in the throat from the front. The Zapruder film taken at the time and place of the assassination shows where the president was looking—to the front and slightly to the right. That was the first shot.

A bullet also struck the president in the back. After he died at Parkland Hospital, his body was shipped to Bethesda Naval Hospital in Maryland, where only military physicians were permitted to examine his body and perform the autopsy. Fortunately, there were two FBI agents present during that time. Agents Siebert and O'Neill wrote a report that was first classified and later declassified, evidently by mistake (based upon our examination of how that happened). In any event, the Siebert-O'Neill report revealed some significant information. The doctors who were performing the autopsy on the president's body in Bethesda found a wound in the president's back.

First of all, they examined his clothing. In the jacket and in the shirt there was a hole, six inches below the shoulder, slightly to the right of the spinal column. In the same place in the president's back there was a hole. They probed it with a finger and with an instrument. They said that the bullet had gone in only a very short distance and stopped, but was not present in the body. They could not figure out what had happened to the bullet. A phone call was made to the doctors at Parkland Hospital to ask if they had any explanation. The doctors there said that after the president died, he was placed on a stretcher and external cardiac massage was administered. His body was struck roughly in the chest area in the hope that his heart would begin to beat again, but the attempt was unsuccessful. Shortly after that a bullet was found on the stretcher. The doctors conducting the autopsy said, in effect, "Well, that explains it. The bullet had entered a very short distance. It was misfired. Perhaps it was a dum-dum. In any event, it was probably dislodged as the president's body was subjected to external cardiac massage." That's the second bullet.

A third bullet was fired. At least one bullet hit Texas Governor John Connally, who was riding with the president. He suffered many wounds. At least one bullet had to have hit him to cause his wounds. (We are dealing with absolute minimums to see if we can make the Warren Commission case stand up.)

A fourth bullet was fired and missed. James Tague, though, wouldn't say it missed; it hit him. It missed the occupants of the presidential limousine, struck a curb, and left behind some metallic material in the curb. Then either that bullet, or portions of the bullet and the curb, struck James Tague in the face, and his face began to bleed from a superficial injury. Other than Governor Connally, who was severely injured, and President Kennedy, who was killed, James Tague was, so far as we know, the only other person wounded in the firing in Dealey Plaza that day. That's four bullets.

A fifth bullet was fired. It struck President Kennedy in his head. That was the shot that killed the president. Five shots. At an absolute minimum, five shots.

A weapon was found on the sixth floor of the Book Depository building. The officer who found it, Deputy Sheriff Seymour Weitzman, described it in detail in a sworn affidavit the next day as a German Mauser 30-caliber. Shortly after that the FBI said that Oswald had purchased an Italian Mannlicher-Carcano, caliber 6.5. So the Dallas police said: "That's what we found yesterday." Overnight the weapon changed its nationality and its size. It is not a very good weapon, the one they ended up with, the Italian Mannlicher-Carcano.

I talked about this case in Milan and Rome. Each time I have mentioned that the Italian Mannlicher-Carcano was the weapon utilized for the precision firing that day, the audience, particularly men in their fifties or more, burst into hysteria. The first time I asked what was funny about that, one man got up and said: "We always thought that the Mannlicher-Carcano was the reason we lost World War II." In any event, the "weapon" was tested for the FBI by the fastest rifleman east of the Mississippi, Robert Frazier. To work the bolt, to get the new round into the chambers, Frazier said, required a minimum of 2.3 seconds without even aiming the telescopic sight, which would require another second. So we have an absolute minimum to work the bolt of this old rusty weapon of 2.3 seconds. An absolute minimum.

Now we have Governor Connally examining the Zapruder film frame by frame. He said that President Kennedy was struck at that certain frame, and that he himself was struck at this certain frame. He swore that he was absolutely sure. Mrs. Connally, who was seated alongside him, corroborated his testimony. If his statements are true, then Governor Connally was struck 1.8 seconds after President Kennedy was struck because the Zapruder film, the Muchmore film, and the Nix film are all clocks. Once you know the speed of the film through the camera (the Zapruder film has 18.3 frames per second), it becomes a clock for the assassination. Therefore when you say "that frame and this frame," you can tell how far apart they are—1.8 seconds. Now with a weapon that requires 2.3 seconds as an absolute minimum for an interval period, having shots 1.8 seconds apart becomes very difficult.

But the Commission never bothered with that question at all, except to say that Governor Connally was probably wrong, that he had had a delayed reaction. He was just struck a glancing blow. The bullet entered his back and shattered his fourth and fifth ribs, causing his chest wall to explode with a huge gaping, sucking hole that almost cost his life. The Commission referred to that as a glancing blow that he hardly noticed.

Now we have problems for the Commission. The most serious problem for the Commission has been provided by the Zapruder film. From the first shot to the last, the Commission conceded, the maximum period of time elapsed is 5.6 seconds. The problem that the Commission has is that you can't get off five shots in 5.6 seconds with a 6.5-caliber Mannlicher-Carcano, and that weapon is the one with which they were going to prove that Lee Harvey Oswald killed the president.

But the Commission started with a preconception, and they utilized the evidence or distorted the evidence to meet that preconception. I'll give you an example. When the Commission was formed on January 12, 1964, J. Lee Rankin, counsel of the Commission, held its first press conference, which explained to the media (the account was published on the front page of the *New York Times* under the headline "Six-Phase Inquiry,") how the commission was organized in six panels. All of the evidence that would reach the Warren Commission would come through those six panels. What were they?

Panel number 1: What did Lee Harvey Oswald do on November 22?
Panel number 2: Oswald's background.

Panel number 3: Oswald in the Marine Corps and Oswald in
the Soviet Union (a strange juxtaposition).

Panel number 4: How Ruby killed Oswald.

Panel number 5: Ruby's background (which we saw they
did splendidly).

Panel number 6: The effectiveness of the Secret Service
that day in providing precautions. (We thought we knew
the answer to that one already.)

Those were the six panels. When I went before the Commission I congratulated it upon its development of an organization. I thought the six panels were fine, but I said: "However, Mr. Chief Justice, I would have added a seventh panel if I was conducting the investigation." He said: "Really? What would you call it?" I said: "I'd call it 'Who killed John Kennedy?' " The only evidence that could come before the Commission, based upon their table of organization, relative to the death of John Kennedy was in Panel 1: What did Lee Harvey Oswald do on November 22? In other words, there has never been a more public, open, cover-up in the history of this country. They said in advance what they were going to do. And they did it.

Let us see now how they handled the evidence in the light of their preconception. How many shots can be fired with the weapon they designated as the murder weapon in 5.6 seconds by one person? Three is the maximum, assuming the weapon is fully loaded. There is time for two interval periods. You cannot get four shots off; it takes too long. With that information the Commission concluded: Lee Harvey Oswald fired three shots. That is the most you can fire with the weapon; that is what he must have done. But then the question is: How do you explain all of the wounds and all of the known results of the bullets? You do it by the development of "the magic bullet theory," which is central to the Commission's conclusion.

This is the magic bullet theory. Lee Harvey Oswald is up on the sixth floor of the Book Depository building with his trusty German-Italian Mannlicher-Mauser 30-caliber 6.5-caliber. Here comes the president's limousine directly in front of the Book Depository building and almost stops as it makes its turn. At this point Oswald can drop the weapon out of the window confident that it will injure someone. But does he even fire at that point? Oh, no. Being somewhat of a sport, he waits until the car speeds up. As it moves rapidly away, Oswald fires the first shot. This bullet strikes the president in the back of the neck, leaving behind a wound six inches below. It exits from his throat, leaving behind a small, neat wound of entrance as it does so. It hangs out there in mid-air for 1.8 seconds until, apparently, it observes Governor Connally seated directly in front. It then strikes Governor Connally in the back, shattering his fourth and fifth ribs. It exits from his right chest wall and makes a sharp right turn, fractures his right wrist, makes a U-turn, and embeds itself in Governor Connally's left thigh, where it remains until external cardiac massage is administered to President Kennedy. Then it falls out of the president's back onto his stretcher.

Is there any wonder that the inventor of that miraculous bullet, Arlen Specter, who was elected district attorney of Philadelphia based upon his development of that theory, has refused to debate with a single critic of the Warren Commission ever since 1964? He was invited to appear on the Geraldo Rivera program with me. He said that he would not go on if I was there, or if Cyril Wecht (forensic pathologist of Pittsburgh) was there, or if anybody who was going to talk about the facts was there. ABC said to him: "We'll tell you what we'll do. If you don't want to debate with them, we'll put them on first. They can say what they want. Then you will have the last forty minutes, all to yourself, to say whatever you want." He said: "I refuse to do that. I'm not going to get involved in that kind of situation." But he accepted Tom Snyder's invitation to appear on his show. A full hour, no debate, and no one asking any intelligent questions. No one was there to ask any intelligent questions.

When the full story is told about the death of John Kennedy and what the media have done in an effort to affect the thinking of the American people, we shall then begin to unravel the role of the CIA disinformation section. We now have hard information for the first time about its role in issuing false statements about the critics of the Warren Report. The government was very active in the period when criticism first began to be voiced. There was not a single lecture that I gave in any college campus or before any church group in this country during which there were not at least two members of the Federal

Bureau of Investigation present with tape recorders. Not one. It's all now available in the National Archives.

I want to talk about one other area regarding the death of John Kennedy, that concerning Jim Garrison, district attorney of New Orleans—the single most maligned public official in this country. Garrison submitted evidence to a grand jury in New Orleans, and they indicted Clay Shaw. This is what was presented to the jury: Garrison's theory that there was a conspiracy to kill John F. Kennedy, Garrison's theory that Clay Shaw was part of that conspiracy, and Garrison's theory that Clay Shaw's motivation was that he was working for the Central Intelligence Agency. The evidence was submitted to the jury. It was the only time an American jury has had an opportunity to examine the evidence regarding the death of John Kennedy.

The twenty-six volumes came into court in New Orleans in a wheelbarrow. I remember it very well. The single bullet theory relies upon the fact that the bullet they have—Commission exhibit 399—is responsible for all of the wounds, a view that Arlen Specter still holds. During the trial Jim Garrison's assistant asked Lieutenant Colonel Pierre Finck, the pathologist who conducted the autopsy of the president for the government, if that one bullet could have caused all the wounds. Finck said: "It's impossible, for the reason that there are more grains of metal still in Governor Connally's wrist than there are missing from that bullet. That bullet could not have done it." Add to that statement the statement of Norman Redlich, assistant counsel to the Warren Commission, that if it is proved that the single bullet theory is not accurate, then he would concede that there was a conspiracy to kill John F. Kennedy, and you can see how central the single bullet theory becomes in an analysis of all of the evidence. And Finck said that that bullet could not have caused the wounds suffered by Governor Connally, certainly not the one in the wrist.

The evidence was presented to the jury. The jury listened closely. Then the jury concluded, number one: That there was a conspiracy to kill John F. Kennedy. It was the only American jury that ever heard the evidence and the only one to reach that conclusion—a historic moment that the press has not yet, of course, reported fully. Conclusion number 2: That the evidence showing Shaw's association with the assassination did not, however, prove his guilt beyond a reasonable doubt. Every juror I talked to (and I talked to them all with a formal questionnaire) believed the nine witnesses who swore that Oswald, David Ferrie, and Clay Shaw were together in Clinton, Louisiana, and elsewhere. Every juror said: "I believe them absolutely. I. believe that Shaw committed perjury when he denied that he knew Lee Harvey Oswald."

Garrison's failure to prove an association between Shaw and the CIA was, however, a central question in the minds of many of the jurors. The jury acquitted Shaw and then Garrison indicted him for perjury for denying that he knew Lee Harvey Oswald. In my view there is no such thing as an open-and-shut criminal case. But we do have nine witnesses believed by every single juror, and every single juror also believed Clay Shaw committed perjury. It *was* a strong case. Then, for the first time, the federal government moved in directly and openly. A federal judge in New Orleans issued an injunction forever prohibiting Jim Garrison from trying Clay Shaw. Such a thing had never happened before in the history of this country. It was unprecedented. That was the end of the case. That was the end of it all.

According to Victor Marchetti, at the Central Intelligence Agency during the time of the Shaw trial it was said (in a meeting with a number of people, including Richard Helms), in essence: "Clay Shaw is ours. Our relationship with him can't be known. We have to do what we can to help him during the trial." What did they do? Isn't it about time, since Victor Marchetti made that statement in early 1974, that some committee of Congress invite him to make the statement under oath and then call Richard Helms and ask him if he and the others said that? Isn't it about time to ask them what the Central Intelligence Agency did to pervert the course of justice in New Orleans? I think it is long past time.

I have been talking about this matter all over the country ever since 1964. The assassination of John Kennedy is not a spectator sport. We have to do things. We have to change the course of this country. We have not had a real election in this country, one that has been decided by ballots instead of bullets, since John Kennedy's head was blown off in Dealey Plaza. Who became president after that? Lyndon Johnson. Then he was elected because John Kennedy was dead. Next Robert Kennedy was killed in the 1968 campaign. Then in 1972, when the polls showed that Nixon could not win because of the strong showing that Wallace appeared to be making, Wallace was removed. *We have not had an election where we have made the decision without the interference of bullets since John Kennedy's head was blown off.* If we do not want to have a country where that is the situation, we will have to do something about it.

We have never before had the opportunity we have now, never. Watergate has brought about a change. The Freedom of Information Act was signed in the wake of Watergate. It says that documents that are in the public domain belong to us, no matter what the CIA and the FBI say. They belong to us. That act was passed by a strong vote of the House and the Senate. It was vetoed by President Ford, who, as Congressman Ford, signed the Warren Commission Report as a member of the Commission.

When the facts are finally disclosed, one thing I believe will stand out with absolute clarity. Gerald Ford and the six other members of the Warren Commission, because they did not take the hard evidence available to them and make it available to those who had the authority to prosecute, are all accessories after the fact in the murder of John F. Kennedy.

What can we do about it? There is a committee called the Citizens Commission of Inquiry comprising just about every responsible critic of the Warren Commission, everyone who has done hard research and others who have been involved in peripheral areas. It started with Marcus Raskin and Richard Barnet, the two codirectors of the Institute for Policy Studies. It contains Bernard Fensterwald, former counsel for committees of the Senate; George O'Toole, former CIA agent who wrote *The Assassination Tapes* (New York: Penthouse Press, 1975); L. Fletcher Prouty; Morton Halperin, former deputy assistant secretary of defense; and many other people.

What we have done under the new Freedom of Information Act (passed by an overwhelming vote over President Ford's veto) is to demand all of the relevant material on the assassination. It's quite clear that the FBI and the CIA and the others are dragging their feet. We'll have to go into court to get the material. But we are confident that we are going to get it.

We are going to analyze that material. I'm teaching at the Law School of the Catholic University of America. The administration there has made it possible for us to have an internship program. Law students will begin getting credit for going through that material as it comes out of the National Archives. That work will be done, and that material is going to be made available to every relevant committee of Congress that has a responsibility to investigate any aspect of the cover-up by the CIA and the FBI.

What you have to do is see to it that your congressperson and your senator understand that it is his or her responsibility to fight for such an investigation. If you think that this is a matter that belongs on the agenda of the American people, you have to put it on the agenda. When Gerald Ford or any other candidate for the nomination of his or her party comes to any place where you are, this question must be raised and raised forcefully until we know where that candidate stands. If we do this together with the new Freedom of Information Act and the Citizens Commission of Inquiry, I believe that we are going to bring out the facts regarding the cover-up of the assassination of John Kennedy, the cover-up by the FBI, by the CIA, and by the Warren Commission. I believe that through an examination of the cover-up, we will be able to follow footsteps right back into the conspiracy that killed John F. Kennedy.

This can only be done if we force the apparatus of government to work for us in an effort to secure the facts rather than to do what they have done since November 22, 1963—work in an effort to suppress the facts.

The CIA versus Labor

Ernest De Maio

■ A biographical sketch of Ernest De Maio precedes the first of his two presentations at the Conference on the CIA and World Peace contained in this volume.

I DO NOT BELIEVE that there is much distinction between the FBI and the CIA. They are both repressive agencies of big business used mainly against politically advanced individuals and organizations.

In the *New York Times* of February 24, 1974, there is a story that tells how the FBI and Westinghouse Electric Corporation sent a spy into a union local in Tampa, Florida. The labor spy called himself the leader of a "revolutionary" movement called "The Red Star." His assignment was to talk to the workers about this "radical" movement, motivating them to join it. When any joined, he would report them and have them fired. Despite the high rate of unemployment in the area, he got his job at the factory very easily. Although according to the contract there, the last hired are supposed to work on the second shift, he began right on the first shift as a sweeper. This job made it possible for him to be all over the plant and get involved with the workers, telling them about his "revolutionary" organization. He even had a little paper, paid for and published by the FBI. All the articles were extremely "revolutionary."

While he was at this plant, there was a strike that lasted eleven weeks. But nothing that happened during it was satisfactory to him. He claimed that the union was not carrying on the fight the way he thought it should be carried on. He kept saying that there ought to be a little violence. When time came for a settlement, he attacked it because it "wasn't good enough." Fortunately, he did not have much support because he was suspect immediately. Every worker has to suspect a person who begins working on the first shift and who then, after being in the plant only two weeks, is able to take two weeks off to go to Canada to attend a "revolutionary workers' convention." The important point to understand is why the FBI sent this person into that plant. It was simply to create divisions, to weaken the workers' unity so that they could not carry on effective negotiations with the company, and to give substance to the company's charge that there were Communists in the union.

This story is not an unusual one. The same kind of situation has always existed. It is not always possible to catch this kind of person. Sometimes they get elected to high office in the trade union movement. Unfortunately, much of the trade union bureaucracy in the United States is very bad. They have accepted CIA money. They have used that money in France, for instance, to set up the Force Ouvrière, to cause divisions in the French labor movement.

Our government has been in the dirty business of splitting unions all over the world, including here in the United States. If we believe that the real, basic power in society is based upon those who create the wealth in that society (that is, the working class), we shall understand why dividing, corrupting, and misleading the workers is a business that the monopolies have been involved in for a long time. It is because of this belief that I don't get discouraged about all the "dirty tricks." I think that they are a fact of life that we have to go through. We shall learn to separate the agents of the enemy from those who have kept faith with the people.

Revolutionary changes are taking place all over the world. When they begin to happen in this country, we shall see some big struggles here. Unfortunately, the power of the trade unions in this country has been used not to lead the people, but to mislead them. This situation has been caused by many elements. One of the most important has been the work of government agencies to destroy popular movements in this society. The CIA and the FBI are working hard *not* to unite the people, *not* to give them leadership, *not* to provide them with better government but, rather, to oppress them, to use the power of government against the people. A few years ago, this was done to the student movement, the Black Panthers, and others.

For this reason the primary work to be done is to unite not just the working people, but all the progressive forces of this country. We are now in a very different situation today from the one we were in in the 1930s, when we had a coalition of the Left and Center forces to build the CIO. That coalition was disrupted by the Cold War, with the State Department and the CIA actively engaged in splitting the trade union movements of the world. We have to heal these divisions. And the time is now because this country is in a serious crisis.

The same economists who said in the spring of 1974 that we were not going to have a recession proclaim in the spring of 1975 that we shall be out of it in six months. Maybe, but not likely. The monopolies who control our government will continue to use their power to promote their interests at the people's expense. Large-scale, extraparliamentary activity by organized labor working together in coalition with blacks and other minorities, the peace and environmental forces, and the intellectuals will guarantee progressive changes in America. History has proved that popular success is possible. Let us get on with our work of making it a reality.

The AFL-CIA

Winslow Peck

■ From 1966 to 1969 Winslow Peck served in Turkey and
Vietnam as an intelligence analyst for the United
States Air Force Security Service and the National
Security Agency. His responsibilities in these positions ranged from supervision of a large number of
information collectors to combat flying. Since 1972
he has been a coordinator for Fifth Estate Security
Education, Inc., a group monitoring abuses of power
by the intelligence community. He is an editor of and
a writer for Counter-Spy magazine and is also research
task force coordinator for the international labor
survey of the Intelligence Documentation Center, Inc.
The material by Mr. Peck that follows is taken from
Counter-Spy, vol. 2, no. 1 (Fall 1974), in which it
appeared in slightly different form as "Clandestine
Enforcement of U.S. Foreign Labor Policy." Mr. Peck's
presentation at the Conference on the CIA and World
Peace was based on this Counter-Spy article.

FOREIGN POLICY COMPRISES the aggregate of the activities of a
government conducted for the purpose of achieving its international objectives. Of these policies the most important, besides
global military strategy, are those that support, maintain, and
encourage the growth of the political economy. With the rapid
internationalization of the U.S. political economy at the end of
World War II, the dominant sector of the American political
economy, and thus the main determinant of foreign economic
policy, has been the transnational, or multinational, corporation.

Strategists for the multinational corporations foresee a time
when world industry will be ruled by 300 or fewer global giants

competing across continents. Even today these multinationals often have greater revenues than the countries in which they operate. The scale of international industrial development has far surpassed the scale of international political development, a discrepancy that ruthless companies can and often have exploited. In *Management and Machiavelli,* Anthony Jay states that "future students of the twentieth century will find the history of a firm like General Motors a great deal more important than the history of a nation like Switzerland." This view, that the corporation is more important than countries, is shared by many top executives of multinational corporations because their companies provide security, incentives, and jobs for millions of people.

To maintain this view and achieve their foreign economic goals, the multinationals have used and continue to use all ways and means available to them: their vast resources of capital, manpower, communications, etc.; their independence of national trade and currency restrictions; and their ability to dominate and manipulate international labor relations.

One of the most strategic resources available to the multinational corporations is intelligence. Intelligence that can not only monitor trade and rival corporate interests, but that can also collect information on anticorporate forces, including the objectives of Soviet communism, the nationalism of the states in which the multinationals operate, the national liberation movements of the Third World, and the aspirations of foreign labor itself. And intelligence that can clandestinely enforce foreign policy and act in secret against these forces.

The multinational corporations each maintain their own vast intelligence networks, as well as being able to call upon various private and independent intelligence organizations, but the most important intelligence resource available to them is the Central Intelligence Agency.

The CIA, besides serving as the major evaluator of information for our government and as a participant, along with the rest of the intelligence community and the military services, in war and counterinsurgency operations, has from the beginning of its existence supplied strategic information to the multinationals, assisted in their internal security and acted as *their* agents enforcing *their* foreign policy objectives, especially those targeted against international labor. The CIA and the multinational corporations have also served each other as recruiting pools for executives and operatives. Although factions have developed within the CIA opposed to specific objectives of foreign policy as suggested by the multinationals or the conduct of those policies, in the arena of foreign labor policy it is virtually impossible to distinguish between the objectives of the CIA and those of the multinational corporations.[1]

The CIA, acting as an agent of the multinational corporations, has infiltrated international labor organizations, established proprietary international labor fronts, and manipulated the AFL-CIO and the free trade union confederations of Europe, Latin America, Africa, and Asia.

The U.S. political economy, dominated by the multinational corporations, has since the end of World War II been in competition with Soviet communism for world hegemony, and the primary foreign policy objective for operations by the CIA has been to maintain foreign labor within the camp of our political economy. The strategy for this goal of the multinationals has centered upon the CIA and other departments and agencies of our government and has fostered and promoted fanatical anticommunism in the ranks of foreign and domestic labor.

In fostering this fanatical anticommunism, the CIA has been able to establish a pro-CIA infrastructure in foreign labor. This infrastructure has been used to gather information on foreign workers, governments, and Third World national liberation movements. This infrastructure has been used also as one front to attack those movements; to undermine the foreign and domestic labor policies of other governments—especially Europe and Japan—whose political economies, although aligned with ours, are in competition with ours; and to thwart any nationalist tendencies on the part of Third World governments that threaten the multinational corporations' holdings. This infrastructure has also been used to dampen the aspirations of foreign labor by manipulating labor relations in favor of management.

The International Labor Structure

The major international labor organization in existence today is the International Labor Organization (ILO). The ILO is an intergovernmental specialized agency of the United Nations and is similar to UNESCO, the World Health Organization, and the Food and Agriculture Organization. Each national delegation to the ILO is comprised of labor, government, and industry officials. The UN charter provided that "co-ordination between the Specialized Agencies and the UN be of the closest kind, with the Specialized Agencies providing reports for the Economic and Social Council which will permit the Council to discharge the responsibility given it by the United Nations Charter, of co-ordinating international action in the area of economic and social policy."

Article 62-3 of the UN Charter gives the Economic and Social Council (ECOSOC) the power to "prepare draft conventions for submission to the General Assembly." Article 63-1 gives ECOSOC the power "to make arrangements with members of the UN and its specialized agencies to obtain reports on the steps taken to give effect to its own recommendations. . . ." Thus the recommendations of a specialized agency, such as the ILO, channeled through ECOSOC, and finally to the General Assembly become "conventions" and "treaties." When approved by member nations, the recommendations of the ILO become law in those nations and govern labor relations.

Since its inception the ILO has been an arena of major contention between the Soviet Union and the U.S. The multinational corporations have consistently used the ILO to further their objectives. Not only have CIA operatives assisted the fanatical anticommunist infrastructure in international labor in its attempts to control the ILO, the multinationals have also used the ILO as a propaganda forum extolling the virtues of this infrastructure and its objectives. Of course, the same can be said of the Soviet Union and its allies. The effect has been that the ILO, rather than serving the needs of international labor, has been weakened by becoming an arena of competition between the Soviet Union and the multinationals.

The most effective means of CIA control of the ILO has been the funds provided for its operations by the U.S. government. The threat of suspending funds continues to be used by the CIA and its labor allies.

The Soviet Union dominates the world's largest international labor organization, the World Federation of Trade Unions (WFTU). As a global international, the WFTU purports to represent the working classes the world over. Although its membership figures are somewhat dubious, there is no denying that the WFTU is the largest global international because a single one of its affiliates, the Soviet Union, has more members than all the unions of the other internationals combined. The other member nations of the WFTU are the remainder of the Soviet bloc, four Asian nations—North Korea, North Vietnam, Mongolia, and China—and Cuba and the trade union federations in Italy, France, and India and a number of considerably smaller organizations in approximately 25 to 30 other countries in the Third World.

Established in 1945, the WFTU was *the* international labor organization at the end of World War II and included many American unions that belonged to the CIO before its merger with the AFL. As the Soviet Union began opposing the Marshall Plan for the recovery of Europe, the CIA instigated the withdrawal of the American unions and many European unions from the WFTU by 1949. Two years later the WFTU was ordered out of France, where it was originally established, but the WFTU found a new home in the Soviet sector of Vienna. A year after the signing of the treaty in 1955 recognizing Austria as a soverign state, the WFTU was, however, again asked to leave. Finally it settled in Prague. Today, because of the Sino-Soviet split and disagreements between many of the Communist unions, the WFTU is a house divided.

The World Confederation of Labor (WCL) is the oldest international trade organization in existence today and was until recently the international embodiment of denominational labor organizations. Composed primarily of Christian trade unions, the WCL has in recent years expanded its focus to include workers of all faiths. This universalization and accompanying secularization has, however, seriously weakened the WCL. Only in Latin America and here and there in Europe does the WCL offer a viable alternative to the pro-Eastern WFTU or the pro-Western ICFTU.

The ICFTU

Of the three global union internationals, the International Confederation of Free Trade Unions (ICFTU) is the most heterogeneous. Its members are predominantly oriented toward the

West, although a few unions from unaligned nations are also
members. Among those aligned with the West are representatives of democratic socialist unions of Western Europe; several
socialist-oriented unions of the Third World, especially Africa;
several Christian socialist unions, disaffiliated with the WCL;
and the uncompromising anticommunist unions of North America, including the AFL-CIO until its disaffiliation in May of 1969.

Although originally formed as an anticommunist trade union
international, in recent years, many members of the ICFTU
have increased their contacts with the WFTU, much to the
consternation of the AFL-CIO, which remains uncompromising
on this issue. Only in recent years has the AFL-CIO begun to
favor detente—and then only with conditions.

The ICFTU was formed in London in 1949 in the atmosphere
of deteriorating relations between the Soviet Union and the U.S.
Its avowed purpose from the start was to provide an international framework for the operations of noncommunist trade
unions in the developed nations and to promote and organize
free trade unions in the underdeveloped Third World. The
ICFTU owes its existence in large part to early CIA labor operations designed to split the WFTU, and its early history is replete
with projects being influenced or directly controlled by the CIA.
In recent years, however, there has been some movement to
eliminate the CIA's hold over the ICFTU.

The CIA through its infrastructure in the ICFTU was able
to mobilize ICFTU support for the following:

- —the uprising in East Berlin and other East German cities
  and towns in 1953
- —the uprising in Poznan, Poland, in 1956
- —the Hungarian revolt in October 1956
- —the revolution in Venezuela in January 1958
- —the CIA control of Thailand and Nepal
- —the attempted overthrow of Sukarno in Indonesia in 1956–
  58
- —the overthrow of Nkrumah in Ghana in 1966

The CIA infrastructure in the ICFTU in the early years was
especially successful in mobilizing the ICFTU against the colonial interests of our Western allies, Britain and France. The
ICFTU, guided by the CIA, was instrumental in aiding the
rebels against French colonialism in Algeria and North Africa

in 1956. And again in Aden and Kenya the ICFTU, hand in hand with the CIA, was successful in helping to end British rule.

But the CIA's clandestine affiliation with the ICFTU has not always been one of total cooperation. For instance, the ICFTU's strong stance against fascism in Spain and Greece and against the apartheid governments in southern Africa produced strains on this clandestine relationship. The ICFTU was and is strongly opposed to these governments and took many steps to isolate them internationally, while at the same time elements of the CIA were cooperating with these governments. The CIA was unable, or, perhaps in light of the disreputable natures of these governments, unwilling to mobilize ICFTU support to acquiescence to these governments. The CIA did, however, manage to use the information collected by the ICFTU on the workers' movements in these countries. In this sense, even with the opposition of the ICFTU to the policies of these governments, the ICFTU served as unwitting cover for the CIA's operations.

Decision making within the ICFTU rests in its congress, which meets at least every three years. This congress then elects an executive committee, which in turn elects a president and other officers. A general secretary is also elected by the congress. A subcommittee of the executive board serves to manage matters of urgency between meetings of the executive committee. In its early days during the Cold War, the CIA was successful in having its operatives sit on these councils, but in recent years the CIA has been forced to operate at lower levels. In addition, the ICFTU has several standing committees established to deal with specific problems, such as international trade and women workers. The most important of these committees is the International Solidarity Fund Committee. In the early years this committee was one of the most important elements of CIA infiltration of the ICFTU.

The International Solidarity Fund was established as a response to the uprising in Poland. The Committee went on to raise nearly one million dollars to aid the workers involved in the Hungarian uprising, then to organize many of the refugees into right-wing, anti-Soviet, CIA-controlled organizations.

The CIA was also instrumental in controlling the propaganda services of the ICFTU through the Press Service, the *Free Labour World*—official organ of the ICFTU—and the Organization Department. The latter, while organizing free trade unions throughout the Third World, provided a convenient cover for the CIA as well as funds for the publications of the regional and local unions. These publications were a major source of CIA-generated propaganda during the Cold War and, in many cases, continue to be.

The CIA also worked with the ICFTU in changing the labor legislation of many U.S. allies, such as Japan and France. Whereas the trade union rights of many workers in these countries were restricted and needed the assistance of the ICFTU to pressure these governments to ensure those rights, there is also no denying that restoring those rights favored the U.S.-based multinationals over these countries in international trade relations. It is the latter fact that probably motivated the CIA rather than concern for trade union rights.

The ICFTU's power, and thus the CIA's interest in this organization, does not lie just with its ability to stimulate and coordinate the activities of its affiliated organizations or to organize new unions in the Third World. The ICFTU also makes full use of its consultive status with the UN, the ILO, and other specialized agencies. The ICFTU is also influential with many other international organizations, mainly in the field of education.

Regional Internationals

Early in its history the ICFTU recognized that to carry out its task of establishing, maintaining, and developing free trade unions in the Third World, the differences between the various regions of the world in the economic, political, and cultural structure had to be taken into consideration. For this reason the ICFTU established regional organizations with wide autonomy. These regional organizations hold their own conferences, elect their own governing bodies, and have their own secretariats.

The Asian Regional Organization (ARO) was founded in 1951 with headquarters in New Delhi, India. The Inter-American Regional Organization of Workers (ORIT) was established in January 1951 with its headquarters in Mexico. Also in 1951, the European Regional Organization (ERO) was set up in Brussels, Belgium. The African Regional Organization (AFRO) was established in 1959 in Lagos, Nigeria.

It is primarily through these regional organizations that the CIA has been able to manipulate international labor. For in-

Guide to Abbreviations

AAFLI	Asian-American Free Labor Institute	ECOSOC	Economic and Social Council (UN)
AALC	African-American Labor Center	ERGAS	Workers' Anti-Fascist Group (Greece)
AIFLD	American Institute for Free Labor Development	ERO	European Regional Organization (ICFTU)
AFL	American Federation of Labor	EUFTT	European Union of Film and Television Technicians
AFRO	African Regional Organization (ICFTU)	FO	Force Ouvrière
AID	Agency for Information of Development (U.S. govt.)	FTUC	Free Trade Union Committee
		GSEE	Greek National Trade Union Confederation
AMG	American Military Government (postwar Germany)	ICFTU	International Confederation of Free Trade Unions
ARO	Asian Regional Organization (ICFTU)	IFBWW	International Federation of Building and Wood Workers
AVC	American Veterans Committee		
CIO	Congress of Industrial Organizations	IFCCTE	International Federation of Commercial, Clerical, and Technical Employees
CGT	French Confederation of Labor		
CP	Communist Party		
EAM-ELAS	Greek National Liberation Front (WW II)	IFFTU	International Federation of Free Teachers' Unions

stance, ORIT, the most dominated of the three regionals, was for many years the most effective arm of the CIA in Latin America. A staff report of the Senate Committee on Foreign Relations (July 15, 1968) says ORIT:

> was originally founded for the specific purpose of combatting Communist infiltration of the Latin American labor movement. ORIT has never quite solved the problem of emphasis as between fighting communism and strengthening democratic trade unions. . . . Generally speaking, in ORIT North Americans have emphasized anti-communism; Latin Americans have emphasized democratic trade unionism.

This is one reason for what seems to be a decline in

IFIOGWU	International Federa-tion of Industrial Organizations and General Workers' Unions	ITF	International Trans-port Workers' Fed-eration
IFOCAW	International Fed-eration of Oil, Chemical, and Atomic Workers	ITGWF	International Textile, Garment, and Leather Workers' Federation
IFPAAW	International Federa-tion of Plantation, Agricultural, and Allied Workers	ITS	International Trade Secretariats
IGF	International Graph-ical Federation	IUF	International Union of Food and Allied Workers Associ-ation
ILAB	International Labor Affairs Bureau (U.S. govt.)	MIF	Miners' International Federation
ILGWU	International Ladies' Garment Workers' Union	OSS	Office of Strategic Services
ILO	International Labor Organization (UN)	ORIT	Inter-American Re-gional Organiza-tion (ICFTU)
IMF	International Metal-workers' Federa-tion	PSI	Public Services Inter-national
IOD	International Organi-zations Division (CIA)	PTTI	Postal, Telegraph, and Telephone International
ISLWF	International Shoe and Leather Work-ers' Federation	UADW	Universal Alliance of Diamond Workers
		UAW	United Auto Workers
		WCL	World Confederation of Labor
		WFTU	World Federation of Trade Unions

ORIT prestige in Latin America. More fundamental, per-haps, has been the tendency of ORIT to support US govern-ment policy in Latin America. ORIT endorsed the overthrow of the Arbenz regime in Guatemala and of the Goulart re-gime in Brazil. It supported Burnham over Cheddi Jagan in Guyana, and it approved the U.S. intervention in the Domini-can Republic. To many Latin Americans, this looks like ORIT is an instrument of the U.S. State Department.

If the Senate staff had probed harder, they would have dis-covered that many of the leaders of ORIT have been in the em-ploy or control of the CIA. By the early 1960s, however, ORIT was so thoroughly discredited in Latin America and divided by internal disputes that it was no longer an effective tool for the CIA.

ERO likewise was in the early years during the Cold War infiltrated and controlled by the CIA, but its effectiveness was sharply circumscribed when the national trade union federations in the Common Market countries entrusted the handling of their joint representation in the Common Market to a specialized international, the European Trade Union Secretariat, rather than to ERO.

AFRO has perhaps been the least effective tool for the CIA. After an initial willingness on the part of African unions to cooperate with the CIA—during the period of African independence in the 1950s—the African nations became increasingly suspicious of external interference in their affairs. By the 1960s many African national trade federations had withdrawn from the ICFTU, thus limiting CIA clandestine activities in their countries.

Except for the CIA's success in overthrowing the Sukarno regime in Indonesia in 1965 with the help of ARO and some assistance by ARO in the CIA's activities in Indochina, ARO has been an ineffective tool for CIA manipulation. The vast cultural differences between various parts of Asia, enormous language barriers, and competing economic objectives have limited the amount of cooperation the CIA could expect from ARO.

International Trade Secretariats

Perhaps the most effective international labor tool for the CIA until recent years has been the International Trade Secretariats (ITS), which are organized along specific industrial trade union lines rather than by geographical regions. Rather than negotiating with governments, as do the ICFTU and the regionals, the ITS deal directly with the industries. Thus the ITS are the primary international representatives of the workers with the multinational corporations. This effort to parallel the structure of employers in a highly concentrated internationalized industry has provided the workers with their most effective tool for bargaining. At the same time several of the ITS provided the CIA with its most effective tools of infiltration into the political economies of the Third World. As one well-known observer of CIA operations worldwide has noted, governments come and go but the industrial unions tend to continue throughout. Thus through the ITS, the CIA was able to create its most effective infrastructures.

These ITS are:

—International Federation of Building and Wood Workers, with nearly 3 million members.
—International Federation of Commerical, Clerical, and Technical Employees, with nearly 7 million members.
—International Federation of Chemical and General Workers Unions, with over 3 million members.
—International Secretariat of Entertainment Trade Unions, with almost 500,000 members.
—International Union of Food and Allied Workers' Associations, with nearly 1.5 million members.
—International Graphical Federation, with almost 1 million members.
—International Federation of Journalists, with 60,000 members.
—International Metalworkers' Federation, with almost 11 million members.
—International Federation of Petroleum and Chemical Workers, with over 1 million members.
—International Federation of Plantation, Agricultural and Allied Workers, with over 4 million members.
—Postal, Telegraph, and Telephone International, with over 3 million members.
—Public Services International, with over 4 million members.
—International Federation of Free Teachers' Unions, with over 1 million members.
—International Transport Workers' Federation, with nearly 8 million members.
—International Textile, Garment, and Leather Workers' Federation, with over 4 million members.

In 1967 the International Federation of Oil, Chemical and Atomic Workers revealed in its financial report that it had received $30,000 from the Andrew Hamilton Foundation, a well-known CIA front. In January 1967 this ITS was expelled from Brazil for subversive activities.

Also in 1967 Drew Pearson and Jack Anderson revealed that this same ITS was spending a considerable amount of CIA funds in Indonesia. They also revealed that the Postal, Telegraph, and Telephone International (PTTI) and the International Transport Workers' Federation (IUF) were likewise spending CIA funds.

The International Textile, Garment, and Leather Workers' Federation (ITGWF), formerly the International Ladies' Garment Workers' Union, (ILGWU) was active with CIA in establishing the ICFTU.

Also in that year of revelation about the CIA's involvement with labor, Gerald J. Poulsan of the IUF claimed that his organization had been used by the CIA and that he knew of eight agents in his organization.

Perhaps the most dominated of the ITS is the PTTI. Because this ITS is involved in the strategic area of communications, it has been essential to CIA strategists to control this union. PTTI members were active in controlling communications during several coup d'états in Latin America and are now suspected of playing a substantial role in the 1973 coup in Chile. Joseph Beirne, president of the Communications Workers of America, member of the PTTI, has been of primary importance in securing CIA control of this ITS. Pearson disclosed that Bierne was instrumental in the channeling of CIA funds through his union and the ITS.

Although most of these international labor organizations—the ICFTU, the regionals, and the ITS—are legitimate expressions of trade unionism in the West, there can be no doubt that CIA strategy in targeting labor has included the essential element of infiltration and control of these organizations. Although this infiltration and control was strongest during the Cold War, many remnants of the CIA's infrastructure remain in these organizations. If more evidence comes to light revealing the role of these organizations in the overthrow of the Allende government in Chile, then the only conclusion we can reach is that this infrastructure is still effective and far from neutralized.

From WWII to the Formation of the ICFTU

The roots of CIA targeting of labor can be found in the policies and practices of the CIA's predecessor, the Office of Strategic Services (OSS). The OSS was developed on the doctrine of political pragmatism with agents of the political left, right, and center joined in the struggle against fascism. Thus the OSS contained corporate officials, blueblooded members of the establishment, conservative émigrés from Europe and Asia, liberals, socialists of every persuasion, and communists. The OSS did not fare so well, however, in achieving ideological coexistence. Drew Pearson and Jack Anderson analyzed the OSS executives as being "all picked from the Red baiters." The OSS, they said, "had succeeded in collecting one of the fanciest groups of dilettante diplomats, Wall Street bankers and amateur detectives ever seen in Washington." They further noted that the younger operational types, predominantly from the left of the political spectrum, "have done some of the most heroic work of the war."[2]

One of the major concentrations of left politics in the OSS was the Labor Branch. The Labor Branch was created to work with Socialist trade union groups in the European theater. The Branch was the brainchild of OSS Colonel Heber Blankenhorn, a veteran of army intelligence in World War I, who is credited with developing aerial propaganda campaigns. In the 1930s Blankenhorn had been a staff aid of New York Senator Robert Wagner, who had been instrumental in championing prolabor legislation. As an expert both on labor and intelligence, Blankenhorn later became director of the Senate Civil Liberties Committee investigation of corporate spying on the trade unions of the newly formed CIO and other independent unions. Upon joining OSS, Blankenhorn convinced General William ("Wild Bill") Donovan, head of the OSS, that the European trade unions would constitute the center of anti-Nazi resistance and that the OSS should make a special effort to develop labor contacts of intelligence and resistance operations.

To organize the labor unit, Donovan chose George Bowden, a former Industrial Workers of the World (IWW) organizer who combined a successful tax practice with prominent membership in the National Lawyers Guild. Bowden, in turn, recruited a friend of his from the Chicago bar, a young attorney named Arthur Goldberg, to become the first chief of the new OSS Labor Branch. At Blankenhorn's suggestion, several liberal officials from the National Labor Relations Board were recruited to staff the Labor Branch. Throughout the war, the Labor Branch was an active and vocal voice of political liberalism in the conduct of OSS operations.

The Labor Branch became one of the most important sec-

tions of the OSS, working with major resistance groups in occupied and neutral territory in Europe and North Africa. Toward
the end of the war, however, the more conservative elements of
the OSS managed to co-opt the Labor Branch projects into other
sections of the OSS, but not before the Labor Branch had succeeded in several important operations, including major strikes
in occupied territory. The attempt to organize anti-Nazi strikes
in neutral territory, though, led to the eventual demise of the
Labor Branch by giving fuel to the more conservative elements
of the OSS who were antilabor. As Goldberg would later write,
one of the "mistakes" of the OSS was "the selection by General
Donovan of men for the higher echelons of the organization who
by background and temperament were unsympathetic with Donovan's own conception of the necessity of unstinting cooperation
with the resistance movements."[3]

Throughout the war the OSS Labor Branch and other divi-
sions recruited agents from American unions and from the ITS.
These included Dr. Lazare Teper, a Russian-born economist who
directed the research department of the ILGWU, headed by
David Dubinsky, members of the ITF and members of the PTTI.
The ILGWU also provided the OSS with the services of Serafino
Romualdi. He was an Italian Socialist exile who emigrated to the
U.S. when Mussolini took power in Italy and joined the staff of
the ILGWU. In 1942 Romualdi began work for the Coordinator
of Inter-American Affairs, an intelligence and propaganda
agency headed by Nelson Rockefeller, which competed with the
OSS and the FBI for control of intelligence in the Latin American theater. In July of 1944 Romualdi was sent to Italy with the
rank of major in the OSS to work with Italian labor.

It is in this milieu, toward the end of the war, that we find
the seeds of future CIA policy toward world labor. Not only do
we have the more conservative officials of the OSS, all linked
with the developing multinational corporations, opposed to OSS
cooperation with the more radical elements of the trade unions,
we also begin to find a militant anticommunism on the part of
labor leaders and liberals connected to the OSS. Romualdi, for
instance, began in Italy to manipulate the situation politically
"to strengthen the Socialist forces at the expense of the Communists. We were preparing for the day—which many of us regarded as inevitable—when the Communists would have to be
opposed."[4]

Also in 1944 Goldberg had already begun to oppose the
Communists he had previously been working with closely. For
instance, the Labor Branch had been sending funds and equipment to the French Confederation of Labor (CGT). This resistance group included a Socialist majority and a Communist
minority, which began a campaign to gain control of the trade
union confederation. Goldberg began financing the Socialist
faction. When Goldberg refused to fund the Communist faction
equally, the Communists began a campaign exposing Goldberg's
activities in France.

At the same time, anticommunist labor leaders in the United
States began to intervene in international labor affairs. The
ILGWU, which had supplied many officers for the OSS, had,
throughout the late 1930s and early 1940s, a militant procommunist minority. David Dubinsky, head of the union, had attempted during the war to isolate and combat this grouping
and had succeeded fairly well. He and other anticommunist
union leaders then turned their attention to Europe. Although
anticommunist union leaders within the OSS were beginning
their campaign to oppose the Communists, the leaders in the
United States saw the need for a special agency to oppose the
growing power of the Communists. This power was based on the
fact that the Communists during the war had given the best
leadership to the resistance and therefore were looked to for
future leadership by the majority of the rank and file. The
instrument Dubinsky and other anticommunist trade unionists, including George Meany, chose was the Free Trade Union
Committee (FTUC). The FTUC from the beginning was designed to resist the growth of communism as a world force,
which to American labor leaders was a new and alien element
in the international labor movement.

The FTUC in France

The FTUC was the official foreign policy arm of the AFL, the
most vehement anticommunist trade union grouping in the U.S.,
and towards the end of the war and immediately following
worked closely with the OSS. In late 1945 the FTUC arrived in
Paris headed by Irving Brown. Brown had already been working

in Europe in late 1945 with the Foreign Economic Administration as Director of the Labor and Manpower Division and thus was the United States government's direct liaison with the European labor groups. In this capacity he worked quite closely with the remainder of the OSS which still worked with the labor resistance.

The major problem facing Brown was the strength of the CGT. Brown found the French situation to be "not very encouraging" because, as he frankly admitted, the Communist Party (CP) had a "terrific hold on the CGT. They control whatever is important to control. The opposition forces are weak, lack program and are divided in their strategy." The CP were strong among labor, Brown found, because of their record in the resistance. They claimed 75,000 martyrs; they had a large propaganda machine; and the dire economic circumstances of postwar France allowed the Party to appear "before the masses as their only savior." The masses of the CGT were noncommunist, Brown insisted, and only voted for the party because its leaders appeared as "dynamic trade unionists" and very "dynamic fighters." The Communists were also strong because they received assistance from the WFTU, the international labor organization.[5]

A further problem faced Brown. The majority of the noncommunist CGT leaders had become collaborationist during the wartime pro-Nazi Vichy regime. Their wartime activity compromised them, and the Communists were using this fact to full advantage.

The major group committed to anticommunism was gathered around a small newspaper, *Résistance Ouvrière,* published by the Force Ouvrière (FO). Brown immediately began urging the AFL to finance the activities of the FO against the CP faction of the CGT. The funds for the FO were to be deposited in the account of the Jewish Labor Committee, then headed by Arthur Goldberg, which would serve as a front for the secret transfer of the funds. Throughout 1946 the AFL continued to finance the FO through this secret channel in its opposition to the CP.

Brown's strategy in backing the FO was to split the CGT between noncommunist and Communist forces. Because the CP at this time adopted a program that proved to be a strategic error, Brown was able to report by late 1947 that there would definitely be another national trade union movement in France soon. The error of the CP was that, although they came out of the war in the strongest position in French labor, they soon adopted a policy that other Communists called revisionism. The French Communists supported piece-work and speedups and developed the slogan of "produce, always produce." This program called for great sacrifices on the part of the French workers, who soon opposed the policies of the CP leadership. "The Communists," Brown correctly observed, "are acting as a brake on the economic demands of the workers." This Brown thought would only serve "to strengthen the opposition forces" being organized by him and the FTUC. As historian Gabriel Kolko has noted, the French Communists thus ironically played "a critical role in disciplining the working class and ultimately making it possible for capitalism as an institution to survive and profit in France. Above all, the Communists were the advocates of production, for they above all others could make the workers toil."[6]

In the meantime Brown was consolidating the anticommunist opposition around the FO. By January of 1948 Brown had convinced the AFL to support the FO openly and fully.

In the meantime the CP was mounting a campaign among French workers to oppose the Truman administration's Marshall Plan for the recovery of Europe under U.S. economic and military leadership. Their strategy centered upon an attempt to organize a general strike in the late 1940s and 1950s and to oppose the importation of arms provided by the Marshall Plan. The CP organized a dock workers' strike in 1949–50 that attempted to do just that. But by this time a new force was assisting Brown and the FTUC in its attempt to oppose the CGT.

Brown supported a rightwing group called the Mediterranean Committee. This committee was composed primarily of Corsican criminals active in heroin smuggling. That group hired Italian strikebreakers to unload American arms at Marseilles and other French ports. The money for the strikebreakers came from the newly formed Central Intelligence Agency. Thomas W. Braden, who directed the International Organizations Division (IOD) of the CIA—responsible for funding various CIA programs through such fronts as the trade union internationals and the National Student Association—from 1950 to 1954, wrote in an article in the *Saturday Evening Post* in 1967 about the CIA's early subsidies of Brown's activities in the FTUC. Referring to a receipt for $15,000 in his possession, signed by Brown in 1947, Braden explained that Brown:

> needed it to pay off his strong-arm squads in Mediterranean ports, so that American supplies could be unloaded against the opposition of Communist dock workers. . . . In 1947 the Communist CGT led a strike in Paris which came near to paralyzing the French economy. A takeover of the government was feared. . . . Into this crisis stepped Irving Brown. With funds from Dubinsky's union, they organized *Force Ouvrière*, a non-Communist union. When they ran out of money they appealed to the CIA. Thus began the secret subsidy of free trade unions. . . . Without that subsidy, postwar history might have gone very differently.[7]

Although the funds received by Brown from Braden in 1947 were undoubtedly used to fund the Force Ouvrière, the strike-breaking by the Mediterranean Committee did not occur until 1949–50. By then CIA subsidies had jumped from $15,000 to $2 million per year by Braden's account.

Brown's strategy in France matured during the early 1950s under CIA guidance to include not only propaganda against the CGT and its CP leadership for their policies calling for sacrifices on the part of labor and for their opposition to the Marshall Plan but also an attempt to rehabilitate the Vichyite pro-Nazi labor leaders back into positions of power in French unions. At the same time he began a campaign to blacklist and outlaw the CP leadership in the CGT. Although this plan failed to be accomplished totally, it served as a major point of the strategy of the CIA-controlled FTUC in France during the early 1950s.

The FTUC in Greece

The CIA and the FTUC faced a different problem in other parts of Europe. In Greece the Greek Communists had come to play a major part in the growth of organized labor. During the war the Communists had been the spearhead of the major resistance group, the Greek National Liberation Front (EAM-ELAS), which received help from the OSS. At the same time another resistance group, the conservative republican EDES was being backed by the British. The conflict between these two groups escalated into civil war after Athens was liberated from the Germans in December 1944. When the British installed the exile government of Prime Minister George Pompendrieu, the EAM-ELAS partisans broke into open rebellion. Although a cease-fire was eventually achieved, the Greek civil war led to an important alteration in the operations of the OSS. More conservative OSS officers were sent to replace those working with EAM-ELAS. They carried new orders that "the main target for intelligence operations should now become discovering what the Soviets are doing in the Balkans rather than German operations . . . the German threat was receding. The Soviet danger was already looming."[8]

Greek labor was united in the Greek Confederation of Labor (GSEE) to which four separate groups belonged. One group was headed by a former Nazi collaborator. Another group was led by two men who had left the EAM-ELAS at the start of the civil war. The largest group, in which the Communists were very active, was the Workers' Anti-Fascist Group (ERGAS). The other large group was the pro-Monarchist EREP, which had been allied with the pro-British EDES during the war. It was this group that received the support of the government.

EREP immediately began consolidating its position among the rightwing unions and political parties. By 1946 EREP and the Greek government had managed to depose all the ERGAS leadership from the GSEE. The result was that Greek labor was thrown into chaos. The crisis was temporarily resolved by an agreement between EREP and ERGAS forced by the British. Almost immediately, however, EREP began to sabotage the agreement. Many of the ERGAS leadership had been arrested during the early stages of the civil war, and EREP worked to keep them in jail.

In the early months of 1947 Brown travelled to Greece and began working to evolve a settlement between ERGAS and EREP, a settlement that would leave the ERGAS representation in GSEE at a minimum. Noting that the deteriorating economic conditions in Greece produced favorable conditions for Communist organizing, Brown did all he could to undermine the ERGAS. ERGAS, Brown stressed, was a total CP instrument, "acting in complete support of Russian goals in Greece." If its leaders won power, "this Communist group would destroy free trade unionism." Earlier, however, he had stated that free trade unionism *did not exist* in postwar Greece.[9]

Brown's method of operation was soon quite clear. Anything was justifiable when seeking to oppose Communists in the trade union movement, including cooperation with a government-appointed group that did not have the support of the Greek workers. To achieve world support for this program, Brown emphasized his recommendation that the state end its intervention in the unions and act to raise standards and also that Marshall Plan aid "be conditioned on greater guarantees of democratization of the government." Thus under the cover of reformism, the FTUC was able to continue the support of the EREP and to undermine the ERGAS.

ERGAS was eventually eliminated from GSEE but fighting broke out between rival anticommunist groups. A strike was called in 1947 by the leadership of the EREP that only weakened their position and that of their major opposition. In this milieu pro-fascist elements arose under the appearance of neutrality. Because a fascist takeover of the trade unions would have been embarrassing to the U.S., which backed the government, Brown intervened to reach a compromise between the various factions. As the government in Greece shifted further to the right, however, Brown accused those he had previously supported of putting their personal ambitions ahead of militant anticommunism. This dispute continued throughout the 1950s and early 1960s with those union leaders whom the CIA and Brown had originally supported declaring that Brown was trying to "establish conspiratorial anticommunist organizations under the guise of trade unionism."[10]

The FTUC in Germany

In Germany the older Social Democratic trade union leaders had been persecuted by Hitler and a great void in union leadership and organization existed. Germany had been divided into four zones, each controlled by the various Allied occupation armies. In this context the CIA and the FTUC moved to organize the trade unions and to eliminate "procommunists" from leadership positions of unions formed in the zone supervised by the American Military Government (AMG).

Efforts to rebuild the unions in the American, British, and

French zones were begun by the Free German Trade Union League, which had worked with Goldberg's OSS Labor Branch during the war. These German unions wished to act as a central organizing committee that would rebuild unionism on a democratic basis. But Brown believed that the policies of the AMG were giving an advantage to Communists in gaining control of the local plant organizations. He accused the Manpower Division of the AMG of being procommunist and "party-liners."

The AMG policy was to go slow in rebuilding the trade unions in Germany and to have a policy allowing organizing in single plants only. This policy had the effect of limiting the growth of trade unionism, but the AMG argued that this situation was necessary to ensure democracy in the redevelopment of Germany. But to Brown this policy was procommunist. He then began a campaign to eliminate from the AMG those who opposed his policies. In 1946 he met with several anticommunist union leaders and was convinced that he should back their propaganda efforts. He provided financing for their publications, which were then sent into Germany clandestinely, because official Allied policy forbade external publications.

At the same time Brown began a campaign to have the AMG return the property of the old Socialist unions that the Nazis had confiscated during the war. This situation enabled these unions to build rapidly with an anticommunist perspective.

Toward the end of 1946 Brown vigorously opposed the affiliation of these unions with the WFTU. Brown for the first time began proposing the building of a new anticommunist international union organization. Such a group, he emphasized, would also provide him with "an excellent official function for my presence in Europe."

This proposal caused a major dispute between the CIO, which belonged to the WFTU, and the AFL, which backed Brown. The dispute escalated when the CIA helped distribute an AFL propaganda paper in the Soviet zone. This paper was smuggled into the Soviet Zone by an anticommunist underground organization associated with the newly formed free trade unions.

At about the same time Brown and the FTUC moved to block the establishment of CIO offices in Germany and to purge CIO officials from the AMG. To further the promotion of the unions in Germany, the FTUC tricked the commander of the AMG,

General Lucius Clay, into providing further assistance to the unions by returning more confiscated property and hiring AFL personnel, many of whom were CIA agents, on the U.S. payroll of the AMG to work on propaganda and assistance to the newly formed unions. Clay was opposed somewhat to the growth of the unions, but upon hearing that the AFL favored socializing both the basic industries and public utilities—as an alternative to union development—he changed his mind. Clay said that "as the military representative of a government devoted to the private enterprise system he could not be expected to order or promote socialization in Germany."[11] Clay, then, preferred that the unions rely on their own independent strength rather than on military law. After this time the AMG supported the goals of the FTUC in building the unions.

The criterion for German unions to receive aid and assistance became their degree of anticommunism. In Germany, as throughout Europe, these anticommunist, although leftist, unions became the base of the CIA's infiltration into trade unionism, but this base would remain only regional in scope until Brown's suggestion for a new trade union international was implemented.

The CIO and McCarthyism

Back home in the United States, Arthur Goldberg, through the Jewish Labor Committee, had become general counsel for the CIO. In 1947–49, he engineered the expulsion of the left of the CIO from that organization. Ten unions were accused of being "Communist-dominated," and their expulsion signalled the beginnings of a massive hysteria that reached into every institution in the land and almost backfired on the CIA targeting of labor. Anticommunism became the dominant politic in America during the late 1940s and early 1950s. This trend peaked with McCarthyism.

McCarthyism began by purging the left of the State Department and other branches of government. It even threatened the liberal element of the military and the CIA. Ironically, those threatened in the CIA were predominantly the liberals of the International Organizations Division, which was financing the activities of Brown and the FTUC.

McCarthy had learned that the International Organizations Division had "granted large subsidies to pro-Communist organizations." Actually this division was supporting the noncommunist left, predominantly Social Democratic and Trotskyite, around the world, including the trade unions organized by the FTUC and its successor, the ICFTU. Much of this subsidy would probably have been supplied openly—as it now is—by the State Department had it not been for the dominant political atmosphere of the time: McCarthyism.

Braden, head of the IOD, recalled: "In the early 1950's, when the cold war was really hot, the idea that Congress would have approved many of our projects was about as likely as the John Birch Society's approving Medicare."[12]

Braden's IOD was subjected to special scrutiny because of its obvious political liberalism. Braden's director of trade union operations, for instance, was fired because he had briefly belonged to the Young Communist League in the 1930s. Derogatory reports on IOD personnel were prepared for McCarthy by the FBI and several private corporate intelligence organizations. In the end, however, Allen Dulles, head of the CIA, and other prominent liberals in the government were able to stop the purge of liberalism in the CIA and to stop McCarthyism.

But the effects on trade unions were the same nonetheless. After the purge of the left of the CIO, Goldberg immediately began working to achieve a union between the AFL and the remainder of the CIO, and in 1955 they were merged. The CIA had in the meantime worked with the AFL in creating a new labor international—as per Brown's suggestion—the ICFTU, established in 1949. From 1955 to 1969 the AFL-CIO served as the primary proponent of anticommunism in that body. Throughout that period the ICFTU foreign policy considerations were guided by two elements: the fanatical anticommunism of its North American leaders and the objectives of the Central Intelligence Agency.

Lovestone

Although the roots of the CIA's targeting of labor lie in the espionage war of World War II, we must go back even farther to understand the individuals who brought about this union of CIA anticommunist liberalism and fanatical labor anticommunism. In 1919, two years after the successful Bolshevik Revolution in Russia, the Socialist Party of America held its convention. At that convention the more radical members split from the Socialist Party and began organizing what became the Communist Party–USA. One of the CP's founding members was Jay Lovestone.

Lovestone was born in Lithuania in the late 1890s and came to the U.S. with his parents at the age of ten. He grew up in the leftwing atmosphere of New York's large immigrant Jewish community, where his father was a sexton in a local synagogue. After graduating from the City College of New York, he joined the Socialist Party. After helping to split that party in 1919, he went on to become a member of the executive committee of the newly formed CP–USA. As editor of *The Communist*, the party's theoretical journal, Lovestone remained in the highest party echelons. In a short time he was elected General Secretary of the CP–USA, that organization's highest position.

Those who remember him recall him as an extremely domineering, mysterious, and macho figure. Benjamin Gitlow, a member of the CP who later became disillusioned, remembers in his book *I Confess* that Lovestone "was unmarried, as far as anyone knew, but beyond that not a man in the Party knew anything more about him."

> Lovestone [writes Gitlow] was a veritable Tammany chieftain among us Communists. One of his most successful methods was to call a comrade into his office, tell him extremely confidential information, obtaining in return a solemn promise that the matter would not be disclosed to a soul. In that way he won the support of numerous Party members who believed they were particularly favored by him. . . . Lovestone was a high-pressure super-salesman of communism.[13]

For nine years Lovestone continued to dominate the CP with these tactics, but his downfall from the party ranks occurred in 1928. In May of that year Lovestone journeyed to Moscow for a meeting of the Presidium of the Communist International. At that Congress Lovestone supported the position of Nikolai Bukharin in his struggle for power with Joseph Stalin. Bukharin, who was later executed, wanted to give Communist parties outside the Soviet Union a relatively large degree of independent freedom from the Soviet Communist Party and to pursue within the USSR a gradual approach to communization of the political economy. This position was denounced by Stalin and his supporters as opportunistic and favoring an economic rather than political approach to their goal. In Stalin's view the gradual approach would lead to the demise of world communism.

Stalin's analysis of American capitalism was that it was in a state of disintegration. He believed the CP–USA should prepare for revolution. Lovestone, on the other hand, favored a long-term approach that would include electoral politics. The Lovestone faction within the CPUSA was then accused by their comrades in the Comintern of the heresies of "American exceptionalism" and "revisionism." Stalin himself accused Lovestone of promoting factionalism. When Lovestone replied with a vehement attack on the Soviet leader, Stalin pronounced his fate if he remained in the Communist International He turned to Lovestone and rasped: "There is plenty of room in the cemeteries of the Soviet Union for people like you."

Lovestone, shaking with suppressed anger, stormed back: "Such remarks show you are unfit to be the leader of the Russian working class, much less of the international working class." Lovestone was then arrested and detained in Moscow, but he managed to sneak out. The CPUSA immediately expelled him from the party.[14]

Refusing to give up his position, Lovestone rapidly formed an opposition group called the Communist Party (Opposition). Later he changed the designation to the Independent Communist Labor League and, still later, decided it was best to drop the word "Communist" from the title of his independent movement.

Throughout the 1930s he and his followers were known as "Lovestonites". The Lovestonites continued to preach against the "errors and terrors of Stalin." Gradually a conversion developed in Lovestone's politics from Communist to vehement anticommunist. Disbanding his organization in the late 1930s, he offered his services to labor leaders who were busy fighting the tightly organized Communist factions in their unions. He brought with him several of his lieutenants from the Lovestonites, including Irving Brown, who would later represent the FTUC and the CIA in Europe.

Lovestone first found a niche in the United Auto Workers (UAW). The UAW was split at the time into three major factions: a CP-oriented one, a liberal faction led by Walter Reuther, and a conservative anticommunist faction led by UAW President Home Martin. Martin immediately came under the influence of Lovestone. But Martin and Lovestone's tactics of labeling anyone who opposed them as "Communists" soon earned the ire of the union's members. After Martin tried to hold onto the union leadership by such tactics as threatening members of the Reuther faction at gunpoint, he was deposed and purged along with Lovestone.

After the Lovestonites lost their position in the UAW, they traveled to the International Ladies Garment Workers Union headed by David Dubinsky. Dubinsky was faced with a militant procommunist minority that threatened to disrupt his control of the union. Lovestone personally knew most of the Communists in the New York clothing industry, and was able effectively to aid Dubinsky in combating and isolating his opposition. In 1940 Dubinsky appointed Lovestone to head the ILGWU's International Relations Department. The purpose of this office was to prevent the Communists from grabbing control of the world free trade union movement. Lovestone was instrumental in placing several Lovestonites and other anticommunists in the OSS Labor Branch and other departments to begin working with the trade union resistance in Europe and North Africa. When the AFL formed the FTUC, Lovestone was appointed executive secretary. In this position he dispatched his old friend and ally Irving Brown to Europe. At the same time Lovestone gained greater influence over the AFL's foreign policy. George Meany, secretary-treasurer of the AFL and later president of the AFL and of the AFL-CIO, was a staunch anticommunist who appreciated Lovestone's intimate knowledge of Marxism and his ability to express his anticommunism in communist semantics. Because of this fact Lovestone became the grey eminence behind the AFL and then the AFL-CIO's foreign policy. He, more than any other man, was responsible for shaping that policy, including its allegiance with the CIA.

The *Washington Post* in 1967 said of Lovestone,

Those who know him maintain that he has a totalitarian personality that has simply been carried over from one world to the other. They see him as a man who disillusioned with the god he once worshiped, evokes its image everywhere so that he might continue to curse and flog it in an endless psychological rite of expiation. He views the world, they argue, as being divided into Communists and anti-communist sectors that must inevitably clash in a great final battle.[15]

Although that clash has not come—and is not likely to in this age of detente between the superpowers—and though Lovestone is now retired—his legacy lives on in the vehement anticommunism of the AFL-CIO and its continued ties to the CIA. Ironically, a similar political conversion to anticommunism can be found in the man who for many years shaped the CIA's policies toward international labor and who continues to be a troubleshooter for the Agency, Cord Meyer, Jr.

Meyer

Meyer, the son of a wealthy State Department officer, led a sheltered life in his youth. He attended an exclusive prep school and went on to Yale, where he belonged to the best social clubs, played on the hockey team, and edited the literary magazine, showing a particular affinity for poetry. In September 1942 he graduated summa cum laude and Phi Beta Kappa and was honored as the Yale senior who had "contributed most intellectually to the university." Two weeks after leaving New Haven, Meyer enlisted in the Marine Corps. He served as a machine gun platoon leader in the Pacific until a Japanese grenade rolled into his foxhole and severely wounded the 23-year-old lieutenant. The explosion cost him the vision of his left eye.

Recovering in the hospital, Meyer underwent a spiritual rebirth, dedicating his life to achieving world government under which there would be no wars. In a letter to his parents, while in the hospital, Meyer wrote:

> If there be a God may He give us all the strength and vision we so badly need. . . . I really think, if possible, I should like to make a life's work of doing what little I can in the problems of international cooperation. No matter how small a contribution I should happen to make it would be in the right direction. We cannot continue to make a shambles of this world, and already a blind man can see the shortsighted decisions that point inevitably to that ultimate Armageddon.[16]

Returning to the U.S. to recover from his injuries, Meyer was chosen as one of two wounded veterans to attend the United Nations Founding Conference at San Francisco in April 1945. There he met Charles Bolte, another wounded veteran, who had founded the American Veterans Committee. The AVC was founded as a liberal alternative to the conservative veterans groups founded after World War I. Dedicated to the New Deal and to international peace through the United Nations, the AVC attracted the active support of many influential young men, and its membership grew geometrically after the end of the war.

An early recruit to the AVC, Meyer devoted his energies to the growing movement for effective world government. In early 1947 Meyer formed a new group supporting the concept of a strengthened UN as the key to world peace, the United World Federalists.

By this time Meyer's view of world politics had already been shaped by his experience in the AVC. At the second national convention of the Committee in 1947, a minority supported by the CP–USA attempted to gain control over the AVC. Meyer was a member of the liberal majority and helped lead this faction to a resounding and decisive defeat of the procommunist faction. This battle left him with a strong distaste for Communism. He was particularly disturbed by the Communist line that denounced all proponents of world government as "reactionary plotters" attempting to seek world hegemony for capitalism. At the convention the radical faction had sided with the rightwing southern aristocracy in opposing the veto power of the nations on the U.N. Security Council. Both sides viewed this policy as giving up national sovereignty to an organization that the other side would control.

Meyer was also disturbed by American Cold War politics and the consequent U.S. support for "corrupt and oppressive" regimes in Greece, Turkey, and China. Meyer concluded unhappily that America's anticommunist zeal was obliterating the democratic principles of American foreign policy. At first, he believed that the Soviets should be offered the opportunity to "cooperate in building the institutions of a durable peace." But Meyer's viewpoint would soon change.

Alarmed over the Communist coup in Czechoslovakia and the Soviet blockade of Berlin, he began to doubt the peaceful intent of Moscow. He became especially alarmed over the Soviet view of world government. In 1949 Meyer wrote, "I have to admit that the present leadership in the Kremlin is opposed to the idea of world government. As a matter of fact Moscow radio has spent some time attacking us [the United World Federalists], and it attacked me personally not so long ago as the fig leaf of American imperialism."[17] The following year, a Soviet newspaper described the movement for world government as an attempt to "beautify the boundless expansion of American imperialism."

By the time he testified before the Senate Foreign Relations Committee in February 1950 on a proposal to revise the UN charter, Meyer had become preoccupied with Soviet belligerence. He warned that "we have failed in many respects to meet the ideological challenge and no quantity of bombs can make up for that failure to appeal to the hearts and minds of men." It was the outbreak of the Korean War in June 1950, however, that solidified his decision to take a more active part in fighting a Cold War he had once viewed with skepticism. Several months later, he left the United World Federalists and went into the CIA as assistant to Tom Braden.

Meyer soon wished he had remained in the world government movement, for he became an early target of the McCarthyites and the FBI. The FBI produced a particularly inane derogatory report on this "tall intense young man with a preoccupied smile and wavy brown hair."

But, unlike his colleagues who dejectedly accepted their dismissal from the CIA, Meyer, according to *Esquire* magazine, "fought back doggedly against slurs on his loyalty. . . . Meyer was suspended from the Agency while preparing in his own defense a brief that ran into hundreds of pages. Dulles, who had recruited Meyer to the Agency, stood by his embattled side." He "eventually won his battle against the impugners on Capitol Hill."[18]

When Braden left the CIA in 1954, Meyer succeeded him as chief of the International Organizations Division, responsible for, among other things, the CIA's activities in international labor. Later in the 1960s when the activities of this division were disclosed, the CIA was reorganized and many of the IOD's responsibilities were shifted to the newly formed Covert Action Staff, including labor affairs, which became and still is one of the five divisions of that office. Both the IOD and the Covert

Action Staff came under the direction of Clandestine Services.

But how did this battle with the McCarthyites affect Meyer? The *New York Times* reported in 1967 that a friend recalled, "He was one of the most promising guys. . . . Very sensitive, very intelligent. His whole spirit was one of great humanity. But [after years in the CIA] he got cold warized."[19] Many liberals who came under attack during the McCarthy era later developed a pervasive and sometimes blind anticommunism as a defense against future criticism of their ideological integrity. Meyer was no different. Over the years it became increasingly difficult to remain both a liberal and a CIA officer. The Agency's covert power was consistently exercised on behalf of political repression and dictatorship. Added to this reality is the belief by some of his friends that Meyer had an unsubstantiated belief that the unknown assailant of his ex-wife was a Communist agent and that Communist agents somehow engineered the death of a son in an auto accident. Such is not likely to be the case, but after the death of his ex-wife, Meyer used the friendship *she* had had with Jackie Kennedy to convince the CIA that *he* should be the CIA's liaison with the White House. His briefings to President Kennedy were so replete with the inconsistencies of fanatical anticommunism that the president was often heard to remark to his aides that he was extremely frustrated with Meyer's reports. It should also be noted that Meyer's machismo, like that of Lovestone, is also extreme. In 1974 CIA leaders finally removed him from the decision making process and sent him to be station chief in London.

Goldberg

One other man was also instrumental in the marriage of American labor to the CIA. Arthur J. Goldberg was born in 1908 in Chicago of Jewish parents who had emigrated to the U.S. in the 1890s and settled in that city. He graduated from Northwestern University and then entered the law school there. In 1930 he was graduated *summa cum laude* and granted awards as the best student in his class. As a Doctor of Jurisprudence he went on to edit the *Illinois Law Review,* and in 1937 he qualified for practice before the United States Supreme Court. In 1939 he began to lecture at the John Marshall Law School. After the U.S. entered World War II, Goldberg became head of the OSS Labor Branch. Upon completing his military service he returned to his Chicago law practice. In March 1946 Goldberg wrote that the failure of the U.S. "through ignorance or fear," to give "the democratic forces of the resistance in Europe the help they deserved" limited "the scope and effectiveness of OSS activities in support of our allies in the underground." This statement was in contradiction to Goldberg's own limiting of the scope and effectiveness of OSS activities by not equally funding all factions of the resistance, especially the Communists, who were the majority of that resistance.[20]

By 1948 the liberal faction of the CIO led by Walter Reuther was attempting to purge the Communist forces from that body. As Reuther said, "Exposure, not repression, must be our goal. We must get the Communists out of the political back alleys and walk them up Main Street in the full light of informed opinion." To achieve this goal, the Reuther forces engineered the dismissal of Lee Pressman as CIO general counsel on charges that he was soft on Communism. To replace him, the Reuther forces hired Arthur Goldberg. Goldberg's first duties were to arrange the expulsion of eleven unions from the CIO, thus eliminating the left wing of that body. With this purge accomplished, the stage was set for the CIO's withdrawal from the WFTU, which by that time was firmly against the Marshall Plan. It was Irving Brown's contention, as representative of the FTUC in Europe, that the Marshall Plan and the growth of anti-communist trade unions would never be accomplished so long as some American unions supported the WFTU.

After Goldberg had accomplished the purge of the left of the CIO, he devoted his energies to the liberal defense of trade unions during the McCarthy era and in 1955 developed the mechanism for the merger of the AFL with the CIO. In this step Jay Lovestone as the director of the International Affairs Department of the AFL-CIO became the dominant strategist of American labor's foreign policy interest. And as Drew Pearson and Jack Anderson revealed in 1967: "Lovestone takes orders from Cord Meyer of the CIA. No money for labor [internationally] is spent without Lovestone's approval."[21]

It is debatable whether Lovestone took orders from Meyer or Meyer took orders from Lovestone. Some sources who have

worked with the CIA's labor programs insist that it was Lovestone who determined policy and that the CIA official in charge
merely coordinated the transfer of funds and administration of
resources and the placement of personnel. In either case, both
Lovestone's and Meany's faces are well known to the guards at
the CIA's Langley complex, where they have visited frequently
to coordinate operations.

After the merger Goldberg continued to work as general
counsel for the AFL-CIO and, along with Reuther, was instrumental in getting labor support for John F. Kennedy's election
in 1960. As a reward, Goldberg was appointed secretary of
labor. As a member of the Cabinet, Goldberg was able to continue facilitating the CIA's interface with labor.

The Labor Department maintains labor attachés in embassies overseas. This system of labor attachés developed during
World War II and expanded during the Cold War. Selection of
the labor attachés is officially done by the International Labor
Affairs Bureau, which evolved in 1947. Most of the ILAB's work
involves coordination of policy on international labor matters
with other departments of the government including the CIA.
Its most important responsibilities, however, are the selecting,
training and promoting of labor attachés.

But the AFL-CIO also has a hand in this selection. As Drew
Pearson and Jack Anderson stated: ". . . few labor attachés are
appointed to American embassies abroad without his [Love-
stone's] okay." The labor attachés cooperate quite closely with
the ICFTU in efforts to prevent achievement of Communist objectives. One critic of American international labor policy
thought that labor attachés went too far in these efforts. Aside
from their "legitimate labor information activities," he com-
plained, attachés spent U.S. government money to win supporters for anticommunist policies in foreign lands. Classic examples
of such activities, he expounded, could be found in Japan,
where "elements with the right-wing labor movement are given
free trips to America . . . or in the Philippines, where the U.S.
Embassy from the beginning supported labor leaders of questionable integrity simply because they favored British-American
policies."[22]

The attachés also inform foreign governments, management
of the multinationals, and labor officials about American developments. The attachés "show the flag" and endeavor to have

people abroad think well of the United States. Since Goldberg's tenure as secretary of labor, many labor attachés have received some training in "agent handling," the same training clandestine officers of the CIA receive. In addition, many of the labor officers have been direct employees of the CIA operating under cover. Because of this situation, labor attachés have been the target of militant radicals overseas. Labor attachés have occasionally been kidnapped by foreign revolutionary groups because of their activities with the CIA.

Thus, due to the activities of three men—Jay Lovestone, Cord Meyer, Jr., Arthur Goldberg—and a host of their subordinates, the CIA has managed to implement perhaps its largest and most significant clandestine program—that involving labor. Estimates of the amount of clandestine CIA-controlled funds spent on labor run as high as $100 million a year. With these funds the CIA has been able to manipulate literally millions of workers throughout the world.

Failures and Successes

The contradiction between what a political force attempts to achieve and what it has the capacity to achieve is a major one. This is axiomatic to every field of endeavor, but especially to government policy. Foreign policy objectives are incapacitated by a wide range of forces, including the opposition of enemy states, the competition for decision making power by allied states and subordinate internal forces, the struggle for freedom and independence by neutral states or national liberation forces in allied states or their colonies and neocolonies, the insurgency of internal minority forces, the inadequacies of the state's foreign policy enforcement apparatus—especially public pressure against inhumane or illegal methods of enforcement— and the limited visions, ingenuity, and will of the personalities who are manipulating the foreign policy. There may be no better illustration of this axiom than U.S. foreign labor policy, which, after initial successes immediately following World War II, began a protracted disintegration.

Although the WFTU was harmed by the withdrawal of many unions at the instigation of the CIA, and more recently by the Sino-Soviet split, its strength and unity has fared far better than the ICFTU. The first failure for the CIA labor objectives was the inability to maintain AFL-CIO hegemony in this trade union international. First the national trade union federations in the Third World began to defect. In Africa the more radical trade unions disaffiliated in the late 1950s. Although their nations' independence from colonial control was assisted by the CIA, they soon began to oppose the CIA's meddling in their affairs, labeling this "neocolonialism." They were followed by some trade unions in Asia and Latin America.

The European trade unions, the original base for CIA labor operations, began to oppose the CIA's operations, first because of the CIA's opposition to their nations' colonial interests and then because of the economic and political forces shaping European unity in competition with the U.S. Eventually some of these trade unions entrusted their international affairs to the European Trade Union Secretariat rather than to the ICFTU. Within the ICFTU, those European leaders who cooperated with the CIA were eventually deposed as the trade unions began to make renewed contact with the WFTU in the spirit of detente. Eventually this led to the disaffiliation of the AFL-CIO, which retained a staunch opposition to detente until recent years.

Although failing with the ICFTU, the CIA has had greater success with the International Trade Secretariats. Especially dominating such ITS as the PTTI, where Joseph Beirne, past head of the Communications Workers of America, managed to maintain CIA control, the CIA has been able to continue clandestine intervention in a wide range of affairs in the Third World. Of course, this dominance of the ITS has been ineffective in other conflicts, such as the struggle for power with the Soviets. But in the Third World the ITS have been an effective tool until recent years. Today, after many disclosures about the CIA operating through the ITS, ITS delegations to Third World countries come under close scrutiny by the national police and many of their policies are effectively opposed. But unlike the ICFTU, which became a total failure for CIA policy, the CIA still enjoys some control over the ITS.

A further limitation of the CIA's effectiveness came in a split in union solidarity here at home. In the mid-1960s, the liberal faction of the AFL-CIO, centered around Walter Reuther of the United Auto Workers, began to oppose George Meany on

many issues. The crux of this opposition was Meany and Lovestone's involvement with the CIA. Reuther's brother Victor, in a
speech in 1967 to the Labor Assembly for Peace, revealed the
close association of the AFL-CIO with the CIA. The CIA began
a campaign to balance the revelation with counterrevelations
that Walter Reuther also had accepted and used CIA funds
during the early 1950s. But this tactic was ineffective, however,
and the split widened. Eventually the UAW withdrew from the
AFL-CIO.

In the midst of this battle within the AFL-CIO came the
revelations by Drew Pearson and Jack Anderson of the CIA's
labor programs. The biggest flap came with the *Ramparts* magazine articles focusing on the IOD's funding of the National Student Association and trade unions. The effects on the CIA's
operations after these revelations were unexpected. At first, instead of increased denunciations of the CIA by foreign powers
or the neutralization of CIA programs, the foreign trade unions
in the Third World, in an orgy of opportunism, demanded more
funds from the CIA. But the seeds of discontent were sown, and
eventually the CIA lost more control over these unions.

Labor Proprietaries

By this time the CIA had developed a new mechanism for
labor operations. These new organizations operating under the
cover of "international affiliates" of the AFL-CIO are, in fact,
totally controlled by the CIA and are similar to the CIA's proprietaries such as the airlines Air America and Southern Air
Transport. But to further increase the cover of the "labor proprietaries," the CIA secured overt subsidy for many of their
programs, from the Agency for International Development
(AID), unlike during the McCarthy period when all programs
were covertly funded.

Lovestone, Brown, and Meyer, meeting in the late 1950s,
noted that their operations through the ICFTU and its regional
affiliates were not fulfilling expectations and began to look for
new mechanisms in the labor programs. They found their answer in a project begun by Joseph Beirne.

In the summer of 1959, at Beirne's suggestion, the CWA

brought 19 leaders of Latin American unions affiliated with PTTI to the former CWA educational center at Front Royal, Virginia, for a three-month study conference. After training in United States trade union techniques and an indoctrination that firmly placed these leaders under CIA control, the union leaders were sent back to their own countries and continued for nine months in the pay of the CWA.

The results were so successful in the CIA's view that the AFL-CIO under Lovestone and Meany's direction authorized funds for the creation of a new institute to further this training of cadre and to increase the CIA infrastructure in Third World trade unions. In January 1962 President Kennedy appointed a Labor Advisory Committee for the Alliance for Progress to advise the government on Latin American labor matters. Chaired by George Meany, the Committee was under CIA control from the start. At an early meeting it endorsed a recommendation that the government should participate in the financing of the newly formed American Institute for Free Labor Development (AIFLD), the first of three CIA labor proprietaries. To get the Institute launched as soon as possible, Secretary of Labor Arthur J. Goldberg obtained an advance of $100,000 from the President's Emergency Fund. After that AID included the Institute in its annual appropriations and contracted AIFLD for the work it performs.

From the beginning AIFLD was funded and directed by: labor represented by the AFL-CIO; the government, represented by AID; and the multinational corporations. All are connected and coordinated in this regard by the CIA. At the Executive Council meeting of the AFL-CIO in August 1962, Joseph Beirne recommended that the AFL-CIO contribute $100,000 per year to the Institute and that the affiliated international unions make financial contributions in $5,000 units.

Funds from AID have constituted over 90 percent of AIFLD's funding; nearly two-thirds of AID funding for Latin American programs has gone to AIFLD. In addition loans have been provided to AIFLD from the Inter-American Development Bank, pension and welfare funds of the unions associated with the AFL-CIO, and various other government and private loan agencies. And the CIA has continued its subsidies clandestinely whenever official AID or AFL-CIO funding for projects would be embarrassing to the government. Additional funding for

AIFLD projects has come from certain Latin American countries.

In addition, funding for AIFLD has come from multinational corporations that have, along with the AFL-CIO and the CIA, controlled AIFLD from the start. At a meeting at the Link Club in New York in October 1962, George Meany, Arthur Goldberg, and Serafino Romualdi enlisted the assistance of scores of businessmen to support AIFLD. Since that time approximately 95 business establishments, primarily multinational corporations, have contributed to AIFLD's programs.

These multinationals have included the Kennecott Copper Corporation, ITT, Pan American World Airways, Standard Oil of New Jersey, the Anaconda Company, International Paper Company, Standard Fruit Company, IBM World Trade Corporation, Coca-Cola Export Corporation, the Chase Manhattan Bank, Pfizer International, and others with extensive interests in Latin America. Leading these has been W. R. Grace & Company, headed by J. Peter Grace, who was President of AIFLD until the Reuther-Meany dispute forced him to resign to the less public position of chairman of the board.

Grace set the record straight on the purpose of AIFLD when he said:

> We need to understand that today the choice in Latin America is between democracy and communism. We must bear in mind that we cannot allow communist propaganda to divide us as between liberals and conservatives, as between business and labor, or between the American people and their government. Above all, we have to act together as Americans defending our interests abroad. . . . The American Institute for Free Labor Development is an outstanding example of a national consensus effectively at work for the national interests of the United States. . . . In this organization we also have a successful joint venture that the communist forces cannot possibly hope to match.[23]

Besides such CIA channels as Joseph Beirne, secretary-treasurer, running this "successful joint venture," the first executive director of AIFLD was Serafino Romualdi. He was succeeded by William D. Doherty, Jr., who had previously directed AIFLD's Social Projects Department. Before that Doherty was the CIA's inter-American representative of the PTTI. Several other CIA people from the PTTI and the CWA also came over to AIFLD when it was formed. Today a CIA case officer is undercover in almost every AIFLD office abroad.

Through AIFLD's training program at Front Royal, Virginia, the CIA has managed to train almost 200,000 Latin American labor leaders. Although many of these have just engaged in legitimate trade union activities in their home countries, many have also been available as CIA agents or have cooperated with the CIA's objectives. Where the CIA's programs of operating through the ICFTU, and its regional organizations and the ITS's have been limited, the activities of AIFLD have supplied the agency with its greatest number of operatives and thus increased its effects on the entire labor movement and the political atmosphere in Latin America.

Significant clandestine operations of the CIA labor proprietary AIFLD have included:

—recruitment of AIFLD agents from among the supporters of Cuban dictator Batista after his overthrow by Castro
—involvement in the overthrow of Cheddi Jagan in Guyana in 1967
—involvement in the overthrow of Juan Bosch in the Dominican Republic and support for the U.S. troop intervention in 1965
—involvement in the overthrow of the Goulart regime in Brazil in 1964
—involvement in the overthrow of the Allende government in Chile in 1973

In 1965 the second CIA labor proprietary was established, the African-American Labor Center (AALC). Irving Brown was appointed its first executive director. AALC is similar to AIFLD in structure and programs and has attempted to increase CIA influence in African labor affairs after the serious defeats for the CIA in keeping African unions in the ICFTU. The major thrusts of the AALC have been in undermining WFTU (Soviet) and, recently, Chinese influence in African labor, co-opting the Pan-Africanism expressed by those unions that withdrew from the ICFTU and, more recently, attempting to change the labor relations of the government of South Africa away from apartheid to a system less embarrassing to U.S. foreign policy. The AALC has been involved in many clandestine activities in Africa, including involvement in the revolution in Ethiopia. AALC has also been instrumental in promoting population control in Africa.

In 1968 the third CIA labor proprietary was established, the Asian-American Free Labor Institute (AAFLI). Executive Director of AAFLI is Morris Paladino, who was previously active with the CIA and AIFLD in undermining Allende in Chile. Active all over Asia, AAFLI is primarily involved in increasing labor support for the dictatorships in the Philippines, South Korea, Turkey, and South Vietnam.

Status

Through the 1960s and early 1970s, these CIA labor proprietaries have been most successful in enforcing the foreign policy objectives of the multinational corporations in the Third World, especially in those countries ruled by dictatorships. But today the shape of the CIA's labor programs is weak. George Meany is old and facing increased opposition (even from his wife) for his involvement with the CIA. Lovestone has retired. Brown has been thoroughly discredited in most parts of the world. Meyer has been put out to pasture. The CIA's programs are being increasingly exposed. The CIA itself has been weakened from bureaucratic infighting, the effects of Watergate, and world opinion. But weakened as it is, we can expect the CIA to continue its dirty tricks in the labor movement as long as it has the power for clandestine operations.

George Meany and the AFL-CIO pose the theory that the one force capable of resisting the goals of the multinational corporation is the multinational union. But as most people of the world now know, the AFL-CIO has, on the international level, been practically synonymous with the CIA, defender of the multinationals, and Meany's theories are hardly reputable. It is not for mere humor that throughout the world the organization he heads is now known not as the AFL-CIO but as the AFL-CIA.

Notes

The CIA against Cambodia

1. Statement quoted in appendix to Roger M. Smith, *Cambodia's Foreign Policy* (Ithaca: Cornell University Press, 1965), pp. 236–238.
2. Norodom Sihanouk as related to Wilfred Burchett, *My War with the CIA* (London: Penguin, 1973), p. 75.
3. Malcolm Salmon, *Focus on Indo-China* (Hanoi: Foreign Languages Publishing House, 1961), p. 255.
4. Wilfred Burchett, *The Second Indochina War* (New York: International, 1970), p. 44.
5. Ibid.; Malcolm Caldwell and Lek Tan, *Cambodia in the Southeast Asian War* (New York: Monthly Review Press, 1973), p. 103; Sihanouk as related to Burchett, *My War with the CIA*, p. 105.

South Vietnam's Police and Prison System: The U.S. Connection

1. See insert by Congressman Ron Dellums, *Congressional Record*, April 3, 1974, p. E.2041. To the figure of $1.49 billion he gives should be added $179.5 million additional military aid.
2. Congressional Research Service, Library of Congress, *Summary, Public Safety Program—Vietnam*, April 24, 1972, Chart 3: "National Police Manpower," dated Feb. 1972.
3. Ibid.
4. Ibid.
5. Ibid., p. 2.
6. *CORDS Newsletter*, no. 72 (Feb. 28, 1973), by Office of the Director, Civil Operations and Rural Development Support, Saigon, p. 20.
7. *Summary*, Chart 7: "National Police Command—Training," dated Feb. 1972.

8. U.S. Congress, Hearings before the House Committee on Government Operations, July 15, 16, 19, 21, and August 2, 1971, *U.S. Assistance Programs in Vietnam*, p. 5.

9. *Summary*, Chart 2: "Vietnam Public Safety Program U.S. Dollar Funding," dated Feb. 1972.

10. *U.S. Assistance*. See testimony of former Phoenix agent K. Barton Osborn, beginning on p. 315, for a description of CIA role in police and prison system. Note also admission by pacification chief William Colby in same hearings that interrogation centers "are advised by another element of our mission there" (p. 197).

11. Sen. Edward Kennedy, *Prisons and Political Prisoners in South Vietnam*, statement entered in *Congressional Record*, p. S. 10208.

12. *U.S. Assistance*, p. 197.

13. *Summary*, Chart 8: "National Police Detention Population," dated Feb. 1972.

14. *Prisons*, p. S.10206.

15. U.S. Congress, Senate Appropriations Committee, *Foreign Assistance and Related Programs Appropriation Bill, 1974*, report no. 93–620, issued by Senator Inouye, December 13, 1973, p. 27.

16. Frank E. Walton, "The Rehabilitation System of Vietnam, A Report Prepared by Public Safety Division, United States Operations Mission to Vietnam," October 1, 1963, p. 29.

17. Frank E. Walton, Chief, Public Safety Division, United States Operations Mission to Vietnam, "National Police Plan for Vietnam," March 1962, pp. 21–22.

18. Ibid., p. 22. Emphasis in original.

19. "National Police Plan," p. 30, gives Walton's 62,850 recommendation. *Summary*, Chart 3: "National Police Power," gives actual figure of 59,999.

20. "National Police Plan," pp. 24–26.

21. *Summary*, Chart 4: "Republic of Vietnam—National Police Command," dated Feb. 1972.

22. *Summary*, Chart 1: "Public Safety Directorate," dated Feb. 1972.

23. "Agency for International Development Fiscal Year 1974 Project Budget Submission to the Congress," dated June 1972, pp. 324–34.

24. Letter to Representative Marvin Esch, from Matthew J. Harvey, Assistant Administrator for Legislative Affairs, Agency for International Development, November 23, 1973.

25. *Escalation, American Options and President Nixon's War Moves* (National Security Study Memorandum #1), inserted by Representative Ronald Dellums in *Congressional Record*, May 10,

1972, beginning p. E.4975, and May 11, 1972, beginning p. E.5009. This note refers to quote appearing May 10, 1972, p. E.4995.

26. *Escalation*, p. E.5048.

27. Ibid., p. E.5047.

28. *U.S. Assistance*, p. 210.

29. *Escalation*, p. E.4995.

30. Department of State, Bureau of Public Affairs, Office of Media Services, *Vietnam Information Notes*, no. 14, July 1969, p. 3.

31. *Escalation*, p. E.4995.

32. Ibid., p. E.5048.

33. "Agency for International Development," p. 332.

34. *U.S. Assistance*, p. 321.

35. Ibid.

36. Republic of Vietnam, Ministry of Information, *Vietnam 1967–71: Toward Peace and Prosperity* (Saigon: 1971), p. 52.

37. Ibid.

38. *U.S. Assistance*, p. 183.

39. Ibid., p. 314.

40. Ibid.

41. *Summary*, p. 7.

42. *Escalation*, p. E.4995.

43. Ibid., p. E.5047.

44. *U.S. Assistance*, p. 189.

45. *Prisons*, p. S.10207.

46. *U.S. Assistance*, p. 193.

47. Ibid., p. 192.

48. Ibid., p. 183.

49. Ibid., p. 203. Emphasis added.

50. Letter to Representative Lee Hamilton, from John A. Hannah, Director, Agency for International Development, May 29, 1973.

51. See "Official Telegram from Operation Phoenix—April 5, 1973," inserted by Representative Abzug into hearings held by the House Subcommittee on Asian and Pacific Affairs on September 13, 1973, entitled *The Treatment of Political Prisoners in South Vietnam by the Government of the Republic of South Vietnam*, p. 8.

52. Office of Civil Operations, Public Safety Division, Saigon, Vietnam, Section II—Registration Plans, "National Identity Registration Project (ID Card)," April 1, 1967. Emphasis added.

53. *Summary*, p. 5.

54. Ibid.
55. "Agency for International Development," pp. 332, 330.
56. *CORDS Newsletter*, p. 20.
57. See note 28.
58. *U.S. Assistance*, p. 199.
59. Ibid.
60. Letter to Marcel Naville, President, International Red Cross, from Idar Rimestad, U.S. Ambassador in Charge of the United States Mission to International Organizations, December 7, 1970.
61. Representative Peter Frelinghuysen, *Ambassador Martin's Real Problem: Is Anyone Listening?*, inserted in the Congressional Record, April 4, 1974, beginning p. E.2116.
62. U.S. State Department, Bureau of Public Affairs, Public Information Series, *Civilian Prisoners in South Vietnam*, P–423, December 6, 1973.
63. Contract reprinted in Holmes Brown and Don Luce, *Hostages of War* (1322 18th St., NW, Washington, D.C. 20036, Indochina Mobile Education Project), p. 43.
64. Letter to Chaplain John Steinbruck, from Francis L. Garrett, Rear Admiral, CHC, U.S. Navy, Chief of Chaplains, Pers–9–Mr, September 5, 1973.
65. *Indochina Policy Questions: A Statement from the Department of State*, answers to twelve questions put by Senator Edward Kennedy, inserted by him in the *Congressional Record*, May 25, 1974

Surveillance and Mind Control

1. Harold D. Lasswell, "The Garrison State," *American Journal of Sociology* 46 (1941): 457.
2. Lasswell, p. 460. See also Herbert Marcuse, *One-Dimensional Man* (Boston: Beacon Press, 1964), passim.
3. Hearings before the Subcommittee on Constitutional Rights, Committee of the Judiciary, U.S. Senate, 92nd Congress, 1st Session, *Federal Data Banks, Computers and the Bill of Rights* (23–25 February, 2–17 March 1971), Part I, pp. 213, 267, 861.
4. Ibid., pp. 186, 154, and passim. See especially the testimony of former Army intelligence officer Captain Christopher Pyle, pp. 147–244. It was Pyle's January 1970 *Washington Monthly* article that blew the whistle on the Army's blanket surveillance program.

5. Ibid., Arthur R. Miller's statement, p. 9.

6. Ibid., p. 13.

7. Ibid., Ralph Stein's testimony, p. 244.

8. Ibid., p. 244ff., esp. pp. 247–77; the organizations are listed on pp. 264–65.

9. Ibid., pp. 252–53, 271.

10. Ibid., p. 254.

11. Ibid., pp. 196–97.

12. "Congressman Reveals 'Wired Nation' Study; Rep. William S. Moorhead (D-Pa.) Calls It a 'Big Brother' Plan; Nixon Advisor Says Idea Was Rejected," *Los Angeles Times*, November 1, 1972. Information on the rejected program for testing school children is found in the above-mentioned Hearings in testimony by John A. Sullivan of the American Friends Service Committee; see "American Liberty and Repression: an AFSC Review," pp. 366–67. For information on computerized records of children, see Nat Hentoff, "The Secret File on D. Isaacs, Age Eight," *Village Voice*, February 15, 1973; and Hentoff, "B. F. Skinner for Director of the FBI?" *Village Voice*, February 22, 1973. See also Paul Cowan, Nick Egleson, and Nat Hentoff, *State Secrets: Police Surveillance in America* (New York: Holt, Rinehart, and Winston, 1973), and Sarah Carey, *Law and Disorder III: State and Federal Performance Under Title I of the Omnibus Crime Control and Safe Streets Act of 1968* (available from the Lawyers' Committee for Civil Rights Under Law, Suite 520, 733 15th Street, NW, Washington, D.C. 20005).

13. Theodore Berland, "Up to Our Ears in Noise," in *The Crisis of Survival: The Famine of Resources, Nuclear War, Overpopulation, Pollution*, edited by *The Progressive* (New York: William Morrow, 1970), pp. 92–106.

14. See the suppressed original version of the Keldgord Report, *Coordinated California Corrections*, State of California, Department of Corrections (1971), which includes the Medical Committee of Human Rights Statement at the California Department of Corrections Conference on Prison Violence, held at Davis, November 19, 1971. This statement is available from the Medical Committee for Human Rights. See also John La Stala, "Atascadero: Dachau for Queers," *The Advocate*, April 25, 1972, pp. 11–13; Ed Opton, Jr., "Report on Medical Facility at Vacaville," prepared for the California Department of Corrections on Prison Violence, 19 November 1971 (mimeo), p. 3. In addition, see Nicholas Kittrie, *The Right to Be Different: Deviance and Enforced Therapy* (Baltimore: Johns Hopkins, 1971); Hearings before the Subcommittee on Health, Committee on

Labor and Public Welfare, U.S. Senate, 93rd Congress, 1st Session, *Quality of Health Care: Human Experimentation* (March 7–8, 1973), Part 3, which focuses "on the use of prisoners as subjects of medical research."

15. James V. McConnell, "Criminals Can Be Brainwashed—Now," *Psychology Today*, April 1970, p. 74. See also Jessica Mitford, *Kind and Usual Punishment: The Prison Business* (New York: Alfred A. Knopf, 1973).

16. M. H. Brown, quoted by Dr. Peter Breggin, "The Return of Lobotomy and Psychosurgery," entered into the *Congressional Record* by Rep. Cornelius Gallagher, February 24, 1972, E.1602–E.1612, esp. p. 1606. See also M. Hunter Brown and Jack Lighthill, "Selective Anterior Cingulotomy: A Psychosurgical Evaluation," *Journal of Neurosurgery* 29 (1968): 513–19; Stephen Chorover, "The Pacification of the Brain," *Psychology Today*, May 1974; Constance Holder, "Psychosurgery or Laundered Lobotomies," *Science*, March 16, 1973, pp. 1009–12. The most important volume, however, relating to psychosurgery and electrical stimulation of the brain is Hearings before the Subcommittee on Health, Committee on Labor and Public Welfare, U.S. Senate, 93rd Congress, 1st Session, *Quality of Health Care: Human Experimentation* (February 23, March 6, 1973), Part 2. This volume includes testimony by Drs. Breggin, Brown, Robert G. Heath, and O. J. Andy among others as well as important references and reprints of significant articles. See also the 18 June 1973 Hearings before this same subcommittee, *Psychosurgery in Veterans Administration Hospitals: An Examination of the Extent of Psychosurgery . . . for the Purpose of Modification of Behavior.*

17. Joe Hunt, "The Politics of Psychosurgery," *Rough Times* (formerly *The Radical Therapist*), November–December 1973, p. 6. Vernon Mark, W. H. Sweet, and Frank Ervin, letter to the editor, "Role of brain disease in riots and urban violence," *American Medical Association Journal*, 1967, p. 895; and George P. Anna, "Mark Denies Racism Charge, Believes Violence Ubiquitous," *Medical Tribune and Medical News*, January 2, 1974, p. 1ff. See also Vernon H. Mark and Frank R. Ervin, *Violence and the Brain* (New York: Harper & Row, 1970).

18. For facts about psychosurgery and children see Breggin, *Congressional Record*, E.1607 and passim.; O. J. Andy, "Thalamotomy in Hyperactive and Aggressive Behavior," *Confin. Neurol.* 32 (1970): 322–25; and the 1973 Hearings cited earlier. The international opposition to psychosurgery and to torture by physicians has been spearheaded by Dr. Peter Breggin in the United

States and Dr. Anthony Storr, professor of psychiatry at Warneford Hospital, Heathington, Oxford, England. Dr. Storr is the author of an important paper that surveys the "abuses of psychiatry" from an international perspective.

19. Breggin, *Congressional Record*, E.1609 and "Probing the Brain," *Newsweek*, June 21, 1971. See also Robert G. Heath, "Electrical Self-Stimulation of the Brain in Man," in R. Ulrich, T. Stachnick, and J. Mabry, eds., *Control of Human Behavior* (Glenview, Ill.: Scott, Foresman, 1966).

20. José Delgado, *Physical Control of the Mind: Toward a Psychocivilized Society* (New York: Harper & Row, 1970), pp. 97, 168–69, 221–23, 259.

21. Karen Waggoner, "Psychocivilization or Electroligarchy: Dr. Delgado's Amazing World of ESB," *Yale Alumni Magazine*, January 1970.

22. Quoted in Ruth Tebbets, "The Next Step in Law Enforcement: Electronic Brain Control," *Pacifica News Service* (mimeo, n.d.), p. 1.

23. Ibid. See also Perry London, *Behavior Control* (New York: Harper & Row, 1969), pp. 221–22; Joseph Meyer, "Criminal Deterrence Transponder Systems," IEE, *Transactions on Aerospace and Electronic Systems*, January 1971; Robert Barkan, "Science Fiction or Tomorrow's US," *Guardian*, October 27, 1971.

24. Warren Susman, "The Radicalism of Exposure," *Studies on the Left* 3 (1963): 72–73.

25. I am grateful to my friend Clare Coss, playwright and psychotherapist, for reference to the game Stone Witch and many valuable suggestions throughout this paper. I am also grateful to Gerald Markowitz, Claudia Koonz, and Carroll Smith-Rosenberg for their helpful readings and sustaining friendship.

The AFL-CIA

1. Principal policy makers for CIA labor operations have been the Agency's Director of Operations (Clandestine Services) along with his chief of the International Affairs Division; the AFL-CIO's George Meany and Jay Lovestone; and officers of certain multinational corporations.

2. Quoted in R. Harris Smith, *OSS* (Berkeley: University of California Press, 1972), p. 17.

3. Quoted in ibid., p. 17.

4. Serafino Romualdi, *Presidents and Peons* (New York: Funk & Wagnalls, 1967), p. 22.

5. Memorandum from Irving Brown to Abraham Bluestein, November 22, 1945, Florence Thorne MSS, State Historical Society of Wisconsin, Madison, Wis.

6. Gabriel Kolko, *The Limits of Power* (New York: Harper & Row, 1972).

7. Thomas W. Braden, "I'm Glad the CIA Is Immoral," *Saturday Evening Post,* vol. 240 (May 20, 1967), p. 10, 14.

8. Smith, *OSS,* p. 127.

9. Ronald Radosh, *American Labor and United States Foreign Policy* (New York: Random House, 1969), p. 341.

10. Ibid., p. 327.

11. Ibid., p. 325.

12. Braden, p. 10.

13. Quoted in Dan Kurzman, "Jay Lovestone Once Told Off Stalin, Now Directs Vast Anti-Red Activity," *Washington Post,* December 30, 1965.

14. Ibid.

15. Ibid.

16. Quoted in Smith, *OSS,* p. 372.

17. Cord Meyer, Jr., "A Plea for World Government," *The Annals of the American Academy of Political and Social Science* 264 (July 1949): 12.

18. "These Men Run the CIA," *Esquire,* vol. 65, no. 5 (May 1966), p. 167.

19. "A Hidden Liberal: Cord Meyer, Jr.," *New York Times,* 30 March 1967, p. 30.

20. Smith, *OSS,* p. 17.

21. Drew Pearson and Jack Anderson, "CIA Figures in Reuther-Meany Rift," *Washington Post,* 24 February 1967.

22. Ibid.

23. "An address by J. Peter Grace," printed in booklet form by the AIFLD, September 16, 1965.

INDEX

279